PERFORMING WALES

PEOPLE, MEMORY AND PLACE

LISA LEWIS

UNIVERSITY OF WALES PRESS
CARDIFF

www.uwp.co.uk

British Library Cataloguing-in-Publication Data
A catalogue record for this book is available from the British Library.

ISBN: 978-1-78683-242-9
e-ISBN: 978-1-78683-243-6

The right of Lisa Lewis to be identified as author of this work has been asserted in accordance with sections 77 and 79 of the Copyright, Designs and Patents Act 1988.

The University of Wales Press acknowledges the financial support of the University of South Wales.

Typeset by Marie Doherty
Printed by CPI Antony Rowe, Melksham

PERFORMING WALES

For Mum,
ac i gofio am fy nhad,
Illtyd Lewis (1927–2008)

CONTENTS

PAM YR YSGRIFENNAIS YN SAESNEG

Llyfr ar y modd y perfformir diwylliant yw hwn. Rhan annatod o bron bob math ar berfformiad diwylliannol yw'r modd y cyfryngir ac yr ymgorfforir y perfformiad hwnnw'n ieithyddol, ac y mae'r gyfrol hon yn canolbwyntio ar y profiad diwylliannol i Gymry Cymraeg. Serch hynny, fe benderfynais ysgrifennu'n Saesneg a hynny oherwydd fy mod am rannu gyda chynulleidfa ddi-Gymraeg y ffenest ar y byd a rydd y Gymraeg a'r diwylliant cyfrwng Cymraeg i mi fel rhan naturiol o'r profiad o fod yn siaradwr Cymraeg. Yn ffrâm i'r drafodaeth ar ddiwylliant Cymraeg fan yma defnyddiaf y ddisgyblaeth amwys a elwir yn astudiaethau perfformio, maes addas ar gyfer trin a thrafod diwylliant a'r perfformiad ohono yn gyffredinol. Bydd ysgolheigion sy'n dilyn disgwrs astudiaethau perfformio yn gyfarwydd iawn, go debyg, â'r cysyniadau a drafodir yma, tra bydd deiliaid y diwylliant cyfrwng Cymraeg yn deall rhagor o lawer nac a goleddir yn y llyfr hwn am deithi'r diwylliant hwnnw. Y mae'r newydd-deb, i ryw raddau, i'w ganfod yn y cyfuniad o ddamcaniaethau astudiaethau perfformio a'r achosion diwylliannol penodol y penderfynais eu trafod.

Yn ogystal â rhannu profiad un iaith trwy gyfrwng iaith fwyafrifol a chymdeithasol-ormesol, rwyf ar brydiau yn y drafodaeth yn ymdrechu i dynnu ynghyd agweddau ar y profiad dwyieithog ac yn ystyried y berthynas ryng-ieithyddol (*interlinguistic*) mewn perthynas â diwylliant. Fel un a fagwyd mewn cartref dwyieithog, yr wyf yn gyfarwydd iawn â deialog drawsieithog y Gymraeg a'r Saesneg; fe'i seriwyd ynof. Dyma, felly, ymdrech i rannu agweddau ar drywydd mewnol profiad diwylliannol un iaith yn y llall, a rhwng un profiad ieithyddol-ddiwylliannol a'r llall, fel rhan o barhad y ddeialog honno a fu'n rhan mor ganolog o'm magwraeth ddiwylliannol. Rwyf yn ddwys ymwybodol o ryngberthynas y Gymraeg a'r Saesneg yn yr hunaniaeth Gymreig, ond yn naturiol, fe rydd defnydd o'r Gymraeg berspectif a phrofiad penodol i'r siaradwr nad yw ar gael i'r sawl nad yw'n medru'r Gymraeg, a chaiff hyn ddylanwad ar yr hyn a ysytyrir yn bwnc trafodaeth.

Sylwais, wrth ysgrifennu am bethau tebyg yn y Gymraeg a'r Saesneg, fy mod yn gorfod cydnabod cyfyngderau un ffrâm iethyddolddiwylliannol neu'r llall. Er enghraifft, mae oblygiadau trafod gorthrwm ieithyddol a'i effeithiau yn y Gymraeg yn wahanol i'w drafod yn Saesneg, a'r rhagdybiaethau sy'n llywio'r drafodaeth yn y naill iaith a'r llall yn peri bod ystyr y gwaith yn aml yn wahanol. Gwahaniaeth yw hwn na all y cyfieithiad ddygymod ag e. Fe berthyn perthnasau grym yn amlwg i ddefnydd iaith ac i fynegaint ieithyddol, ac mewn ymateb i'r grymoedd hynny, yn ddigon eironig, yr wyf yn ysgrifennu'n Saesneg, mewn ymdrech i agor y drws ar drafodaeth ddiwylliannol o fath arbennig. Ni allaf fod yn sicr y bydd hynny'n llwyddo, oherwydd wrth gyfathrebu ryw elfen o'm profiad diwylliannol Cymraeg yn Saesneg, nid oes sicrwydd y caiff ei ddeall.

Yr wyf yn gyfarwydd iawn â'r trafodaethau ysgolheigaidd ar berfformio yng Nghymru yn y Gymraeg a'r Saesneg, a'r modd y bydd y trywydd Saesneg yn aml yn diystyru i raddau helaeth gynnwys y traddodiad Cymraeg, heb sôn am ei hanes a'i gyd-destun cymdeithasol. Rhai blynyddoedd yn ôl, clywais athro o brifysgol yn Lloegr yn traddodi darlith ar ddrama Gymreig mewn cynhadledd yng Nghymru fel pe na bai'r iaith Gymraeg yn bodoli. Y mae'r llyfr hwn hefyd yn ymateb i'r 'diffyg ymwybyddiaeth' hwnnw mewn cynulleidfa benodol.

Nodyn ar enwau llefydd
Yn gyffredinol, defnyddir enwau llefydd Cymraeg (ac felly Caerffili nid Caerphilly). Fodd bynnag, lle mae enw Saesneg penodol ar le (e.e. Swansea ar gyfer Abertawe) defnyddir y fersiwn Saesneg er mwyn eglurdeb.

WHY I HAVE WRITTEN IN ENGLISH

This book considers the way in which culture is performed. An intrinsic part of almost every form of cultural performance is the way in which that performance is mediated and incorporated linguistically, and the emphasis in this book, to a large extent, is on cultural experience for the Welsh speaker. Even so, I have chosen to write in English due to a desire to share the window on the world provided by Welsh language and culture as a natural part of being a Welsh speaker. The volume attempts to use approaches from performance studies as a frame for the discussion on Welsh culture – a particularly suitable optic for discussions about culture and its performance. Those who follow the discourses of performance studies will be familiar with the concepts discussed, while participants of Welsh-medium culture will understand vastly more about the experience of the culture than I am able to capture here. Any claim to originality is related to the bringing together of theoretical discussions within performance studies with specific cultural case studies that I have chosen to explore.

As well as sharing the experience of one language, Welsh, through the medium of another majority and socially powerful language, English, I attempt to bring together in this discussion aspects of the bilingual experience, and consider the interlinguistic relationship of the two languages. As someone who was raised in a bilingual home, I am acutely aware of the dialogue across and between languages; it is imprinted in me. This then is an attempt to share some of the internal characteristics of one linguistic experience in the other, and between one cultural-linguistic experience and the other, as a continuation of the dialogue that has been so central to my own cultural upbringing. I am deeply conscious of the interrelationship of the Welsh and English languages in Welsh identity; however, the Welsh language provides a specific cultural perspective that is not entirely accessible to those who have no Welsh at all, and this has a bearing on the cultural focus of the book.

I have noticed, in writing about similar things in both Welsh and English, that I have had to acknowledge the constraints of one cultural-linguistic frame or the other. For example, the implications of discussing linguistic oppression in Welsh and in English are somehow different, and the preconceptions that govern the discussion in one language or the other often produce a different meaning in the work. This is a difference that translation is unable to manage. There are power relationships clearly present in language use and in linguistic expression within specific cultural and social contexts and, ironically enough, it is in response to those forces that I am writing in English, in the hope of opening a door on a cultural discussion of a particular kind. In communicating something of my Welsh language cultural experience through the medium of English, there is no certainty that it will be understood or accepted.

I am very familiar with the scholarly discussions on performance in Wales in Welsh and in English, and the way in which the English language discussion frequently disregards the content of the Welsh performative tradition, let alone its history and social context. Some years ago I heard a professor from an English university deliver a lecture on Welsh drama as though the Welsh language never existed. This book is an attempt to respond to this 'not reached for' aspect.[1]

Note on place names
Place names are in Welsh as a general rule, especially where current English spelling is a variant of the Welsh (thus Caerffili rather than Caerphilly). However, where there is a distinct English version of the name (e.g. Swansea for Abertawe), I have used the English version for the sake of clarity.

---

[1] Raymond Williams, *Problems in Materialism and Culture* (London: Verso, 1980), p. 43.

LIST OF ILLUSTRATIONS

ACKNOWLEDGEMENTS

This book was written over many years and there are numerous friends and colleagues whom I would like to thank for their invaluable advice and encouragement during the process of researching and writing.

I would like to thank my colleagues at the University of South Wales for their unstinting support over the years. Several sections of this book were researched and written with the support of the Theatre and Media Drama research unit and the Centre for Media and Culture in Small Nations at the University of South Wales. I am indebted to colleagues in these centres for their collegial and scholarly support, especially former centre leaders Steve Blandford and David Barlow and research unit leader Richard Hand, as well as current leaders Ruth McElroy and Paul Carr. I would also like to thank Christina Papagiannouli for her support. I am grateful to Owain Kerton and staff at Research and Innovation Services, USW, for their encouragement and backing.

I would like to thank my colleagues Sêra Moore Williams, Rhiannon Williams and Matthew Davies, with whom I teach and research through the medium of Welsh, and who have provided years of discussion and analysis of theatre and performance in Wales. *Diolch i chi am y drafodaeth ac am fod yng nghalon y gwaith.* I am extremely grateful to Helen Davies for her unswerving support, advice and endless optimism.

There are colleagues further afield to whom I'm grateful for allowing me the time to indulge in discussing some of the most difficult aspects of this book – in particular, I'm grateful to Anwen Jones and Aparna Sharma for the opportunity to discuss at length. I would also like to thank my former colleague Mike Pearson, whose influence has had a strong bearing on this work.

I am grateful to Betty Belanus and staff at the Smithsonian Centre for Folklife and Cultural Heritage for the opportunity to experience the Smithsonian Folklife Festival and to participate in it in 2008 and 2009. To Matthew Davies, with whom I have collaborated over many years in his former capacity as education officer at Amgueddfa Cymru/ Museum Wales, I am extremely grateful. I would also like to extend my thanks to Amgueddfa Cymru/National Museum Wales, especially current and former staff and in particular Nia Williams, Steve Burrow, and Ken Brassil. I am grateful to Amgueddfa Cymru for the time spent on a Strategic Insight Partnership at Sain Ffagan Amgueddfa Werin Cymru.

I would like to acknowledge and thank all photographers and copyright holders of the images shown herein for permission to publish them as part of this book. In particular, I would like to thank Bedwyr Williams for allowing me to show his own images of his artwork *Tafarn yr Iorwerth Peate*, Betty Belanus and the Smithsonian Institution for images of the Smithsonian Folklife Festival 2009, Diane Walker, Llancaiach Fawr Manor and Banbury Photography for the image of interpreters at Llancaiach Fawr Manor, Sarah Griffiths of Castell Henllys, Parc Cenedlaethol Arfordir Cymru, Sally Donovan, Amgueddfa Cymru/National Museum Wales for permission to publish images of museum sites, National Theatre Wales, WildWorks and Theatr Genedlaethol Cymru for production photographs and Catrin Rogers (NTW), Emma Hogg (WildWorks) and Mair Jones (ThGC) for their assistance, Mike Pearson for permission to show images from the Brith Gof Archive (National Library of Wales), Margaret Ames for permission to show images from the Cliff McLucas Archive (National Library of Wales), and Eddie Ladd for the image of her production work. To the photographers Simon Clode, Banbury Photography, Marian Delyth, Toby Farrow, Ian Kingsnorth and Keith Morris, thank you for your essential work of capturing the fleeting moments that compose performance and for permission to use the images here. I am grateful to National Library of Wales staff for their assistance, as ever, especially Emyr Evans.

To staff at the University of Wales Press I am extremely grateful. In particular, I would like to thank Llion Wigley for his enthusiasm, endless patience and support.

Finally, I would like to thank my family for their forbearance and support. To my son, who has watched this book being researched and written, I am grateful for his infinite patience – *diolch i ti Twm am dy amynedd ac am gefnogi Mam*; and my heartfelt thanks to Rhys, *f'enaid hoff cytûn*, without whom writing this book would not have been possible.

INTRODUCTION

This book uses the frame of performance studies to discuss the way in which certain aspects of Welsh culture are constituted and to examine how these aspects of culture contribute to a shared sense of identity through performance. Acknowledging that 'Welsh culture' is a loaded concept, the discussion does not seek to define or delimit culture per se, but is written from a specific point of view and in relation to my own experience and understanding of Welsh culture. Therefore, the discussion is not about all Welsh cultures or all of Welsh culture; rather, it is a particular view of my own experience of culture. My understanding of it, as examined here, is based on my experience of Welsh cultural performances, those moments in which time, event and participants are structured in such a way that it is possible to name and define them and subsequently to examine the way they are composed and how they operate. These highly structured moments serve as doorways into an experience of what it is to be of this place, at a certain moment in time. In this endeavour, culture is not considered to be a thing – an object – that is separate or above social relationships; rather, it is to be found being continuously enacted, or transacted, between people. In taking this position, I am following Dwight Conquergood's articulation of the complexity of culture and the necessary emplacement of the researcher/participant:

> This view of culture as a swirling constellation of energies with cross-drafts, wind pressures, and choppy air currents, can help blast researchers free from positivistic moorings because culture can no longer be grasped so much as it needs to be felt and engaged. With this notion of culture, knowledge derived from systematic investigation is displaced by understanding that comes from experience – from getting caught up, or plunging into, the hurly burly of social life.[1]

To pull apart the constituent elements of culture *as* performance one must be alert to the part one played in the performance itself. Many of the accounts I provide here are offered from my own position as participant, though this does not necessarily mean that they are closed or unique readings. My voice is merely one out of the multitude of voices that might express experiences of, and that participate in, a variety of forms of 'Welsh culture' in the widest possible sense. I am not seeking to offer a singular and definitive picture in which Welsh culture is absolute; in this kind of analysis, which usually depends on physical emplacement, I am limited by my own experience.

I have chosen to do this because I am interested in the flow of culture – between people, between artist, artwork and recipient, between institution and public, between people and place, and in particular in relation to memory and its role in the formation of culture. More specifically, within the academy, I am interested in the situatedness of the researcher as a constituent of and participant in culture. Conquergood has written about the challenge of performance studies in terms of refusing an 'apartheid of knowledges, that plays out inside the academy as the difference between thinking and doing, interpreting and making, conceptualizing and creating'. He describes this division of theory and practice as a 'rigged choice' that causes a split in understanding between the 'abstraction' of theory on the one hand and 'the nourishing ground of participatory experience' on the other. Rather, performance studies scholars are encouraged to speak from between these positions, 'to turn, and return, insistently, to the crossroads.'[2] In the spirit of Conquergood's call for an in-between position, this book attempts to reach a position of discourse between, on the one hand, practice and participation, including live events and fieldwork, and on the other, related theory and criticism. Performance studies facilitates this stance because it is open to the multitudinous and variegated ways in which performance is discussed as both theory and practice, or to use Elin Diamond's well-known phrase, as both 'a doing and a thing done.'[3] It is a field of converging approaches and methods that encourages interdisciplinarity, and while its proponents have celebrated its openness, there is also acknowledgment of the fact that it inevitably invites contestation.[4] Its possibilities stem from the fact that it operates as a discursive field, one in which the parameters are continually and frequently revised, and informed and influenced by other fields and disciplines, from the initial influence of ethnography, anthropology, folklore and linguistics, to the realms of sociology, psychoanalysis, postcolonial theory, queer theory and feminist theory, amongst a growing list of approaches and their bearing on what performance might be. In a Welsh context, performance studies can be a conduit for considering cultural expression and production that is not necessarily dependent on the written word and for critically encountering the performative nature of Welsh culture. Performance studies reminds us of the implications of voicing cultural contributions that may not have been focused on widely, adding to and enriching the discourses around identity and self-representation, and in this sense it is a field that can be inherently political, releasing us from the constraints of frameworks of knowledge that pay no heed to our own cultural performances. This is especially relevant in the context of 'minority' cultures and languages that by definition are smaller, more fragile, and more peripheral only insofar as they are situated next to the normative certainty of the majority language and culture, from the central vantage point of which the world is seemingly defined.

With this in mind, much of the activity represented in this book involves practical explorations of certain events, performative activities and customs that happened over a period of time. These represent three broad forms, loosely corresponding to the three main sections of this book, focusing on the museum, festival and theatre as performances of culture. Each section includes descriptions of works participated in, or seen, at various events and sites such as Sain Ffagan Amgueddfa Werin Cymru / St Fagan's National Museum of History, and other Amgueddfa Cymru / National Museum Wales sites, the National Eisteddfod of Wales, the Smithsonian Folklife Festival (specifically the Wales exhibit in 2009), several heritage sites, and numerous re-enactment events. In the final chapter, which looks at theatre, the performances discussed are mostly based on my experience as audience member.

Culture as performance

The emphasis on performance in the study of culture, introduced by anthropologist Victor Turner in the 1980s, signified a rejection of the concept of culture as fixed or somehow extrinsic to basic human behaviour.[5] While Clifford Geertz had already argued (in 1973),[6] that culture operates as a symbolic system unique to humans, in which meanings are publicly shared and form the collective property of a group, Turner emphasises the way in which humans construct culture through their performances, and was the first to posit that performances constitute culture rather than being an external field of referents or objects that humans deal with. In Turner's position culture is therefore *in* the performance itself, *in* the field of human relations that constructs it. Here, performance is a process that discloses the way in which 'cultural specialists'[7] know and understand their worlds and may operate as a critical apparatus for discussing social structures and for reshaping cultural forms. Turner postulates that cultural performances produce a set of 'meta-languages' enabling a group's expression, and more importantly, that they facilitate a process of understanding in order to instigate change within the group.[8] In this way, the structures and functions of cultural performances are both reflective and reflexive, for in performance, the performer reveals herself to the community and with the community. Thus, cultural performances may be political in the sense that they do not simply reflect things as they are or continue with a representation that is unquestionable, as they may induce self-awareness, and knowledge of the group for the group.

Acknowledging that culture is a diverse and difficult area to define, I am adopting Dwight Conquergood's stance that performance can be a valid way of resolving the issues arising from the complexity and scope of culture. Considering the performative nature of culture involves dwelling on the way people continuously enact or 'transact' culture.[9] Writing of the transaction of culture through the medium of performance, Conquergood asks what the conceptual consequences may be of considering 'culture as a *verb*, instead of a *noun*, process instead of product' (p. 96), reflecting the consequences of the performative turn in anthropology and the subsequent shift from cultural performance or 'performance of culture' to the study of culture *as* performance. Explaining the focus on performance as an agent of culture rather than an act of culture, Conquergood elaborates on the reflexive turning back upon the conduct of enquiry, and the way in which the doing of anthropology is discussed as performance. It is in this context that he suggests that in order to study and understand cultures, we need only be alert to what they display of themselves, their publicly accessible 'expressions', or 'peaks' of social experience, that 'function as prismatic lenses through which one can glimpse the inner dynamics and depths of culture' (pp. 18–19). Consideration of these matters ensures that

4

the active processes of culture are encountered. In a further article, Conquergood defines the cultural features that can be highlighted by a performance-centred approach to culture as 'process', 'play', 'poetics' and 'power', offered in opposition to the features of logical positivism, such as structure, system, distance and objectivity.[10] Process, play, poetics and power are features that enable us to concentrate on how culture works to bind the group. 'Play' centres on the improvisational and experimental aspects of culture, 'process' emphasises its emergent, contingent and dynamic properties and 'power' refers to its political, historical and ideological aspects as a site of struggle. It is 'poetics' above all, however, that emphasises the invented or imagined nature of human realities and the concept of culture and people as creative. It is in the context of 'poetics' that reflexive genres such as rituals, festivals, spectacles, dramas, and celebrations 'hold out the promise of reimagining and refashioning the world' (p. 83). Within the context of performance as poetics, Conquergood charts the shifting meanings of the word performance in ethnography and cultural studies in terms of a move from performance as *mimesis* to performance as *poiesis*, and then to *kinesis*, or 'performance as imitation, construction, dynamism'.[11] Conquergood locates a shift in the definition of performance away from imitation (*mimesis*) and towards construction (*poiesis*) in Victor Turner's later work, where the focus is on the capacity of performance to make, or to enable becoming.[12] According to Conquergood, this emphasis on performance as making influences and enables the stance of performance as *kinesis* or transformation, 'as a decentring agency of movement, struggle, disruption, and centrifugal force' (p. 57). This is represented by Homi Bhabha's use of 'the performative' to describe actions bound up with defining group identity, that is situated in opposition to 'the pedagogical', used to refer to the master discourses of nationhood.[13] For Conquergood, the shift from 'Turner's emphatic view of performance as making, not faking' to 'Bhabha's politically urgent view of performance as *breaking and remaking*', is 'a move from cultural *invention* to *intervention*.'[14] Underpinning this view is a critique of the dominance of the textual object and of textuality as the main focus of study, referred to by Edward Said as 'textual attitude', the tendency 'to prefer the schematic authority of the text to the disorientations of direct encounters with the human'.[15] While a textual model, according to Conquergood, emphasises the objective frame of knowledge, ('privileges distance, detachment, and disclosure as ways of knowing'), a performance model is inherently participatory and operates through close proximity ('immediacy, involvement and intimacy as modes of understanding'),[16] enabling us to take note of the non-verbal and the embodied dimensions of cultural practice as human interaction.

Culture in Wales has been involved in constructing and defining nationness in the absence of the apparatus of state structures and it has also been deeply involved in the process of performance as *kinesis* in response to social and political realities; this has tended to take place in the sphere of civil disobedience and protestation – in ruptures which have historical meaning – rather than in the respectability of the bourgeois public sphere, for example through mainstream theatre, journalism or media broadcasting (to the extent that this domain of influence has fully existed in Wales). This book centres on the processes of *poiesis*, of making culture, while recognising that in situations where performance is used as a form of becoming, the stance of performance as *kinesis*, as impetus for change, is always potentially present. The conception of culture as creative, as an enabling force for reimagining the world and for rendering it anew, is a critically important stance in relation to cultures that strive to find a voice in a world of over-arching and dominant 'national' structures (or nations) that impart totalising, homogenous conceptions of identity. This tendency towards a creative reimagining through culture is analysed by Jane Aaron as a characteristically Welsh response to 'threatening attacks on Welsh identity'. Acknowledging that opposing threats to identity and being is a fundamental human response, Aaron suggests that it would be unlikely for Welsh culture to be unique in this respect. She states, however, that 'not all cultures react similarly' and describes the golden ages of English culture which took place during periods of economic and political success, the complete opposite of a creative imagination 'fired in defiance of threats to its future', which 'flourishes despite the absence of a supportive context.'[17] Drawing on evolutionary biologist Richard Dawkins's concept of the meme, Aaron explores the idea that cultures produce repetitive patterns that are perpetually reproduced 'from person to person and from generation to generation' (p. 2). She argues that culture in the Welsh context has drawn on a sense of resistance for its survival and that a pattern has evolved in which 'the Welsh become a people strongly culturally activated in opposition to a threat of extinction' (p. 2). This does not necessarily mean that the Welsh, in their cultural works, have always succumbed to a romantic agony borne of defeat or that they have merely lamented the failures without recourse to self-determination. In their cultural responses, the Welsh have revealed a consideration of culture as creative and enabling, a force through which we may forge the world in a new way and this has become a valuable asset, socially, culturally and politically. The emphasis on 'becoming' has a track history in the writing on Welsh culture. As a manifestation of the desire or the will towards developing a national identity that is constantly on the brink of coming into being, it is occasionally perceived as a nationalist impetus towards developing nationhood. For others, the moment of creative redefinition entails calling 'Wales' into question and examining why it is that we are perpetually summoning its existence into being, or reinventing it. The historical stance of the latter position problematises the hope of the former, or at least positions it as an unstable reality (an invented tradition) that can be upended by the firm historical grasp of objective reality.

It is not the perpetual re-making of Welsh culture in and of itself that is under consideration here, however. Rather, it is the relationship between culture as performance and the way in which performance shapes our understanding of place and memory and therefore our ability to make relevant statements regarding our identity. Making statements regarding whom we are is a recurrent theme in Welsh culture over the centuries and one that emerges more fully in Welsh writing in English during the twentieth century. The discussion in this book is not intended to separate Welsh and English medium articulations of Welsh identity as though they were specifically different forms of identity, though it does acknowledge that the historical connotations of collective memory entail foregrounding, to an extent, the role of Welsh-language culture in relation to social history. The discussion also attempts to recognise fully the way in which both Welsh and English languages have impacted on each other as a medium of cultural expression and how they continue to do so.[18] It is worth noting something here about the nature of Welsh-language communities in Wales. While there are many areas in Wales where the Welsh language is spoken widely and without conscious effort, this experience is diminishing due to a variety of factors that impinge on language use. In other areas, the majority of Welsh speakers exist in language communities formed through specific networks, some of them remote

(schools, clubs, sports teams and other forms of communities including the chapel, which operate across towns and cities) so that even in
an urban context where there are many Welsh speakers, the individual
finds herself part of different linguistic communities.[19] This means
that for a child brought up in a Welsh city, as I was, to speak Welsh is
both a natural aspect of life and at the same time a conscious decision.

I have outlined some of the reasons for writing this book in English
rather than in Welsh in the preface. I reiterate some of it here as it has
a bearing on the critical stance taken. Welsh-language culture has not
been forthcoming in translating itself to the world because, historically, this has not been required of it. Living comfortably within its
own confines, it has existed in and for the people who participate
in it. There are specific examples where the performance of culture
has attempted to exceed the confines of its own sphere, such as the
National Eisteddfod of Wales in the Victorian era, where a self-
conscious performance of Welsh culture became a response to the
denigration of the Welsh language and people in the mid nineteenth
century. In general, however, such performances have been attempts
from within the culture to claim that its participants are part of a
broader identity set (Welsh and British, for example) and have involved
a degree of cultural translation, or rather, a performance of Welshness
in English. The reasons for writing this book in English as opposed to
Welsh are twofold. In the first instance, it is with a little hope that it
may contribute towards a conception of Welsh culture in English as
inclusive of the Welsh language and secondly, with reference to my
own field, it is to press the case for an inclusion of Welsh-language culture in the consideration of theatre and performance across the British
Isles and beyond. What I am writing 'against' here is the inability to
consider the Welsh-language dimension in discussing Welsh culture
as it appears in English-language scholarship about theatre and performance. While it is true that there has been very little translation of
seminal Welsh-language texts, either plays or monographs, into other
languages, the omission of the Welsh-language dimension is a consequence of life on what is considered to be a cultural periphery. With
the exception of material written by scholars working in Wales, there
have been very few texts that deal with Welsh theatre and performance
that include a consideration of the Welsh-language dimension in any
detail.[20] This results in either a sweeping inclusiveness, in which there
is a token reference to Welsh-language forms, or a kind of universalism

in the way the narrative of British theatre and drama is told, one that
privileges a stance in which Britishness is equated with Englishness and
is oblivious to that which it omits. Raymond Williams noted that 'in
certain areas, there will be in certain periods, practices and meanings
which are not reached for. There will be areas of practice and meaning which, almost by definition from its own limited character, or in
its profound deformation, the dominant culture is unable in any real
terms to recognize.' [21] Some of the practices looked at in this book are
specific performances that may not be widely recognised, and even
if they are, they might be considered to be too remote or peripheral to be placed within the broader and apparently weightier canvas
of British culture. Consequently, such performances are not widely
explored outside Welsh-language discourse. In this book, the focus on
culture as performance serves to highlight the residual practices of a
certain people in a certain place in such a way as to examine what it
is that performance does in relation to notions of memory and place.
The intention is to reveal the inner depths of a culture and to reflect
on the tension between that which is continually performed, perhaps
in the guise of tradition, and its emergent and changing meaning(s),
elucidating a constant cultural shift between past and present and the
way in which this relationship is constituted through performance.

On Terminology

There has been some discussion by theatre and performance
scholars writing through the medium of Welsh and English about
Welsh-language terminology used to define the field, and some focus
on the use of terms seemingly translated from English (e.g. *perfformiad*
for 'performance'). By extension there has been a relegation of the
concepts associated with terms such as *perfformiad*, *theatr*, *drama*,
to the sphere of imported cultural constructs. [22] The English word
'performance' became assimilated into discussions in French and in
German in the 1970s, during the emergence of the discourse around
performance, enabling the description in both languages of a social
activity for which there was no equivalent term available. [23] The relationship between Welsh and English is more porous, however, and a
degree of translation and adaptation between them is to be expected in
the adoption of terms to discuss historically indigenous performance
practices, whatever they may be. Notwithstanding the intercultural

dynamics of languages that reside together, it is interesting to note the complex linguistic interrelationships between the word *perfformiad* (performance) and etymologically related Welsh words. But first, let me start by describing an anthropologist's tracing of the English term.

Victor Turner, with whom Richard Schechner constructed some of the first iterations in the field of performance studies as an inter-disciplinary field, provides a detailed etymological analysis of the word 'performance' in his book *From Ritual to Theatre, The Human Seriousness of Play* (1982). Tracing the derivation of the word from the Old French *parfournir* (to complete, bring to completion, accomplish), Turner writes of the centrality of the concept of experience to performance and follows the roots of the word 'experience' back to the hypothetical Indo-European base root *per-*, 'to attempt, venture, risk', from whence comes the Greek *peira*, 'experience'.[24] He explains how the English word 'experience' derives more directly, via Middle English and Old French, from the Latin *experientia*, meaning 'trial, proof, experiment', and that closely associated to it is the Latin *periclum*, or *periculum*, 'trial, danger, peril' (p. 17). Turner also associates the verbal root *per-* to part of a phonetically similar group, related to a central concept meaning 'forward or 'through'. In addition, 'experiment', like 'experience', is derived from the Latin *expeiri*, 'to try or test'. Placed together, this plethora of words associated with experience suggests, for Turner, 'a journey, a test (of self, of suppositions about others), a ritual passage, an exposure to peril or risk, a source of fear' (p. 18). In drawing attention to the process of performance as an opportunity to expose that which is usually hidden, Turner discloses the meaning of performance as that which draws back the veil on aspects of experience that are particularly difficult to access amongst the daily habits of everyday life.

Through a consideration of relative terms, Turner's etymological account opens up a space for us to note the clear points of contact with associated Welsh words. The influence of Latin in the Welsh language enables us to trace the explicit relationships between words and to note similarities in cognate words. There are in fact many similarities and shared meanings in words relating to performance, experience and risk in both Latin and Welsh, which share the etymological roots of the word *perfformiad*. For instance, the Latin *periclum* or *periculum* (trial, danger, peril), gives us in Welsh the word *perygl* (danger), and also *cwlwm* (knot); the Latin verb *expeiri* (try, test) gives us *peiriant* (machine), which is itself formed from the Welsh verb *peri* (to make happen, to force, to impel), which is related to the phonetic group above whose meaning is to 'go forward' or 'through'. *Perfformiad*, first appearing in written form in 1863, was not used exclusively to refer to theatrical performance (*theatr* appears much earlier in 1604 in scholarly writing and dictionaries, though used specifically in reference to the site of performance).[25] The fact that *perfformiad* shares its etymological roots with the flexible Welsh word *peri* opens up a landscape of potential where the implications for performance are diverse and more fluid than the specific connotation of the enactment of a play. For *peri* has three significant meanings: to create, form or make, used to refer to a changed state or quality of person or thing; to cause something to be made, to produce; and to make ready, prepare, arrange, provide, obtain, get, keep, maintain, order.[26] While remaining alert to the pitfalls of etymological dogmatism, it is interesting and worthwhile to consider the inflection these associated words and meanings may lend to a consideration of the role of performance in Welsh culture, and the role of performance in the formation of identity in a particular place and time. These kinds of associations have implications for a consideration of Welsh culture as performative, for *perfformiad*, as relation or reflection of *peri* (impel, make happen, create, form, produce), helps to emphasise culture as a shifting entity which defines us, and constitutes culture in the performance as a process of going forward or through, not only in reference to the durational qualities of an art form or event defined in time and space, but in terms of the experiential nature of the venture, of living through a different quality of time, one that by definition is marked as separate and distinct, during which we reflect and respond to the performance as a cultural process. It also signifies a quest for change, to make a situation different. *Perfformiad* is likewise haunted by the association with *perygl* (danger), which emphasises the relationship with risk implicit in the moment of performance, its unpredictability; it refers to the fact that performance in the moment, in time and space, accesses the condition of life, of living, now, and all the uncertainty involved in the condition of being, and perhaps the risks involved in change. And *cwlwm* (knot) could be adopted to refer to the binding of performer and witness, performers to one another, and along with space and place, of community together, implicit in the performance venture. Finally, *perfformiad* as distant relation of *peiriant* (machine) retains the sense of compulsion, of being compelled to make, of being compelled to watch, of performance as something in which we must be invested, as well as its workings within culture and as culture. These approximate relationships between cognate words should be kept in mind in relation to the approach to culture as performance taken in this book. I also use a network of theoretical positions that cluster around notions of people, memory and place, and these are the specific lenses through which I hope to examine and understand the way in which Welsh culture is constituted as performance. The first chapter is an overview of some of these positions.

PEOPLE, MEMORY AND PLACE: IDEAS FOR A CONSIDERATION OF WELSH PERFORMANCE

1

Cenedl: people

In considering Wales as an entity and the Welsh people as a body, I am referring to all who reside in Wales and understand the place as culturally, linguistically and historically unique, whatever our background, wherever we have come from. In this context, Welsh culture is as diverse as the people who constitute it. Coming from Cardiff, I am acutely conscious of the deep intercultural and transcultural relationships that have defined the city's cultural milieu and of the role of the Welsh language in this. In my deliberations on Welsh culture I do not mean to exclude any version or conception of Welshness; it is merely that my own positionality is critical to the way I understand and talk about culture as a performative act in which I have participated.

The Welsh term *cenedl*, used to signify nation, actually alludes to the people as a people and is a reminder of the importance of dwelling on the civic in discourses around nationhood and nationness. Historian Prys Morgan locates the change from a conception of people as *cenedl* (kin-group) to something approximating the present use of the word to denote 'nation' during the late twelfth century, a shift that was a consequence of recurrent historical invasions and the subsequent need to become 'more keenly aware of a kinship or nationality that was superior to . . . loyalty to local dynasty.'[1] This slippage in the meaning of the term *cenedl*, literally kindred, tribe or clan, to the idea of nation as separate entity, is indicative of the increasingly ambivalent relationship, historically, between the notion of what constitutes a people and the idea of nationhood. Morgan writes of the turn in historiography that has seen a focus on the role of imagination, mythology and images in the constitution of 'modern nations states, or groups' and the attempt to understand the role of human activity in their construction.[2] This historiographic turn runs against the idea of the nation state as an entity that has inadvertently been established in an organic way over centuries, an idea often associated with a modern revival of Welsh nationness. Morgan acknowledges that some would describe Wales as having an inevitable physical unity based on its geography and a historical and linguistic unity based on the fact that the majority of the population spoke Welsh until approximately the turn of the twentieth century.[3] His focus, however, is on the role of mythology and imagination in the definition of Wales over the centuries and, in particular, during times of crisis. In this analysis, the sustaining power of the creative impulse has been imperative in maintaining the existence of a country/people that has not always had a political state.

Similarly Timothy Brennan, in his examination of 'the national longing for form', refers to nation as being both 'historically determined' (the modern nation state) and 'something more ancient and nebulous – the *natio*' – a local community, domicile, family, or condition of belonging'.[4] He quotes Raymond Williams, who emphasises the need to distinguish between these meanings and suggests a strong connection between 'nation' and 'native', for 'we are born into relationships which are typically settled in place', a form of association of 'fundamental human and natural importance'. In this context, the notional jump from emplaced relationships to the concept of nation state 'is entirely artificial'.[5] Referring to Anderson's *Imagined Communities*[6] as one of the few texts to focus on the concept of the nation as an imagined formation, Brennan comments on how it is 'rare in English to see 'nation-ness' talked about as an imaginative vision – as a topic worthy of full fictional realization'.[7] The difference with the treatment and conceptualisation of nationness in Welsh culture could not be starker, for in the Welsh context it is often explicitly evoked through symbol and metaphor and forged into being as a cultural imaginary. Even when the nation is conceived as a political and civic entity, it is hardly ever claimed as a wholly political reality, partly because the discussion must dwell instead on the concept and processes of *becoming* a nation.

That the performance of Welsh nationness has not really been tethered to a consideration of the state, and has manifested itself primarily in and through cultural means, suggests that the people involved in it have foregone the impetus towards self-determination through state citizenship, constructing a sense of cultural identity that rests on performances of difference.

Writing about Welsh identity in the early 1980s, in the aftermath of the 1979 referendum in which Wales voted against devolution, Raymond Williams remarks on a 'national feeling' that constitutes a kind of 'common perception' of Welsh identity as 'primarily cultural – in language, customs, kinship and community – rather than in any modern sense political.'[8] Even so, 'nationhood', though relegated to the realms of culture, perhaps due to the political situation at the time, is nevertheless understood to be a historical possibility and its revival is perceived to be, according to Williams, an almost inevitable social shift, a 'working through of history, among now radically dislocated as well as subordinated people, rather than the fortunate re-emergence of a subdued essence' (p. 22).

In a more complex consideration of the tripartite relationship of Wales, Britain and the people, Welsh philosopher J. R. Jones (1911–70) deconstructs the forces that bind these entities together as those of *gwladwriaeth* (state) and *cenedl* (nation). Jones defines human communities by a number of bonds, some of which are essential for binding people as national community: namely, a defined territory, the specific language or languages of the territory and the amassing of the territory under a sovereign state. According to Jones, a community formed by only two of these bonds – say territory and language – and lacking its own state systems, is a community of 'People', and the basis of their formation is 'the interpenetration' of language and land.[9] He outlines the meaning and the implication of this interpenetration between the external formational ties of space and the internal formational forces of a People's 'spirit' in terms of language as a bearer of tradition and heritage, rather than simply a means of communication. Consequently, the relationship of language and land can be explained in terms of a subjective interpenetration within people and an objective interpenetration in society. This view enables Jones to state: 'Tafell o groen naturiol y ddaear sy'n gorwedd rhwng Lloegr a Môr Iwerddon. Ynom y mae hi'n "Gymru".' ('It is a natural piece of the earth's crust that lies between England and the Irish Sea. It is within us that it is "Wales"').

Furthermore, he sees that the poetic tendency of the act of naming the land in Welsh culture reveals the way in which the ties of people and place are interwoven; 'it is as though they see and discuss and love the land through the mirror of their language.'[10] The 'mirror of their language' suggests a conscious playing out of the awareness of place in the cultural performances structured in and through language and leads to the assumption that language itself is understood as a performative stance. This is language operating in such a way that it represents the relationship of people and place, evoking a deep, embodied awareness of place as cultural construct.

While the establishment of the National Assembly for Wales in 1998 causes us to reflect again on Jones's definition of people and nation, perhaps forcing a partial re-definition of the argument in so far as we can say that Wales now has some of the operational structures of state, and operates (or does not) as 'nation' within the British Isles,[11] it is not an easy task to postulate as to the long term cultural impact of devolution, especially in terms of the impact on cultural and civic national identity.[12] Because of this, and mindful of the tensions between definitions of nation and people, I have chosen to adopt Homi K. Bhabha's word 'nationness' to refer to the binding social and cultural aspects that define a people or nation. This is nation 'constructed through and out of cultural text and context, and specific to its locality',[13] a distinct formation related to the cultural experience of a group of people in a particular location, defined further as a 'form of living the *locality* of culture'.[14] Expounding the idea of nationness as 'a form of social and textual affiliation', as opposed to a historicism that defines a people, nation or national culture as 'an empirical sociological category', Bhabha describes a category of thought that permits consideration of the strategies and methods of cultural identification by which a people (or a nation) are made the subjects of certain 'social and literary narratives' (p. 140). It is within the production of the nation as a process of narration that Bhabha perceives a division 'between the continuist, accumulative temporality of the pedagogical, and the repetitious, recursive strategy of the performative', stating that 'it is through this process of splitting that the conceptual ambivalence of modern society becomes the site of *writing the nation*' (pp. 145–6). Drawing on Anderson's concept of nation as imagined community Bhabha perceives the idea of the imagined community originating in the past and gliding 'into a limitless future', as well as its quality of historic newness, as proof of an inherent ambivalence in the idea of the nation. The pedagogical and the performative are conceptions that describe the ways in which the nation perceives itself as 'immemorial' as well as new. The pedagogical tendency is present in social practices and institutions that represent the nation as timeless, while the performative inclination is present in the representation of the nation in daily life; the former dictates what the nation is, while the later conveys or expresses it. The performative tendency is potentially disruptive, however, because the ambivalence of the situation has the potential for other cultural identities to emerge, and this is where Bhabha perceives an opportunity for minority discourse to enter into and interrogate the seemingly ironclad narrative of the nation state.

In this book, I use 'nationness' to refer to a sense of identity aimed for or revealed by certain performances of culture that are significant in relation to the binding of a community as people. The aim in this is not to obfuscate the desire for political determination, which I associate with the basic conditions of living and with the civic, but to linger on the performance of culture and the way it relates to ideas of nationness as embodied in people.

Cof: memory

Un funud fach cyn elo'r haul o'r wybren, un funud fwyn cyn elo'r hwyr
  i'w hynt
I gofio am y pethau anghofiedig, ar goll yn awr yn llwch yr amser gynt.
WALDO WILLIAMS[15]

Performances that are closely bound up with definitions of culture, such as the museum exhibit, the festival or the theatrical performance, serve a function as channels for the embodiment of culture in their audiences. The way this operates is complex and involves processes of remembering together, that is, ways of using memory in which certain groups are bound together. Performances that embody memory are at the centre of a people's collective memory, the memory between people that sustains their communal identity. This form of memory is repeatedly performed through speech, gesture and movement acts and in art formations. Social anthropologist Paul Connerton refers to such performances found in both traditional and modern societies as 'acts of transfer', in which communal memory is perpetuated through the experience of 'remembering in common', itself enabled through repetition (often in embodied forms) that capture knowledge of the past and images of the past in the form of performance.[16] This book attempts to analyse some examples of 'remembering in common' encapsulated in various cultural performances. In focusing on these acts of remembering we can examine the concept of performance as a network of relationships played out in order to sustain the memory of the group or community. The experience of culture as artistic or ritualised form, represented and lived through again and again in and through performance, provides distinct snapshots of the ideas and responses of a group of people at a certain time. These are glimpses of a community's ideas and beliefs in relation to their social group and of their ways of remembrance as a set of shared ideas, beliefs and meanings. Performance is a rich and diverse complex of bodily practices and customs that relate or retell what we might have lived through together as a group. What we might have 'lived through' is a reference to what we might share as collective memory, though collective memory is not only constituted of what might have been literally 'lived through', for it can also include that which has been transmitted through intergenerational memory, or according to the social structures that constitute 'tradition'.

The theory of collective memory put forward by Maurice Halbwachs (1877–1945) enables an analysis of the nature of cultural remembering and how this operates in terms of collective memory. Halbwachs's theory defines memory as being dependent on *cadres sociaux* (social frameworks), even in the case of what is perceived by the individual to be their own personal memory, which is, according to Halbwach's theory, part of a collective phenomenon of memory.[17] The theory of collective memory is based on two distinct points, firstly that collective memory is the memory of the individual and that it operates within a sociocultural context, and secondly that collective memory includes cultural transmission and the creation of tradition, or the formation and awareness of a shared past. According to the theory, we experience things as part of a specific social group and also bear witness or recall many shared experiences, as well as individual ones, in the context of a network of social relations which elevates itself from the material to the symbolic. This is how people generate symbolic imaginaries, ways of thinking and experiencing that are formed through language and other communicative practices and this is also how our memories are guided by social and cultural ways of thinking. Having established that shared memories are imperative for a group's cohesion, Halbwachs claims not only that memories establish a group's identity and unity, but that the group also has the effect of establishing and stabilizing memory. Accordingly, the dynamics of the group itself and whether it remains as a group are connected to the memory process. Should a group disperse then the memories that bind its members together would also be lost. In this context, it is social interaction that enables a group to retain its memories. In the process of ascertaining what keeps people together in groups, Halbwachs differentiates between history and memory, distinguishing between 'collective memory' and 'historiography', where collective memory works towards sustaining group identity, whereas history or historical memory work towards disarming notions of identity. While collective memories are plural, historical memory attempts to establish a singular framework; and while collective memory is involved in the continuation of tradition (i.e. no change), the historical is occupied with defining it.

In contemporary Western society, which appears to be driven by the idea of individual gain, the concept of communal memory might appear to be an archaic construct. Aleida Assmann reveals how this is an illusion, for once memories are linked between individuals and verbalised, then 'the individual's memories are fused with the intersubjective symbolic system of language and are, strictly speaking, no longer a purely exclusive and unalienable property.'[18] Assmann emphasises the importance of the externalisation of memory for its collective nature. That is, individual memories are bound up with language and images, and to such an extent that drawing a line between individual and communal memory is not only difficult but also problematical. In language, memories are pliable and we can confirm or dispute them; once written, they become part of the archive, making them accessible to a wider group.

In theatre and performance scholarship, memory emerges as a regular constituent of discourse, as it does in the practice of performance. This is rooted in theatre's essential use of time and the way in which time in the theatre is linked to the experience of being alive, reflected in Clov's repeated line in Beckett's *Endgame*, 'something is taking its course.'[19] Joseph Roach, having analysed definitions of performance from Victor Turner, Richard Bauman and Richard Schechner, comes to the conclusion that performance 'stands in for an elusive entity that it is not but that it must vainly aspire both to embody and to replace', which in turn results in 'the abiding yet vexed affinities between performance and memory, out of which blossom the most florid nostalgias for authenticity and origin'.[20] Elaborating on theorist-director Herbert Blau's dictum, 'Where memory is, theatre is',[21] Roach explains that performances carry within them 'the memory of otherwise forgotten substitutions'; that is, through performance, communities refer to their own past and thereby confirm who they are before others, which may also include a performance of who they are not (with reference to other cultures, nations, classes, races etc.). What is more, the form that these 'abiding yet vexed affinities' between performance and memory might take varies according to the cultural context of performance. Rather than merely referring to a substitution, theatre might also recall that which has disappeared, is absent or residual, a condition referred to by Marvin Carlson as a 'ghostly quality, this sense of something coming back in the theatre', which enables theatre to operate as 'the repository of cultural memory'.[22] Not only does theatre shift and change to the present circumstances, in a similar way to cultural memory, it is, according to Carlson, 'always ghosted by previous experiences and associations while these ghosts are simultaneously shifted and modified by the process of recycling and recollection' (p. 2). Reflecting on the dynamics of this theatrical ghosting, Carlson references Elin Diamond's emphasis on repetition in the terminology associated with performance. Diamond draws attention to the interdependence of performance and experience, elaborates on the preponderance of verbs that describe a re-visitation of events ('*re*member, *re*inscribe, *re*configure, *re*store') and reveals the fact that performance incorporates traces of previous, other performances and 'the possibility of something that *exceeds* our knowledge, that alters the shape of sites and imagines new unsuspected modes of being'.[23] Carlson's ghosting and Diamond's repetition point to the uniqueness of each performance as a distinct entity that binds together current and previous experience in a new moment of cultural reflection and understanding that is internalised as memory. The change in awareness instigated by performance, an understanding that is referred to as a transformation,[24] is described by Aleida Assmann as a memory (*Erinnerung*) process: 'Something internalizes itself in us, and only afterwards do we become conscious of it'.[25] While memory associated with knowledge and thinking, the cognitive aspect of memory, may be reproduced, the contents of this internalised memory process may never be so consciously reproduced or learned. This transformational awareness, when it happens, usually represents the apotheosis of the experience of performance and is ultimately affirming. This is because performance enables the participant to enter into a moment of time that is framed, where the awareness of temporality is heightened. It is in such moments of reflection that the interplay between past and present takes place. This is the space between tradition and memory, between life and death, so central to cultural performances. In the context of embodied practices and their significance for cultural identity, Diana Taylor defines performance as resting 'on the notion of ghosting, that visualization that continues to act politically even as it exceeds the live.'[26] Resisting the archival notion of capturing and encompassing the event, Taylor defines the moment of performance as a powerful concatenation of performer, performed and witness calling something into being, which she describes as 'a (quasi-magical) invocational practice. It provokes emotions it claims only to represent, evokes memories and grief that belong to some other body. It conjures up and makes visible not just the live but the powerful army of the always already living.' (p. 143) The idea of the memorialisation of the past through an evocation of living presence, whether in relation to the community who remember or a notional past presence, is a common thread in the commemorative cultural processes of many cultures. In Welsh-language culture, the formation of group identity in relation to cultural memory has been referred to as *cwmwl tystion* (cloud of witnesses), a concept probably taken from the biblical letter to the Hebrews in which the author refers to 'all these witnesses to faith around us like a cloud.'[27] Welsh philosopher J. R. Jones, in his essay on the idea of the nation, uses Waldo Williams's poem *Pa beth yw dyn?* (What is man?) as a starting point for deconstructing the way in which the concept of nation is created through memory: '*Beth yw bod yn genedl? / Dawn yn nwfn y galon. / Beth yw gwladgarwch? / Cadw tŷ mewn cwmwl tystion.*' (What is being a nation? A talent / Springing in the heart. / And love of country? Keeping house / Among a cloud of witnesses.)[28] According to Jones, 'keeping house among a cloud of witnesses' involves the process of *ymglywed*, a reflexive feeling of the past and an understanding of the relationship it has with the present and within daily life. His question centres on what it is that gives our life a separate identity and how it is that we follow our duties, conscious that this is a part of the daily existence of our own specific community of people. The answer is partly to be found in our daily space, or 'the theatre of our work', for in this territory, we 'keep house together',[29] and we do so in relation to our conception of the past: 'You keep your house surrounded by witnesses, not from flesh and blood, but a 'cloud of witnesses' – witnesses in the mind, witnesses from the past.' (p. 138). Thus, 'the cloud of witnesses' of a nation or people is its history. It provides the subject with a degree of certainty and stability and promotes the condition 'of working in the disappearing present, *as if under the gaze of the eternal past*; the idea that this generation was not left disconnected and without witness, *but that eyes from the past are looking at it*' (p. 138). What exactly are the witnesses from past generations witness to? For Jones, they are 'witnesses to who they are as a People – witnesses to their national identity. Here the past operates as a kind of memory' (p. 138). This type of memory is also to be found in examples of Welsh culture, and Jones refers to *Y Trioedd Cymreig* (The Welsh Triads), which operate as a form of memory for the people.[30] Wales's repertoire of culturally specific performative traditions, from the bardic tradition to the Eisteddfod, from oratory and preaching to ballad singing and *cerdd dant*, incorporates memory as a constituent element, as though the art form is a technology for memory, bringing it forth, declaring it and letting it form itself as part of the repertoire.[31] Here, memory takes on special properties as an art form, as is the case with most oral traditions, but it is also in the Welsh context firmly embedded into the written and embodied landscapes of literature. For Jones, *cof cenedl* (the memory of a people/nation) 'is a memory which is neither personal, individual, or genealogical, of the kind that binds a family together, but rather, a memory that spans the ages'.[32] Wary of the pitfalls of personifying the nation, Jones defines it as a collective entity, stating that in understanding 'memory' as the act of remembrance, it is not the nation that remembers, but rather the people who constitute it. Furthermore, national memory is not to be found in the process of remembering but in the content of that which is remembered. The secret of being a *cenedl* is somehow to 'stand within the track' of this history, for being outside it implies the ruin or decline of nationness: 'When the past of a People disappears from their view so that they are unable to know the pathway to it any more, they won't know from where they came, or what People they are. They won't have witnesses to who they are' (p. 139). According to Jones, there are two possible ways of resisting this decline and they both relate to ways of encountering the past: '*ymglywed echblyg*' (explicit feeling), to be found where people are fully aware of their cultural and historical context, and '*ymglywed ymhlyg*' (implicit feeling), involving the use of national symbols and in particular national and cultural institutions to mediate the national memory as a perpetual background to life (p. 140). In Jones's philosophy memory and place are inherent in the construction of a community of people and in defining nationness as a specific cultural marker of difference. In this process, memory and place do not operate as objective entities but rather as a web of symbolic formations, encapsulated in the phrase 'cloud of witnesses', folded together in an entanglement of people, memory and place, each one inextricably bound to the other. Operating in this context, performance is not necessarily bound to buildings and territories; rather, the way it is carried out insists on the importance of the situated nature of embodied practices. In seeking out performance composed of these interconnections between people, memory and place, one must be alert to the context in which such points of contact are made.

In an article on 'Welsh Culture' (1975) Raymond Williams seeks 'the real identity, the real culture' and states that it is worth walking around 'the Folk Museum at St Fagan's' with this question in mind. In the process of walking through the site, visiting the re-erected buildings from all over Wales, Williams explains how one can sense a connection with the past:

> Inside the houses are the old furniture, the old utensils, the old tools. You can touch the handle of a shovel and, closing your eyes, feel a life connecting with you: the lives of men and women whose genes we still carry; the labour now dissolved into what may seem a natural landscape of high field and culvert and lane.[33]

Here, access to Welsh culture is based on an empathetic connection with the people who have gone before us, represented – presented to us in their absence – in the vacant historical houses at St Fagan's National History Museum, where touching an artefact is a form of being in touch with our predecessors. Williams is referring to a nostalgic impulse that necessitates a performative gesture in order to get going and is not without criticism for this stance, which he counterpoints with the realisation of the place in which the museum is built: 'And then you look up at the big house on the mound, in whose park this image . . . has been rebuilt' (p. 5; in reference to St Fagan's Castle, historic summer home of the Earl of Plymouth, the family who donated the property and the land to Cardiff in lieu of death taxes). As an example of how place is associated with power, throwing its shadow over the culturally binding activity that takes place within it, this statement is an important reminder of the necessity of examining the relationships inherent in the performance of culture and of being alert to the wider context in which such performances take place.

Lle: Place

> 'There are places in Wales I don't go:
> Reservoirs that are the subconscious
> Of a people, troubled far down
> With gravestones, chapels, villages even'
> R. S. THOMAS[34]

It is not possible to consider culture as performance without examining ideas regarding the spatial and notions of place. The tangle of identity, cultural memory and emplacement is located in the concept of 'place', a space or site loaded with significance, which is sometimes contested and almost always problematical. I emphasise place rather than space because it represents the way through which we identify with each other and with our locality in the embodied practices of daily living – 'place' as space that has been made by us. This is 'embodied space' as referred to by anthropologist Setha Low, a space dependent on the material and conceptual interface of body, space and culture,[35] or as in Stuart Rockefeller's work and ideas, a locality constituted of movement patterns, where 'places . . . are not in the landscape, but simultaneously in the land, people's minds, customs, bodily practices'.[36] Embodiment plays a crucial part in the bearing of place on memory. According to philosopher Edward Casey, our understanding of ourselves is held together by reference to our memory of ourselves and of our relationships with other people, an understanding fundamentally rooted in conceptions of place. The answer to why it is that place can be so powerful in matters of memory is to be found in the centrality of the physical experience of living in and between places, in aspects of place 'in its landscape character', by which Casey is referring to the sensory experience of inhabiting space, a concept overlooked because of the preoccupation with time and the fixation with site. Casey refers to this fixation as the 'triumph of site over place', or 'place levelled down to metrically determinate dimensions', a stance that he charts from Descartes until the present day.[37] For Casey, the embodiment of remembering suggests that memory is located *in place*: 'As embodied existence opens onto place, indeed *takes place in place* and nowhere else, so our memory of what we experience in place is likewise place-specific: it is bound to place as to its own basis' (p. 182). Since bodily movements are our way of orienting ourselves in space, Casey sets outs to trace 'the corporeal basis of remembering' (p. 189), an approach that enables him to describe place as a 'mise en scène for remembered events', in which our memories are situated and in which they 'can deploy themselves' based on a recollection in *place* (p. 189). Developing from this, Casey introduces the concept of remembering as 'an activity of *re-emplacing*', that is, of re-experiencing past places, rather than re-experiencing the past in a more general sense, and of the body that remembers as 'a *body moving back in (to) place*' (p. 202).

In Welsh-language culture the relationship with place is often profoundly embodied and the emplaced body a recurrent motif, famously so in T. H. Parry Williams's poem 'Bro' (1954), where the poet imagines forward to his own death and, in the process, revisits his childhood home and conceives of his end as a fracturing of his own emplacement in and across the square mile of his upbringing. Here, memory is place itself and the cessation of memory in the poet's own death reveals itself as a scar on the lake and a crack in the schoolhouse wall, and so on: '*Mae darnau ohonof ar wasgar ar hyd y fro*' (there are pieces of myself scattered across *y fro*).[38] Similarly in Waldo Williams's poem 'Cymru'n Un', ('Wales as One'), the self becomes the locus of the nation: '*Ynof mae Cymru'n un. / Y modd nis gwn. / Chwiliais drwy gyntedd maith fy mod, a chael / Denuydd cymdogaeth – o'r Hiraethog hwn / A'i lengar liw.*' (In me Wales is one. / How, I know not. / All the fore-courts of my being I've searched, and found / The stuff of neighbourhood. From this longing one, so / Steeped in literature').[39] J. R. Jones's concept of the interpenetration of language and land also assumes an intrinsic and deep-rooted relationship between the land that has been inhabited (and therefore worked upon) for generations and the language spoken by those dwelling there. Its problematic aspect is that it negates more complex conditions of living and cultural and linguistic shifts, while its aim is actually to safeguard ways of life for a minority culture. The interpenetration of language and land should not be understood as a crude relationship of language to a point on the map. Rather, the idea points to the rootedness of the individual within community, and their actions, including language, that define place. Jones articulates a problem of belonging that is based on the need for home and roots as locations in time and space that repel meaninglessness. Perceiving the need to belong to people and place as fundamental aspects of the existential search for meaning,[40] Jones posits that being involves making space for oneself, with others. In a seminal essay problematising the 'need for roots', influenced by Simone Weil's writings,[41] Jones establishes that the need for roots exists as a consequence of the fact that humans have severed their closeness with Nature and are free to roam as 'a kind of refugee in the world of definitions of the possibilities of freedom'.[42] The metaphysical location of the need for roots is defined here as the perceived emptiness of human existence, an emptiness by which that existence is perpetually threatened. The human response, according to Jones, is to root oneself in the land of one's *cynefin* (habitat/home), in community, site of the perpetual carrying of the past, and in work. While Jones's concept of the interpenetration of language and land might be misread as essentialism, it could equally be applied to more complex formations of linguistic experience. Language can be positioned as an intrinsic facet of human interaction in space, as in Henri Lefebvre's theory of social space, where language is one of several fundamental human interactions that compose spatial practice. Here, language and land are not static or empty entities, but aspects of our social life charged with meaning. In Lefebvre's exploration of the production of space, space is never inert or transparent, it cannot be in a state of nature untouched by culture and, accordingly, there can be no such thing as an 'empty space':

> Vis-à-vis lived experience, space is neither a mere 'frame', after the fashion of a frame of a painting, nor a form or container of a virtually neutral kind, designed simply to receive whatever is poured into it. Space is social morphology: it is to lived experience what form itself is to the living organism.[43]

In this conception of social space, space is no longer a context for material action but rather a production of the self and the community according to the subject's views and ideas, a projection of the subject/community's identity, and a basis for social interaction at the same time. Thus, space is constituted of social relations and is also perpetually in the process of production: 'Spatial practice consists in a projection onto a (spatial) field of all aspects, elements and moments of social practice' (p. 8). As social practice is constantly unfolding in a continuous stage of becoming, so too is the space which depends upon it, and due to its political nature space cannot be considered or investigated as virtual abstraction:

> If space has an air of neutrality and indifference with regard to its contents and this seems to be 'purely' formal, the epitome of rational abstraction, it is precisely because it has already been the focus of past processes whose traces are not always evident in the landscape. Space has been shaped and moulded from historical and natural elements, but this has been a political process. Space is political and ideological. It is a product literally filled with ideologies.[44]

Political geographer Edward Soja takes the potentials of social/spatial awareness a step further and encourages a consideration of space as site of resistance, categorically refuting the idea of space as a neutral backdrop to any position.[45] It follows that any conception of 'our place', of our own location in the world, is important for our ability to counter the dominant discourses of power, and thus 'spatiality' is a descriptor for the ways in which the social, political and spatial are bound together and spring forth one from the other. Rather than shifting our focus to the realms of the global, such a stance encourages us to contemplate place as local, a standpoint advocated by historian Lucy Lippard in her emphasis on locally situated art. Lippard presents space as a text of all human experience, woven in a certain way in order to form place. She describes place as more than a familiar site, it is somewhere 'seen from the inside', a place that is known and inhabited, with deep meaning and significance.[46] Moreover, she considers identity to be a formation woven into 'place', tied to our relationship with places and the histories they embody. Arguing for a closer consideration of the role of places in the formation of our identities and cultural values, Lippard encourages a relationship to place as a means of countering the trends of the dominant capitalist culture, proclaiming 'the lure of the local' as

> the pull of places that operates in each of us, exposing our politics and our spiritual legacies. It is the geographical component of the psychological need to belong somewhere, one antidote to a prevailing alienation . . . that undertone to modern life that connects it to the past we know so little and the future we are aimlessly concocting. (p. 7)

This sense of place is 'entwined with . . . memory . . . a layered location replete with human histories and memories . . . It is about connections, what surrounds it, what formed it, what happened there, what will happen here' (p. 7), and its development and value through inhabiting is tied to the need for roots; 'the search for homeplace is the mythical search for the axis mundi, for a center, for some place to stand, for something to hang on to' (p. 27). Although this tendency can be read as nostalgic, it does not detract from the fundamental point that the distinctiveness of local cultures is homogenised or eradicated through the commodification of space in the expansion of capitalism, and that clinging to the rock of 'local' identity is one of the last acts of hope for anyone facing the deluge of cultural annihilation. Lippard provides one of the few creative stances from which to renegotiate our sense of place, one that is particularly pertinent for a consideration of place in the performance of culture.

The meshing of place and memory and its importance for cultural identity is also presented forcefully in Pierre Nora's concept of 'realms' or places of memory, discussed in his major work *Les Lieux de mémoire* (*Realms of Memory*), in which he attempts to locate the memory places that are critical for (in his case, French) national identity. These are realms that are both historical realities and imaginary representations, including geographical places, historical figures, monuments and buildings, literary and artistic objects, emblems, commemorations and symbols, all symbolic sites that are crucial to the formation of social and cultural identity: 'they are *lieux* – places, sites, causes – in three senses: material, symbolic, and functional . . . These three aspects of embodied memory . . . always coexist.'[47] Nora distances himself from history that is preoccupied with chronology and teleology above all else and explains how it is that memory (as opposed to history) takes on a 'variety of forms through which cultural communities imagine themselves in diverse representational modes'.[48] Reworking several of the key ideas found in Halbwachs's theory of collective memory, Nora explains that memory is dependent on social context and the act of remembering. Consequently, places of memory are determined by the composition of people constituting the social group. Outlining the reasons for our curiosity regarding those places 'in which memory is crystallized, in which it finds refuge', Nora centres on a turning point in French history and culture, 'in which a sense of rupture with the past is inexplicably bound up with a sense that a rift has occurred in memory'.[49] This rupture evokes a strong sense of memory, which is problematized by its inability to be lived through physically as a perpetuation of tradition: 'there are sites, *lieux de mémoire*, in which a residual sense of continuity remains. *Lieux de mémoire* exist because there are no longer any *milieu de mémoire*, settings in which memory is a real part of everyday experience.' (p. 1). Here, Nora describes the shift away from a place where traditional ways of life were once stable to a situation where the community's links with the past have been destroyed and ways of life are lost. Realms of memory are there to remind us of who we are, as we may no longer live within the 'track' or 'groove' of history as it has been recognised by those before us:

> When certain minorities create protected enclaves as preserves of memory to be jealously safeguarded, they reveal what is true of all *lieux de mémoire*: that without commemorative vigilance, history would soon sweep them away. These bastions buttress our identities, but if what they defended were not threatened, there would be no need for them. If the remembrances they protect were truly living presences in our lives, they would be useless. Conversely, if history did not seize upon memories in order to distort and transform them, to mould them or turn them to stone, they would not turn into *lieux de mémoire*, which emerge in two stages: moments of history are plucked out of the flow of history, then returned to it – no longer quite alive but not yet entirely dead, like shells left on the shore when the sea of living memory has receded. (p. 7)

As *lieux de mémoire* are rooted in the idea that there is no spontaneous memory any more, a plethora of institutional and national structures must be forged in order to sustain memory, such as archives, anniversaries and celebrations. Nora goes so far as to say that 'what we call memory today is therefore not memory but already history. The so-called rekindling of memory is actually its final flicker as it is consumed by history's flames. The need for memory is a need for history' (p. 8). Nora locates the French rupture in the 1930s and the crisis that ensued from the separation of state and nation. Though a different social and historical context, the idea of modernity breaking with tradition is equally applicable to Wales and its recurrent social and cultural crises. Historians such as John Davies, Kenneth O. Morgan and Gwyn A. Williams have described modern Welsh history as being comprised of deeply contradictory experiences, and of the Welsh people having to re-evaluate and redefine their history time and again, with each new iteration emerging from a crisis.[50] As a consequence of each process of re-definition, during which the foundations of identity have been shaken, we have become adept at enshrining symbols of nationness that represent a memory of what was, and often in relation to a way of living no longer inhabited or felt. This is particularly true in relation to symbols of resistance, even though they usually stem from significant political failures. Aleida Assmann writes of the sense of continuity that 'has been broken by conquest, loss, or forgetfulness' as one that 'cannot be retrospectively restored.'[51] Memory, however, is the medium through which we can connect with what has been lost:

> Places of commemoration – where something has been preserved from what has gone forever but can be reactivated through memory – are therefore markers of discontinuity. Something is still present here, but what this demonstrates above all is absence: the present relic denotes an irretrievable past. The sense of the past that arises from places of commemoration is quite different from that which pertains to the firmly established place of generational memory. The former is based on experience of discontinuity, and the latter on experience of continuity. (p. 292)

On the A487 roadside in Ceredigion, on the edge of the village of Llanrhystud, is the remaining gable end of a small cottage. Situated on a bend in the road passengers travelling north to south come face to face with the slogan written on the ruin: '*Cofiwch Dryweryn*' (remember Tryweryn). Tryweryn is the name of the river that ran through the valley of Cwm Celyn and the village of Capel Celyn, not in Ceredigion but in Merionethshire, north Wales, a significant distance away from

1. 'Cofiwch Dryweryn' on the gable-end wall near Llanrhystud.
Photo: Lisa Lewis.

the ruin. The entire Celyn valley, including the village, was flooded in 1965 for the creation by Liverpool Corporation of a reservoir to provide water to Liverpool. The local population of Capel Celyn, mostly tenant farmers, were forcibly evicted from their homes, a process recently described by judge and Labour peer Elystan Morgan as 'an act of rape'.[52] The fact that the people of Wales were powerless in the face of the political might of the English consensus in parliament (for not one Welsh MP supported the Tryweryn Bill through parliament)[53] fuelled both a Welsh protest culture and a political movement, and the charge that Tryweryn gave to a political consciousness in Wales is encapsulated in the inscription on the wall in Llanrhystud, which has since become an unofficial memorial.

The irony of Tryweryn is that the entire community was vanquished not in an open act of warfare, but within the everyday normative confines of British political 'democracy', and as a consequence even the possibility of direct generational memory, the experience of continuity, was forcibly removed from the community, whose members were relocated across the region. At the ruin, the slogan '*Cofiwch Dryweryn*'

31

compels us to remember the injustice, but it also refers to the ruin itself on which it is incongruously inscribed. It draws attention, by association, to the signs of a dilapidated community life, through a ruin that is situated over sixty miles away from the drowned valley. Capel Celyn represents the *milieu de mémoire*, the context in which memory lives and is transmitted between people. Its disappearance necessitates the inscription on the cottage wall as *lieu de mémoire*, which reminds us that not only was Capel Celyn destroyed, but that its way of life is continually lost in the present. Furthermore, the continual re-inscribing of '*Cofiwch Dryweryn*' is a *cri de coeur*, acknowledging the fact that living in line with a meaningful past has been made unviable by the effects of an encroaching and unremitting ideology that eradicates differences. The consequence of this is the destruction of Welsh as a living language in the most indiscriminate way. The phrase has subsequently become the catchphrase for the political consciousness that has since fuelled the move towards political self-determination in Welsh affairs. Thus, the graffito on the wall creates a place of commemoration, the kind that Aleida Assmann refers to as 'what remains when a tradition has ended and an event has lost its context', a place that depends for its survival on a 'story to support it that can replace the lost *milieu*'. And, in turn, the pieces of what remain are used 'to authenticate stories that in turn become reference points for a new cultural memory. The places require explanation, and their relevance and meaning can only be maintained through stories that are continuously transmitted.'[54] The writing on the wall is updated, restored or painted over and over again in an endless process of inscription, and a restoration that has a symbolic function. It is a performance that binds memory in place for a group of people who feel their existence is on the precipice, and thus the perpetrators of this graffito are caretakers rather than culprits.

In order to investigate how memory can be elicited through performance and place, the discussion in forthcoming chapters will navigate its way around distinct areas of culture in which the connection of place and memory intersects with performance. It will seek out discrete moments of performing Wales: in the museum and through heritage activities and exhibitions, in cultural festivals such as the National Eisteddfod and in theatre practice. Running through these cultural performances are issues closely bound up with conceptions of memory that underlie the construction of nationness as a social and cultural bind. These performances are associated with several different spheres and cultural and artistic forms, and they are forms of performance that are distinctly conducive for analysing the reflexivity within them. Museums (chapter 2), along with heritage and all its manifestations in sites, tours, tourism and historical recreations (chapter 3), construct history, they tell of events, peoples, places, pasts and cultural memories, and while historical accuracy and authenticity seems paramount, these are not strictly mimetic sites, objectively displaying history for all to see. Rather, they are made, constructed, placed together in a creation – *poiesis* – that is not necessarily neutral or objective. Relationships between memory, performance and the Museum are far from straightforward. Clearly implicated in the pursuit of memorialisation, the Museum may try its best to represent dissonant voices and memories and yet often projects a cohesive and authoritative picture that conveys, by default, the dominant way in which history is related.

Festivals (chapter 4), such as the National Eisteddfod of Wales, are a distillation of time in its most fleeting nature. The Festival may not hold on to cultural memory in what appear to be the most permanent or stable modes of performance and yet it incorporates and embodies cultural memory in one of the most apparently consistent ('pedagogical') ways, through repeated traditions that disclose the significance of embodiment in cultural memory. That the Festival space is fluid does not detract from the importance of place; here, contested standpoints can be played out within the flexibility of the Festival site, revealing the performative function of culture as a strategy for shifting or contorting the closed narrative upheld by the pedagogic strategies of the nation.

Theatre (chapter 5), as both social and aesthetic event, allows us to dwell and interpret special relationships between communal memory and place, and shows us something of the way in which memory is formed. It is a live practice in which memory is embodied and its analysis as an event provides an opportunity to investigate the constituent elements of theatre performance as inflections of memory. This is particularly true of late twentieth-century Welsh theatre performance, which consciously referenced memory and its processes, and embedded it into its aesthetics, making it a blueprint for early twenty-first century iterations of the relationship between people, memory and place. Whether this latter work is able to channel the same aesthetic implications regarding people, memory and place as did the former is discussed in the final chapter.

AMGUEDDFA: MUSEUM

2

In an article written in 1946, Iorwerth Peate (1902–82), Welsh scholar and poet and first curator of the Welsh Folk Museum at Sain Ffagan, explains that in the majority of European languages the word museum stems from the Greek *mouseion* – home of the Muses.[1] This is a word, in Peate's view, which provides an opportunity for a wide interpretation of the museum's purpose. The Welsh word, *amgueddfa*, does not refer to the seat or home of the Muses but rather to the place of treasures.[2] There is no final consensus on the term, however, and Peate draws on various definitions of *amguedd*, including Edward Williams's in *Cyneirlyfr* (1826), 'our dearest mysteries, our most valuable treasures, our chosen objects'.[3] The suffix '*fa*', denoting the place in which the treasures are kept, was added to *amguedd* in 1800. Despite the prevalence of *amgueddfa* in several dictionaries, numerous other nineteenth century dictionaries and journals had used *cywreinfa*, meaning place of curiosities or rarities (e.g. *y Gywreinfa Brydeinig* in reference to the British Museum).[4] The matter was apparently settled when the Council of the National Museum of Wales decided to adopt the term *amgueddfa* in 1907. Peate describes the use of the term *amgueddfa* as rather unfortunate, as the true value of the museum to society is considerably more extensive than the word suggests (or suggested at the time). According to Peate, the idea of a home for treasures or, in his own words, a 'storehouse of dead things' in which 'so and so's hat and so and so's walking stick' are to be found, is no longer sufficient for a museum that must be of value to the people of Wales.[5] Peate locates the museum's value in its ability to collect and interpret and make understandable to people in general the widest view of Wales, including its geology, biology, zoology, material culture and arts, all of which is underpinned by a strong research capability. Furthermore, Peate explains his belief in the importance of developing an aesthetic understanding in the arts and of creating an interest or curiosity in science and history, all crucial aspects of the museum's purpose, which is to be achieved through sponsorship of music, drama and film events at the museum. Such activities are essential because they would be pedagogical, but equally as important is the idea of taking the museum to the people, so that it is encountered as 'a live, dynamic institution, not a storehouse of dead artefacts locked away throughout the week'. It also needs to be a place where 'craftspeople would come to learn and artists to create', for 'our main work is to build the new Wales and not only to safeguard the old' (p. 16). Peate's view of the museum as essentially participatory, a place where Welshness is constructed as well as studied, places him (in 1946) in the vanguard of a progressive museology. This is not a commonly held view of Peate's work in the context of the critique of the Welsh folk movement and its initial realisation, which was perceived by some as a conservative portrayal of Welsh culture. Nevertheless, Peate's critique of *amgueddfa* as place of treasures is reflective of the tension between views of the traditional museum as static collection representing fixed culture, and the museum as an interactive place in which culture is to be interpreted between cultural participants, that is, in which the museum operates as performative. Underlying this tension are fundamental differences in the way the power relations implicit in modes of collecting, preserving and displaying are thought about and understood. For curators such as Peate, culture is located in the performance, a view that stands in opposition to the traditional mode of collecting and displaying, in which relationships between elements within the display and indeed, between that which is displayed, the owner of the display (the museum establishment or, historically, the aristocrat) and the visitor is encapsulated in a tableau of fixed relations. In this moment of stasis, the objectification at work in the display solidifies certain relationships; the static display is absolute and unquestionable as a representation of culture and dictates the nature of the relationship between the viewer and what it purports to represent. Within such a stringent network of relationships cultural memory is shaped by the identity politics of the exhibit itself. That is, we remember, collectively, what we are taught to accept as the object of display, as well as its meaning and implication for our identity, both as individuals and as a people. The interactive, performative mode, on the other hand, has agency, and enables an emergent understanding of culture in the collaborative act between performers and witnesses. Both conceptions of the museum, what we might call the static and the enactive modes, engage with memory in different ways, and this difference has significant implications for the way in which cultural identity is formed in relation to the museum. The critique of the Welsh Folk Museum at Sain Ffagan, discussed further below, is reflective of different views appertaining to the way in which 'Wales' is projected and received, or performed, in the museum context. Before discussing Sain Ffagan in more depth, I want to look at the way in which the museum operates as social space, and to examine the knot of relations between spatial practices in the museum and the theatre. This deliberation is essential for understanding how the museum operates performatively.

Traditionally, the museum pieces fragments together in a spatial machine that stages the entire collection, ensuring a readable context that renders fragments relevant, explains their meaning and significance and provides order through categorisation. The museum's exhibitionary dynamics is organised according to ideas of cultural display and the power relations embedded in them, and the significance of that which is disclosed is as important as that which is not (missing elements, aspects not addressed, or artefacts kept behind closed doors), as is the contextualisation and re-contextualision of exhibits. Barbara Kirshenblatt-Gimblett elaborates on how meaning at the museum is created by means of the exhibition emplacing together objects taken from their former contexts and displaying relationships between them that would not otherwise be seen. In this way, exhibitions are 'fundamentally theatrical, for they are how museums perform the knowledge they create.'[6] From this point of view, museums are not passive receptacles for the display of historical artefacts, but rather sites charged with the meanings structured by narratives and histories conveyed by the placement of objects in space. Anthropologist Richard Handler refers to this presentation of material culture in the museum as an 'objectification' of culture and identity, displayed in such a way that the very existence and presentation of artefacts seems to point to the reality of the people, nation or culture that made it.[7] This is further substantiated by the spatial nature of the exhibition and the modes of seeing it engenders. The concept of 'world as exhibition' and its manifestation in nineteenth-century exhibitions and fairs established the objective gaze, a way of seeing that represented the authorised discourse behind the exhibit, which also taught the onlooker to receive this authority and to value it as reality. Thus, the techniques of organisation in use in the nineteenth-century museum seemed to reflect self-evident truths presented as though inherent in the artefacts themselves, an aspect that has been elevated by the role the museum has played apropos the nation. Sharon Macdonald writes of the museum's role in representing and projecting nation-state identity in relation to the idea of nation as imagined community. She reveals that 'individual identification with the nation-state couldn't rest on experienced social relations', and that therefore it had to be cultural, 'a matter of shared knowledge and practice, of representation, ritual and symbolism'.[8] Consequently, the concept of having a culture, critical to nationalist discourse, was adopted quickly by museums, which became '"national" expressions of identity' and evidence of 'having a history – the collective equivalent of having an identity' (p. 3). In this way, the nineteenth-century museum established itself as a 'material performative' and its 'physical presence performed national and civic identity and pride' (p. 11). What is more, in its portrayal of material culture as evidence of national distinctiveness, the museum not only projected what is staged within as a collection of national possessions belonging to members of the national community, it performed this in such a way that national identity could be objectified. The exhibition reflects that which is apparently an inherent reality through the objective presentations of the artefacts displayed, a scientifically objective way of seeing what Macdonald refers to as 'a gaze which could "forget" its own positionedness' (p. 5). In referring to this 'performance complex', Macdonald asks the question whether museums in Western Europe, in the context of the shift away from nation-state identity, have become too 'entangled in "old" forms of identity to be able to express "new ones"' (p. 1). The concept of 'the gaze that could forget its own positionedness' reveals the museum's deep-seated involvement in the construction of history, and the problematising of the objective gaze in relation to the nineteenth-century museum's narrative of history. It also exposes the role of theatrical invention in the process of constructing history. According to Donald Preziosi and Claire Farago, museums use 'theatrical effects' in order to 'enhance a belief in the historicity of the objects they collect.'[9] Here, the phrase 'theatrical effects' is used to signify a set of exhibitionary premises that work to inculcate a sense of history, culture and society being 'just so', according to the apparent authenticity of the representation before us, as though it were unquestionable. In this context museums are collections that preserve and conserve the 'fragments and relics of the past', staging them in a way that enhances their 'facticity', which is 'clearly a matter of a certain style of presenting things in what in a given time and place may be *legible as* factual.' (p. 13). That is to say, facts are seen to be facts under the conditions in which they are presented and received as such. Underlying this representation is a concept of the world as imaginary structure that is separate from external reality; the world is a picture, and the human being its subject – a view that appears to be self-evident. In Preziosi and Farago's analysis, theatre is situated as a form of illusion and pretence (the representation of something but not the thing itself), associated with the process of establishing and projecting 'historical truths' in the museum exhibit. Preziosi claims in a further article that 'the stagecraft and the dramaturgy of the modern museum' is rooted in 'two and a half millennium long history in Europe of instrumental technologies of what had once been called the "arts of memory," addressed to the production, formatting, storage, and retrieval of knowledge using material objects and their assemblages.'[10] Secondly, he claims that the museum's dramaturgy is based on a history of 'philosophical and religious controversies often distilled into legally-enforced doctrines, regarding the proper meanings and functions of objects in individual and social life' (p. 82). As a consequence, the museum produces knowledge by staging a network of associations between objects in such a way as to assume connections between them, which Presiozi refers to as 'fielding relationships amongst objects that ostensify individual and collective human relationships' (p. 82), underpinning the belief in the existence of that which the museum purports to signify, such as the spirit, character or mind-set of a people or nation. Subsequently, we need to approach and understand the museum as a place that exists in order to manufacture and sustain belief in the collection and what it is implying in the way it is presented or staged. Preziosi suggests that, in acknowledging this fact, we be mindful of falling in to the trap of 'ghost-catching', that is, of going along with the assumption that national narratives exist outside the institutions and events in which they are being staged, as though such narratives are absolute and pre-exist the institutions that perform them. Rather, we should acknowledge the fact that such narratives are 'co-constructed and co-evolving', and further, that this offers a chance to 'interrogate assumptions made about representation itself' (p. 83). Furthermore, in asking whether museum narratives are successful due to their theatrical or dramatic effectiveness, Presiozi raises questions regarding the implications of such effectiveness in relation to 'truth-value' (p. 86). This assertion goes to the core of the way in which meaning is created in the museum context and raises the question of whether the apparent value of an exhibit is produced by a theatricality that projects it.

The idea that theatre is a false and inauthentic medium harks back to an antitheatrical prejudice that since Plato's time has associated performance with fakery. It is also, specifically in the museum context, associated with the use of nineteenth-century European theatre techniques that influenced a multitude of exhibitionary ventures such as the museum, which adopted the nineteenth-century theatre's mimetic mode. Historically, the museum has borrowed from the theatre since its inception as a public institution, when theatrical modes of presenting were used in order to display people and objects, and theatre crafts such as scene painting were employed for exhibits and staged performances, as in the case of the diorama, a nineteenth-century mobile theatre device taken up by the museum for model display. Invented by Louise Jacques Maude Daguerre (1787–1851), the designer and painter of stage illusions, and Charles Marie Bouton (1781–1853), the diorama emerged in Paris in 1822, and conveyed a theatrical experience via a specially adapted rotating stage depicting dramatic landscapes, painted so as to reflect a gradually changing scene that seemed to come alive before the stationary audience. The diorama is an example that reveals the shared history of both museum and theatre as part of a network of performance sites connected with history and memory that operate according to certain principles relating to the presentation of material and the subject's reading of it.

Tony Bennett argues that the museum's formation needs to be seen in relation to the development of a range of cultural institutions, including the theatre and the fairground, which over time have become disconnected.[11] In his seminal book *The Birth of the Museum* (1995), Bennett locates the museum as part of an 'exhibitionary

complex' developed during the nineteenth century, within which neither the museum movement nor the museum itself should be seen as
isolated or discrete phenomena, but rather as part of a wider complex
of sites, techniques of display and immersive landscapes that emerged
in relation to each other. In Bennett's view, the opposition between different sites was part of the discourse of differentiation through which
the museum came into being in its nineteenth century form, with
laws such as the Museum Act of 1845 and the Public Library Act of
1850 passed in order to bolster notions of order in a period of reform
and as a general counteraction to the 'disorder' of workers' uprisings.
Proclaiming the museum as site of all that is rational and scientific
was partly achieved by ensuring that competing exhibitionary institutions were denounced on account of their 'disorder'. Early museum
reformers' writings on the importance of classification and scientific
objectivity were also important in establishing the museum as a pedagogical imperative for civilizing the masses. Yet the fair, the travelling
menageries and similar fleeting or moveable festivities persisted, forming an environment against which the Museum 'sought to extricate
itself.' These festive and transitory events 'confronted – and affronted
– the Museum as a still extant embodiment of the "irrational" and
"chaotic" disorder that had characterized the Museum's precursors'.[12]
Of those precursors, the late eighteenth- and early nineteenth-century
fair, in particular, was an embodiment of the disorderly forms of
conduct associated with sites of popular assembly, which the development of the public sphere was designed to eradicate. Techniques
of crowd control used in museums and exhibitions were later used
in amusement parks towards the end of the nineteenth century, in an
attempt to subdue the behaviour of fairgoers on one fixed site, where
the experience was not of the fleeting moment but more similar to
walking through a landscaped garden, park or museum, all sites that
became spheres of regulation.[13] That this happened alongside the role
of the Museum in the formation of the bourgeois public sphere was
not accidental; the construction of the public sphere necessitates its
opposing negative, the popular and unruly assembly, and herein lies
the source of the differentiation that is central to Bennett's analysis.[14]
As a 'reformatory of manners', the Museum was designed in a way
that had a civilising effect on the visitor, facilitating the orchestration
of social behaviour in both general and literal movement through its
galleries:

The superimposition of the 'backtelling' structure of evolutionary narratives on to the spatial arrangements of the museum allowed the museum – in its canonical late-nineteenth-century form – to move the visitor forward through an artefactual environment in which the objects displayed and the order of their relations to one another allowed them to serve as props for a performance in which a progressive, civilizing relationship to the self might be formed and worked upon. (p. 186)

Museums became public and social spaces and, eventually, places of representation and of regulation, where the visitor's body had to conform to new norms of public conduct. And although the delight of the museum curio was still present in amongst the scientific intent, it was hidden behind a veil of appropriate decorum. In this way the museum extricated itself from popular entertainments and participated in the construction of the nation state and of national identity, not only through the ideological content of the exhibition, but also through a new politics of participation, producing new habits and patterns of behaviour for its subjects under the guise of what Philip Fisher refers to as, 'the democratization of treasure'.[15] In this process the artefacts and the witness were given specific roles that developed in discrete ways throughout the nineteenth century and well into the twentieth. It isn't until the latter half of the twentieth century that we see a detailed critical awareness of this complicity, described by Helen Rees Leahy as 'the reproduction of unequal social and cultural relations' brought about through the museum.[16] Analyses, such as Peter Vergo's *The New Museology* (1989), Ivan Karp and Stephen D. Lavine's *Exhibiting Cultures: The Poetics and Politics of Museum Display* (1991) and Eilean Hooper-Greenhill's *Museums and the Shaping of Knowledge* (1992), expound on methods of compensating for past and present exclusions in museum representation and practices through expanding access and establishing collaborative practices.[17] *The New Museology*, in particular, pits a new museum paradigm against the museum practices concerned with an authoritative or dominant ideology. This new model asked questions regarding traditional museum approaches to notions of value, meaning, interpretation, representation and authority, and was accompanied at the time by a complex of disparate ideas brought from differing fields, most contentiously, business management models and the adoption of entertainment-led approaches, or what was often referred to as 'Disneyization', perceived as critical for the long-term sustainability of the museum.[18] Within this new model there is a tension between what was seen to be a call for participation and collective ownership of the museum and its story, and an implied dumbing down through the emphasis on popular forms and 'entertainment'. It is in this context that the use of 'live interpretation', including museum theatre, expanded as a medium in Wales and in the countries of the British Isles in the late 1980s, and what was perceived as an experimental interpretative form in the 1970s, emerged as a staple of museum programmes, especially where the focus was on becoming more audience-focused. Within these practices of interpretation, the concept of collective memory as enactive process is brought to the fore. The contentious range of practices defined as interpretive, however, have been perceived as no more than a frivolity in many cases, and attracted criticism for their popularisation of the visitor's experience, as Helen Rees Leahy explains:

> The source of much of this criticism is found in the broad range and quality of work variously described as 'museum theatre', 'living history', 'costumed interpretation' or 'live interpretation'. At one end of the spectrum, performance is certainly deployed more as a marketing tool and a crowd-pleaser than as a serious educational tool . . . the term living history is an umbrella beneath which shelters a range of practices that divide both museum staff and their visitors into two camps; on one side, there are those who regard such activities as legitimate and enjoyable means of enlivening a staid institution; on the other side are those who argue that playacting has no place within the authoritative frame of the museum.[19]

The move away from static museum display towards the visitor's immersion in an experience involving a sensory and emotional engagement heralded a crisis. Would museums tackle the emphasis on lives so as to engage the imagination in a way that might deepen historical understanding and personal and social identity? Or would the emphasis on service culture and the production of an 'experience' reduce historical understanding to such an extent that the museum becomes nothing more than historical amusement park, or at best, a place for nostalgic reminiscence? Museum audiences have grown exponentially since the development of participatory story-based interactions, and the problematizing of this medium might have more to do with the loss of hegemonic modes of display and the development of cultural uncertainties (which in turn reflect the decline of the project of the nation-state), than with the process of popularisation in and of itself.

More recently, there has been a renewed emphasis on engaging people as cultural participants as opposed to cultural consumers. Nina Simon has outlined the ideas central to a cultural institution becoming participatory: that of an audience-centred institution being as 'accessible as a shopping mall or train station'; the notion that visitors 'construct their own meaning' from cultural experiences; and the central point, that 'users' voices can inform and invigorate programs'.[20] The renewed emphasis on social engagement, on community involvement at core levels, and on broad cultural understanding in the museum display has had a profound influence on the way contemporary participatory museums are constructed, both as social spheres of interaction, and literally in terms of their architecture and spatiality. Museums are increasingly being designed and built in ways that incorporate some of the most fundamental issues relating to a change in their significance and meaning. Michaela Giebelhausen argues that 'the architecture is the museum: it is precisely the architectural configuration that gives the museum meaning. The architecture determines the viewing conditions both conceptually and physically. It not only frames the exhibits but also shapes our visitor experience.'[21] In museums built to represent their meanings, personal and collective memory becomes an increasingly important factor in the understanding of history. Such museums, built as experiential sites that incorporate the philosophy and significance of the museum into the aesthetics of the building, facilitate a kinaesthetic understanding of history in relation to a personal experience. The Jewish Museum Berlin, for instance, which opened in 2001, is devoted to the principle of site, space, history and building as a philosophical meeting point, as its architect Daniel Liebskind explains: '[it is] conceived as an emblem in which the Invisible and the Visible are the structural features which have been gathered in this space of Berlin and laid bare in an architecture where the unnamed remains the name which keeps still.'[22] In philosophically loaded statements such as these, Liebskind attempts to pry open the relationship between site, place and physical and aesthetic experience of space, history, memory and identity. The museum space is designed to encourage a physical journey in which the visitor experiences emotionally some of the key notions underlying the architecture. Built along three axes, forming a crossroads between 'the axis of exile and emigration', 'the axis of the holocaust' and 'the axis of continuity', the visitor is offered several directions that determine their experience of the museum. The axis of exile and emigration ends in a disconcerting garden where the floor undulates around forty-nine pillars. The axis of the holocaust leads the visitor into a concrete cell, open to the sky, with a metal ladder embedded out of reach in the concrete wall. The third axis, of continuity, leads the visitor up a white staircase into a collection representing the Jewish history of Berlin since the Middle Ages, where each floor is punctuated by 'memory voids', 'empty' spaces that host installations, such as the artwork *Shalechet* (Falling Leaves) by Israeli artist Menashe Kadishman, in which the floor is covered by thousands of small iron pieces, similar to padlocks, on to which faces have been engraved or scratched. Orientating oneself inside a structure that is designed as a fractured Star of David, with so much happening physically and emotionally, the visitor clings to the views of the city outside through the window slits placed at incongruous angles. Liebskind elaborates on this re-framing of our sensibilities as 'our perception of space and structure, and of our own vantage point' being 'no longer a matter of course', but rather, 'a new experience' (p. 57). Similarly, the presence of the National Museum of the American Indian (NMAI), which opened in 2004, on the National Mall in Washington DC, is made all the more unique by its striking architecture and mission history. The entire building and collection was conceived, designed and curated by Native peoples from the Western Hemisphere, and its architecture incorporates Native philosophies and sensibilities into the building itself.[23] On entering, the visitor is struck by the round open space – a symbolic circle demarcated by changes in floor colouring, encircled by a round sitting area for approximately 300 people and enclosed by a bronze basket-weave fence. This is a performance space, rarely empty, around which a circular movement of visitors turns, and the living heart of the building, holding the site together. It is at once a civic space and one of celebration, protest, and lamentation (where ceremonies for the repatriation of remains are performed). In one respect, it appears as though there is nothing here as one enters; there are no collections of artefacts until the visitor ascends to the second and third floors, and even then, the premise of the collection is the articulation of living cultures by native communities, for these are items subsumed by a sense of living culture, continuity and 'survivance'.[24] The museum functions as a forum for debate, a site for performances of solidarity between minorities, and the starting point for rallies and marches by American Indians, at the very heart of the American capital and within view of the US Capitol Building.

The new museum's move towards the immersive, kinaesthetic experience and the forum for change places it in the realm of the site-specific, where meaning takes place in and through interactions between human and non-human agents, including the site itself. As such it appears to problematise the modern museum as bounded site where meanings are fixed rather than contingent, though interactive and immersive aspects are not without precedent in the history of the modern museum. Indeed, the European folk museum movement, which emerged in the 1890s in Scandinavia, with its emphasis on cultural process as much as product, has greatly influenced the museum as cultural site.[25] Despite its roots in the Romantic Movement and the centrality of concerns regarding the preservation of national culture that has been so pervasive in the movement as a whole, the folk museum as a site has operated sophisticated modes of interpretation based on participation, partly as a consequence of its investment in the creation of a national culture. The folk museum site and the nature of its large-scale outdoor exhibit, usually encompassing a range of buildings and artefacts in an approximate representation of how they 'once were', complicated the relationship between the museum as collection and museum as interactive site. While the buildings constitute the collection, and artefacts (often reproduced) are emplaced in an apparently holistic display context within them – staged in order to be read as if they were remnants of a national identity already implied by the museum – the meaning gained from the museum exhibit is predicated on interaction with the exhibit itself. In this process, the participant has a certain agency, and the exhibit is open to a degree of interpretation, even if the content of the display is strongly prescribed. In this performative relationship, which plays out with fluidity between participants on the open site, changes are enabled in the parameters of the museum experience and the understanding and representation of identity at the museum is open to negotiation.

In Wales, Sain Ffagan Amgueddfa Werin Cymru, or in English, St Fagan's National Museum of History, hereafter called Sain Ffagan, the first folk museum in mainland Britain, which opened on 1 July 1948, and one of the seven museums across Wales that now comprise

Amgueddfa Cymru (National Museum Wales), includes an open-air site with buildings removed from their original locations throughout Wales, each one restored, rebuilt and set as it might have been during a particular period in its lifespan.[26] The range of buildings and the museum setting might point to a specific historical interpretation of a people and their history, but the site itself is pliable, and open to a variety of interpretations and responses, as the history of performance at this museum reveals. This is partly due to the museum's site-specificity – by which I do not refer explicitly to the relocated houses taken from elsewhere, but rather to the place itself, which is a palimpsest, making Sain Ffagan a remarkable museum in terms of the way it performs the relationship of people, memory and place.

Sain Ffagan Amgueddfa Werin Cymru / St Fagan's National Museum of History: people, memory and place

> Nid oes a'm hetyb ond tipiadau'r cloc
> Ai oddi cartref pawb? . . . dic doc, dic doc.
> Iorwerth Peate, 'Y Gegin Gynt yn yr
> Amgueddfa Genedlaethol'.[27]

People

Writing in 1948, to mark the tercentenary of the Battle of St Fagan's, Iorwerth Peate optimistically describes the success of the campaign to establish the Welsh Folk Museum in terms of 'a new security for Welsh culture'.[28] In *Amgueddfeydd Gwerin / Folk Museums* (1948), he writes about the importance of portraying the ways of life of a people and of instilling in them awareness and pride in a shared identity: 'the chief aim of all men called to service in museums is . . . to awaken the best in the national spirit' (pp. 10–11). The notion of a national spirit, the means by which a people pass on their traditions and their culture to successive generations, along with the idea of a common language as a binding force and a defining factor in making a people distinct, were central concepts in the formation of the field of folklore in the late nineteenth century. Anthropologist Richard Bauman writes of the emergence of the concept of folklore as part of a 'unified vision of language, culture, literature and ideology'[29] that served romantic nationalism, and explains how folklore as a discipline has been defined through history 'in terms of a principal focus on the traditional remnants of earlier periods, still to be found in those sectors of society that have been outdistanced by the dominant culture.'[30] He refers to Raymond Williams's association of folklore with latent yet enduring cultures: 'experiences, meanings and values which cannot be verified or cannot be expressed in terms of the dominant culture, [but] are nevertheless lived and practiced on the basis of the residue – cultural as well as social – of some previous social formation.'[31] In this context, the study of folk culture was part of a progressive movement by intellectuals, one which is described by Peter Burke as 'a revolt against the centre by the cultural periphery of Europe . . . towards self-definition and liberation in regional or national terms.'[32] What might have been at one time progressive, however, had, by the end of the nineteenth century, partly fallen into a predictable form based on a romantic tendency to look to the past.[33] Mark Sandberg reflects on this shift in relation to the Scandinavian model and suggests that folk museums appear to be at the 'opposite end of the cultural spectrum from spectacles associated with modernity', emphasising a nostalgic drive and a desire 'for simpler, more coherent cultural forms in a time of rapid urbanization, industrialization, and commodification.'[34] Not only was the Scandinavian model the prototype for a Welsh folk museum, but the idea of focusing on the traditional forms of culture prior to industrialisation as an essential part of the safeguarding of culture was prevalent in Peate's writings around the establishment of Sain Ffagan. These writings reveal the drive towards defending the nation from the onslaught of mechanical progress and the seemingly inevitable decline of civilisation that might follow. Folk culture or folklife is implicit in this process because it is a representative of the smaller ways of life that stand against the monopoly of commerce, big business and industry and the subsequent erosion of tradition:

> The present 'push towards barbarism' (a fair definition of the age of the machine) represents the dissolution of civilization, the regular emigration from the countryside and the great wart-like growth of suburbia. But the machine the development of our towns is based upon, or the automatism, will not create tradition. That which is handed down from generation to generation is the multitude of basic skills that belong to individual men. We are concerned with skills, with the handmade, with spiritual belief, with the pre-megalopolitan. Our present mechanical civilization is not absolute . . . My belief is that if our civilization

is to be saved, the study of the 'small tribe', its social order, its abilities, its spiritual beliefs and aspirations, will play an essential part in its rescue.[35]

The folk museum was therefore to involve itself with 'pulling man out of barbarism', equated with urban progress, and was ultimately to be a place that was to have a civilising effect (pp. 22–3). Rather than being a repository of middle-class manners, Peate's museum was idealised as a space in which the visitor would bear witness to the ideal of *gwareiddiad mewn natur* (civilisation in nature), represented by the folk ways of the pre-industrialised Welsh people. The aim was to safeguard culture from the homogenising onslaught of certain social factors relating to commercial and industrial developments.[36] It is possible to read this as a form of nostalgia, manifested in a compulsion to dwell on pre-industrialised rural traditions and crafts and aspects of culture unaffected by heavy industry, as well as the social context that accompanied it, but this would be far too glib a response to Peate's work. If the history of a people before the advent of the industrial revolution is so critical to a certain portrayal of life and culture, one needs to ask why exactly this is. Peate was not drawing a blunt line in the sand between pre-industrial and industrial history, or concocting a portrayal of the people as a rural Welsh-speaking peasantry on the one hand, and on the other a hardened, industrial society in which the Welsh language was in decline. The Welsh Folk Museum project was an attempt to represent the people of Wales before the industrial revolution, a period of history that represented a cataclysmic shift in their belief systems and cultural values. Historian Kenneth O. Morgan writes of the buoyancy of Welsh culture in the final decades of the nineteenth century, the vitality of the linguistic community and its role as the language of debate and discussion, and the apparent strength of the Nonconformist culture inextricably linked to the language, residing alongside other social factors that threatened to undermine Welsh language and culture. This explains in part Peate's compounding of 'national spirit' with the Welsh language and his emphasis on the museum's role in educating and enlightening, so that people who may not have recourse to traditional folkways of Welsh life, including the Welsh language and all that it represents, could be provided with the opportunity to learn about it. While the number of Welsh speakers was higher in 1900 than ever before, census information showed that it was decreasing consistently as a percentage of the population. Between 1880 and 1930 the decline of the language and culture across the most populated areas of the country was critical. In 1800 Wales was an agricultural country with a population of approximately 500,000; by 1911 it had been utterly transformed into an industrial and in some areas a heavily urbanised country with a population over 2,500,000.[37] This is even more striking when we consider the industrialised areas alone; for example, the population of Glamorgan grew by 253 per cent between 1861 and 1911, a shift reflected in the linguistic change that took place from a primarily Welsh-speaking population to a majority English-speaking one. The same could be said in regard to religion, as Nonconformist culture was slowly secularised from the inside, as it were, and gave way by the end of the 1930s to a materialistic humanism. This decline in the Welsh language and in Nonconformity was compounded by the efforts of the Welsh people to conform to ideas of liberal respectability, partly in response to the damning indictment of the Royal Commission into Education in Wales (1847) – the Blue Books, which painted Welsh culture as backward or semi-civilised, a position that was inadvertently assimilated by the Welsh people. The Blue Books report was itself a response to the encroaching sense of Welshness as a threatening difference felt by the British establishment following a series of social and political revolts across Wales in the early nineteenth century, a difference that was encapsulated in the Welsh language. One of the responses to the Blue Books' portrayal of the Welsh was the position assumed by the Nonconformists, who assimilated the ideal of *y werin bobl*, the moral, cultured (and classless) folk. This course entailed a performance of Welshness that located its authenticity in the rural, in Nonconformity and in simple living represented by the Welsh cottage, or *bwthyn*, the dwelling place in which tradition was not only passed down but represented by the space itself – in its very walls and the techniques used to build it. It is described by Daniel G. Williams as 'the sacred space in which the assumed characteristics of the Welsh – particularly their religion and the language – were preserved and transmitted', and is encapsulated in the popular nineteenth century folk song, 'Y Bwythyn Bach To Gwellt' (The Little Thatched Cottage), which came to represent for the Welsh émigré to the industrial heartlands the very essence of the Welshness that they had left behind.[38] The mythology of the *gwerin*, which arose from the differentiation between rural living and the demographic shift to the centres of industry is, however, far removed from the research into rural communities and their ways of life that Peate spent the greater part of his life completing. This was a lifelong study that acknowledged, in an almost autoethnographic way, the centrality of his own upbringing as a native of Llanbrynmair in Powys and a product of 'Traddodiad Llanbrynmair' (the Llanbrynmair tradition), a radical tradition in which a spirit of independence thrived. Connected with the Independent branch of Nonconformity, the tradition celebrated the basic Christian principles of freedom and love, though in accordance with its independent nature it was not dogmatically aligned with religion per se. Peate was also highly conscious of his own displacement from his native square mile, a move that he associated with the burgeoning Welsh middle class:

> For the first time in its long history, Wales developed a middle class of 'black coats', the children of rural craftsmen and farmers who turned their backs on their fathers' world and expected an easy life in the world of town and industry. I, being one of them, do not blame them. It was not their fault. Their society did not call for their services in rural life and there was no future for them in it. But the truth is that the rural life has been bled almost to death.[39]

It was this awareness that paved the way for a fraught and contradictory experience of Welshness presented at the Welsh Folk Museum, which was to represent and encapsulate the rural Wales forsaken by those who were dislocated from their square miles. Peate's life work, the elevation of folk culture and of museum studies in Wales, was a consequence of this impulse to embody that which was being lost. This was not a regressive stance. In relation to the effects of industrialisation, Peate made an interesting comparison between the situation in Wales and in England. The middle classes were not a new phenomenon in England, which also had laws protecting the English language. In Wales, on the other hand, 'the machine grew stronger than man in a country where there was no legal support for his language'.[40] Fully acknowledging that no culture is static, a matter which he discusses in detail at the beginning of his book *Diwylliant Gwerin Cymru*, Peate was staring squarely at the crisis facing Wales as a consequence of the fundamental changes being wrought to its culture and society since the advent of mass industrialisation.

One of Peate's main contributions, *The Welsh House*, is an investigation of the Welsh folk dwelling and how it 'varies according to the climatic and geographical conditions of the locality in which it is found *and also according to the social condition of its occupant or builder and his economic status*'.[41] Peate does not attempt an analysis of a particular kind of architecture; rather, he focuses on the houses of the people – all the houses, of all times, that belong to the people of Wales (pp. 4–5). He writes with precision and detail and presents several hypotheses, some of which have since been disproved, such as his theory on the development of the longhouse.[42] There is no connotation of the folk as a sweeping, romanticised category of people here, however, and Peate emphasizes the comprehensive view of folk (*gwerin*) as signifying all people. Nevertheless, the problematics of the term folk have haunted the museum at Sain Ffagan and have forced a trajectory of evolving names, finally arriving at a point where the museum's English name is National Museum of History, while the Welsh remains steadfastly Amgueddfa Werin Cymru ('Welsh Folk Museum'). This difference is partly located in the difference of meaning between the Welsh word *gwerin* and the English *folk*. Peate was apparently the first to use the term 'folk culture' in a British context (in the paper 'Welsh Folk Culture', 1932), and must have felt considerable responsibility for its use (and what he designated its misuse).[43] He remained acutely aware of the debate around the term and contributed to it, referring to the confusion surrounding its usage in many papers.[44] In an essay entitled 'Astudio bywyd gwerin: a'i ran mewn amddiffyn gwareiddiad' (Studying folk life: and its part in defending civilisation), written in 1958, he addresses head on what he considers to be the misuse of the term folk and advocates the use of the word *gwerin*: 'Perhaps because I have come from a nation that places no emphasis on class differences . . . I find myself considering the significance of these words laughable . . . Folk life is the life of all society, and folk culture is the culture of the entire nation.'[45] Emphasising the fact that he uses folklore as an essentially anthropological term that refers to 'all people', Peate is claiming the study of folk culture as explicitly related to the modern world and relevant to it. Rejecting outright the definition of folk society as 'discrete' and 'homogenous in terms of race and tradition' (p. 12), he repudiates the idea that folk is limited to relationships of blood or marriage,[46] and reiterates his view that the study of folk life is a study of the ways of life of communities and nations

unaffected by 'high industrialisation' (p. 12). His vision for imple-
menting such an inclusive view of all people included approaching
the museum as a space of 'social activity', and he cites as an example
a Communist meeting being held at Trondheim's folk museum and
the use of churches for religious services, amongst other activities
that reveal the museum as a social space in which culture is enacted:
'Politics, religion, music, drama, dances, crafts, art, architecture, agriculture, dress, furniture – all these are found in Scandinavian folk
museums. This is an attempt to bring the museum to the core of all
life, banishing completely the old idea that it is merely a repository
for the dry bones of a dead culture.'[47]

However, Peate's definition of folk culture and its performance
was unable to provide a view of the increasing hybridity in Welsh
culture or to consider the way in which culture and identity in Wales
were manifested following the industrial revolution. This was to be
damaging to any consideration of the role of the Welsh language and
its social significance in either industrial or post-industrial contexts,
and detrimental to the way the relationship of Welsh and other languages, especially English, were initially portrayed at Sain Ffagan. It
also inadvertently perpetuated the idea that folk was synonymous with
the Welsh-speaking, rather than the people of Wales as a whole. The
importance of the monoglot Welsh speaker to the continuation of
culture was discussed by Peate in several instances, with bilingualism
perceived as dangerous to the long-term survival of the lesser spoken
language. The reason for this lack of emphasis on linguistic interactions
is complex and seems to run against his own view of 'folk' as inclusive
of all peoples. It is deeply connected to the period in which the Welsh
Folk Museum was established (1948), a moment in history when the
life of the people became an important consideration in museum representation and interpretation. There was more to Sain Ffagan than
representing the people in general, however. Historian John Davies
refers to the government's policy of ensuring a Britain that was 'totally
united' around the time of the Second World War, and of the subsequent strengthening of British identity having a devastating effect on
Welsh-language culture.[48] In this context a portrayal of Welshness in
terms of its 'people', and in a way that clearly differentiated between
the Welsh people and the British state, was all the more urgent. At a
time when British cultural assimilation was being driven through on
the tides of the war effort, the emphasis on safeguarding Welsh culture

at Sain Ffagan was a cultural imperative. In his writings Peate talks of the importance of tracing the 'organic continuity' between past and present:

> It may be well to preserve objects because they represent a past that has utterly vanished ... but it is of more importance that a museum should preserve objects capable of yielding some lesson of use for our own time. And still more important is the preservation of arts, industries and customs, which from their truly national character afford the firmest foundation for the national life of the future.[49]

Peate's vision was to perform the Wales that continued to be under threat and to sustain its continuity through a repetitive performance that served to consolidate the existence of that which is being performed, or at least educate the visitor in its importance. In this way the performance of folk culture was part of a movement not only to define and delineate culture through mimesis, but also to perpetuate it. Sain Ffagan was an attempt to articulate, within an immersive environment, a culture that was wholly peripheral to British definitions of 'the nation'. The museum came to be established, however, before the vestiges of the picturesque had fallen away from modes of museum representation. Nineteenth-century museum reforms had set about transforming European museums from the closed institutions of the ruling classes into politically driven operations committed to the education and moral improvement of the masses, but the process of democratising the museum required more than simply opening up the treasure chest for all to see, because what was inside was neither related nor necessarily of inherent value to working people. Such a process would require a shift in the way the museum operated as social space for the representation of people and their cultures. This did not happen until the post-war period, during which the European folk museum shifted towards a more cogent social representation. The vestiges of the picturesque element remained, however, and even now continue to haunt the folk museum. This is partly due to the view of the folk museum in contemporary imagination as a site portraying rural, or vernacular, life and culture. In many ways, the Welsh Folk Museum at Sain Ffagan and Peate's work in general became a touchstone for the folk movement in general. Peate was a central figure in the development of folklore studies in Europe and Sain Ffagan became

2. A rural view of Kennixton farmhouse and fields at Sain
Ffagan Amgueddfa Werin Cymru (with kind permission
of Amgueddfa Cymru/National Museum Wales).
Photo: Lisa Lewis.

an important early example of the open-air folk museum. The roots
of such an enterprise grew out of the establishment in 1932 at the
National Museum of a Sub-department of Folk Culture and Industries,
led by Peate and dedicated to the development and understanding
of Welsh culture. Following its establishment, a large collection of
objects, which since 1926, had formed the basis of a 'Welsh Bygones'
exhibition at the National Museum, became the focus of a National
Folk Collection, organised in new gallery spaces.[50] These included four
room displays from the traditional Welsh farmhouse of the eighteenth
and nineteenth century – Cegin (Kitchen), Bwtri or llaethdy (Dairy),
Cegin orau or Siambr (Parlour), and Ystafell Wely (Bedroom), as well
as a smithy and a turner's workshop.[51] The movement towards a larger
Folk Museum was characterised at first by the language of cultural
revivalism, but also reflected the significant discourse around the changing purpose of the museum. This was to be 'a home for new life and
not a collection of dry bones' and within it 'every national virtue' was
to be gathered together 'until it becomes in Welsh history . . . a means
of uniting every movement in our land into the national identity . . .

so that we may, by drinking of its living well, quench our thirst ready for our national purpose in the future.'[52] It is hardly surprising that Sain Ffagan has been perceived by some as a cultural island, an enclave for the representation of Welsh culture that at the time of its inception absolved the National Museum of Wales of the responsibility to define and present Welsh culture more broadly across its entire collections, thereby affirming the normative British narrative of the National Museum of Wales itself, a matter discussed in more depth by Peter Lord in relation to visual art.[53] In his book, *The Aesthetics of Relevance*, written in 1992, Lord laments the fact that Sain Ffagan 'locks Wales into a perpetual rural past', ghettoizing is 'as a narrowly defined folk culture . . . an increasingly potent force against the living culture', which had the added unfortunate effect of portraying the nation as passive (p. 40). In 1948, the establishment of Sain Ffagan could be read as a response to the significant changes in the social, economic and cultural life of the Welsh people by its portrayal of life before the enormous social impact of industrialisation in Wales, but it did not, initially, represent the tensions underlying the change, nor its consequences.

Historian Dai Smith has berated the folk tradition in Wales because it has ignored the processes of industrialisation and urbanisation that, along with the English-speaking working-class traditions that accompanied them, were responsible for forging a modern Welsh identity. In his view, the Welsh folk tradition chose to focus instead on 'wholeness and harmony, and continuity, and distinctiveness, and togetherness, and uniqueness' presented through sites such as Sain Ffagan.[54] Likewise, Hywel Francis, deploring the 1980s heritage boom, writes of Sain Ffagan: 'It's all about Welsh dance, music, costume, barns, crafts, coracles, carts and idyllic sterilized whitewashed cottages. But no word, as far as I can see, about land-ownership and social control except revealingly (?) in the first sentence of its guidebook where the earl of Plymouth's 'generosity' is acknowledged in giving and selling land and property to the museum!'[55] This critique has continued to weigh on the museum, the implication being always that the old folkways portrayed bear no relation to the life of the living; even when elements of later industrialisation and urbanisation have been introduced, it is as though the museum's origins in the folk movement cannot be shaken. Again, the picturesque element, and the general view of Sain Ffagan as a site that celebrates *y bwthyn Cymreig* has stifled the museum's possibilities of opening up a contemporaneous interpretation of what it means to be Welsh, despite repeated efforts by numerous curators and keepers to dispel this perception.

Tony Bennett makes a powerful assertion regarding the way in which museums, in seeking to portray 'the people', employ processes that end up sentimentalising them: 'the terms in which the ways of life of such classes are represented are often so mortgaged to the dominant culture that "the people" are encountered usually only in those massively idealised and deeply regressive forms which stalk the middle-class imagination.'[56] This is significant in relation to the evolution of Sain Ffagan, and many of the historical critiques of its direction and purpose have centred on the museum seemingly pandering to a kind of middle-class imagination associated with linguistic nationalism. The fact that the majority of the population spoke Welsh up to 1911 suggests that this critique is not fair – to portray Welsh culture and life prior to 1900 one would have to consider the central role of the Welsh language to the people of the time. The fact that Peate was concerned with preserving Welsh culture prior to industrialisation ensured that the portrayal of Welsh culture was inevitably rooted in the Welsh language, and as his emphasis on the performance of culture was a central tenet of the folk museum, one is at a loss to understand what the linguistic representation on site could be, other than Welsh. The discontent voiced by numerous critics regarding the absence of Welsh industrial history is understandable, but including it wholly was never part of Peate's project.

The re-framing of the representation of Welsh life to include elements of industrial society instigated by J. Geraint Jenkins (1929–2009), curator at Sain Ffagan from 1987 to 1991,[57] was welcomed by many. It could only ever be partial, however, a nod towards industrial society in so far as it impacted on village life or smaller industrial communities, as the semi-rural site at Sain Ffagan is unable to represent the world of heavy industry.[58] There is also a sense in which the reconstruction of industrial buildings is arguably inappropriate or incongruous in terms of representational authenticity, and this has a bearing on the interpretation. For instance, Rhydycar terrace from Merthyr, which in its original location stood opposite the ironworks in a heavily polluted industrialised area and backed on to the cholera-infested Glamorganshire canal, is inevitably presented out of context in the picturesque parkland of the museum site. The way in which the terraced houses have been rebuilt and 'dressed' in a timeline successfully references the industrial past, but unless the visitor is able to read the houses with the expert knowledge of a curator, they would not be able to deduce the relevant information regarding their original context.[59] The sense of absence encountered as we enter these houses suggests that something else is required in order to remind us of their original context.

Memory

> 'To it will come school-children for tuition, architects, artists and crafts-men for inspiration, country men and women "to cross the bridge of memories", colliers and quarrymen to view anew their wider heritage, and townsfolk to discover the permanence of Welsh life.'
> IORWERTH PEATE, *AMGUEDDFEYDD GWERIN.*[60]

Peate's reference to visitors crossing 'the bridge of memories' suggests a vision based on a personal and somatic experience of the open-air site, in which the visitor participates in a series of negotiations regard-ing their own particular memories and a more general and collective sense of memory related to the people as a cultural group. On site, various buildings from different periods in time are set in a congruent relationship with one another, a practice that is important to the suc-cess of the open-air museum, as the experience this generates for the visitor is one of strolling through a familiar environment, for instance a rural village, providing a unity of place that supports the authenticity of the experience within each house. Thus, the tollhouse is situated at a crossroads, and the baker's, the tailor's, the post office, village stores, cockpit and school are situated around a village field or green. The walkways, roads, fields and forestry all combine to create a structured environment, where the visitor inadvertently creates a meaningful sense of place for the buildings. Other buildings and structures are situated further afield – the mill and the tannery, the church and the chapel, in a kind of rural isolation. The combination of buildings and the disparate timeframes involved in their interpretation make this a representation of a village and a countryside depicting a generic past, and a collection that actively encourages the visitor, through the phys-ical act of walking the site and entering houses, to perform a square mile into being. There is also a pleasure associated with the sense of trespass and the experience of moving between time frames (between buildings). There are no costumed guides here, though there are extremely knowledgeable caretakers placed within the buildings, which reinforces the sense of the vacant rather than the inhabited house, and the understanding of the empty houses as a collection of artefacts rather than a theatrical representation. And yet, despite the fact that this is a place where historical and conservational expertise is all, the delight in the representation and the excitement of immersion enhances the somatic experience of the site. At Sain Ffagan we re-live memories: our own (of home), and of the idealised home. Gaston Bachelard describes our dreams of the house in which we were born as 'the well-tempered matter of the material paradise . . . the environment in which the protective beings live,'[61] and states that a house 'constitutes a body of images that give mankind proofs or illusions of stability' (p. 17). As well as fulfilling the function of representing a specific home, the houses represent all our homes, the homes and buildings of the people of Wales and our collective sense of communal memory relating to our ancestors. These, 'our' houses, are protected, and doubly so; they are protected both as heritage conservation and as an encompassing representation of nationness, the process of rebuilding and interpreting them anew giving them especial value. Peate's work on the Welsh house presents it as both a component of Welsh life and an expression of it; as a product of geography, climate and a particular society, the Welsh cottage or farmhouse is 'true architecture', which 'knows no time: it represents the past, present and future.'[62] Peate understands the Welsh house in terms of an organic and natural evolution of place according to the inhabitant's basic needs, which is an illustration of the steadfastness of folk life. The timeless quality of the house is grounded in its utilitarian and elemental nature as a dwelling place, and despite what Peate perceives as the lack of a distinct Welsh architectural tradition, the cultural connection is felt in relation to the understanding of the life and the living that has taken place within it.[63] This is the experience we glimpse when moving through the reconstructed house. Reminiscing about our own past within it – an act of empathetic recollection – challenges the assumption that visitors are passive consumers. This aspect is elaborated on in Gaynor Bagnall's research into heritage sites and open-air museums. Bagnall arrives at a definition of the visitors' participation in acts of reminiscence as being 'informed by performativity', and proceeds to establish that 'the relationship between visitors and the sites is based as much on emotion and imagination as it is on cognition.'[64] Visitors actively construct their own understanding of the past represented at these sites and do so by mapping their consumption physically, emotionally and imaginatively. The visitor experience is enabled by this embodied mapping, which in turn facilitates a connection between personal and cultural memories in a specific location. Sain Ffagan is suffused with this form of mapping based on the visitor's own personal associations with the buildings, and many of the houses retain specific meanings and memories relating to the visitor's experience of place – our square mile, region or area of origin. Demographic shifts across Wales and across generations due to work, education and familial connections have left an imprint on many Welsh families, enabling them to trace some close connection with at least one building within the collection. It is the impact of industrialisation in Wales that ensures this connection for the visitor, and the accompanying sense of 'returning home'. The connections between visitors and houses are active points of memory, so that even before the inclusion of buildings from the industrial south, the role of industry in social history was present in the visitor's awareness of their connection with a rural building even though they might be from an industrial area themselves. The visitor's agency in acts of remembrance relating to the houses and their areas of origin is probably responsible for the most evocative performances on site. Rhydycar terrace, the one building that provides a concrete sense of continuity (from 1805, through 1855, 1895, 1925, 1955 to 1985) and one of the most popular, enables strong reminiscences, especially through the very last house in the terrace, which explicitly references the miner's strike of 1984. The ties between Welsh visitors and the last house, in terms of its significance, situate the preceding houses in the terrace, set in earlier time frames, in a more meaningful context, the house within 'living memory' helping to convey the communal memory related to the preceding timeframes depicted. According to Bagnall, emotional realism is key to such an experience, a process of engaging the emotions through imagination in order to engender and facilitate real feelings and a sense of authenticity. While capable of providing a deep empathetic response, realism is a form that hides itself well. It is a representational practice in which we have accepted the fact that we will not acknowledge its presence as a convention, thereby colluding in its affect. The verisimilitude brought about by the accurate representation in each house can induce real

3. Rhydycar Terrace, showing houses set twenty-five years apart,
Sain Ffagan Amgueddfa Werin Cymru (with kind permission
of Amgueddfa Cymru/National Museum Wales)
Photo: Lisa Lewis.

feelings and responses, and Bagnall acknowledges that the visitors'
emotional mapping may result in various readings of the museum and,
interestingly, that the physicality of the experience can lead visitors to
believe that they 'really were consuming the past or getting a good
sense of what life was like in the past' (p. 89). The empathetic response
brought about by the immersive nature of the open-air museum, which
allows for the prominence of the personal story or recollection, enables
the formation of a memory to take precedence over, or at least sit side
by side with, the more general historical context portrayed. Such
responses are as valuable in terms of a democratisation of interpretation as they are potentially problematical as generalisations of historic
events. The task for the museum is to recognise this tension in the
open-air experience, while ensuring the facilitation of an engaging
interpretation. Such a balancing act is not easy because the persuasive-
ness of realism is strong, and our pleasure in being complicit in the
game is so great that it is easy to forget that the houses, in the past, did

not stand where they are now situated, were not dressed exactly as they are now and for the most part were built in drastically different landscapes and social circumstances. In crossing the threshold of a historic house, we invoke the assumed experience of doing so centuries ago, and this is supported by the mimetic representation, which we believe gives us a sense of the actual experience. This is the impulse that provokes the desire to see the empty house populated by human subjects, if only to appease our understanding that it was once a working house. This is a somatic response based on our awareness and memory of distinct places as constructed through habitual bodily practices. At the same time the performative response is subject to the imaginative act of remembering the human activity that once took place in the house, and for this reason some people would prefer not to unhinge the imaginative endeavour through the immediacy of human contact, which would effectively remove it from the realm of reverie and into an all too real dramatic presentation. While the static building is fixed and mute, an apparent remnant from history, the fear is that human agency might impair its apparent authenticity by self-consciously drawing the interpretation into the realms of pretence, or by exposing the fact that the site is predicated on the idea of the copy (such is the expectation that theatre will taint the experience through its inauthenticity). Instances of costumed interpretation, however, give no reason to believe that involving such interpreters would heighten a sense of pretence. On the contrary, it is feasible to imagine that they might assist in critically unmasking the pretence of the site itself by drawing attention to the importance of personal memory in the construction of history.

Aleida Assmann points out that the memory theories of Maurice Halbwachs and Pierre Nora 'emphasize the constructivist, identity-forming character of memory, and affirm its right over a neutral historiography'.[65] Discussing the opposition between memory and history in relation to contemporary curatorial practice, which is particularly relevant in the context of the participatory museum, she states that 'there is no such thing as historiography without some form of memory work; whether overtly or not, it cannot wholly avoid interpretation, partiality, and identity' (p. 123). Referring to the journal *History and Memory*, founded in 1989, as an exemplar of this relationship, within which the line between history and memory is blurred, Assmann suggests that the polarisation of history and memory is as problematic as their equation and that they 'should be grasped as two complementary modes of cultural memory' (p. 123). If we abandon the dichotomy of history versus memory and use instead the phrase 'cultural memory', one of Assmann's variants on the more generic collective memory, within which there is a broad range of forms of cultural remembering, including historical memory, we step closer to acknowledging that history and historiography are but two modes of reference and are accompanied by other media, such as performance, literature, arts, religion, myth and other cultural forms. This conception of cultural memory as composed of a variety of forms is of significance for the process of attempting to understand the immersive and participatory museum as a performance of culture, and the role of memory in sustaining cultural histories within it. Sain Ffagan, as site of memory, might be described as a place representing the transition in Welsh culture between *milieu de mémoire* and *lieu de mémoire*. According to Nora, when cultural frames and social contexts change dramatically, objects of older times ('bygones'), can become national treasures, representations of ways of life that we no longer occupy but which are meaningful to us because they represent cultural memory. Nora describes the *lieu de mémoire* as a hybrid place 'compounded of life and death, of the temporal and the eternal', and although its purpose is 'to stop time, to inhibit forgetting, to fix a state of things, to immortalize death, and to materialize the immaterial', *lieux de mémoire* advance 'only because of their capacity for change, their ability to resurrect old meanings and generate new ones along with new and unforeseeable connections'.[66] This capacity for change is true of Sain Ffagan, and it is part of the history of the museum's continuous revision of itself, including its change in terms of title and implied remit, from Welsh Folk Museum to Museum of Welsh Life, and to National Museum of History, representing the shift towards a more comprehensive view of the history of Wales.[67] This view is encapsulated in the emphasis on participation and inclusion in Amgueddfa Cymru's most recent iteration of its aims and objectives.[68] In this, the museum is concerned with opening up the process of constructing history, and of enabling an awareness of the methods involved in history-making, an aspect of the museum's historiography that is incorporated into its own participatory interpretation and education policies in the 'Making History' project (2014–18) that accompanies a major rebuild of the museum.[69]

Place

Sain Ffagan interprets the collection of 'authentic' buildings on land previously owned by the earl of Plymouth and donated to the people of Wales. This was largely agricultural land bordering the village of Sain Ffagan, within which a few buildings were located, namely the Elizabethan 'castle' built in 1580 and used by the Plymouth family in the nineteenth century as a summer residence, and Llwyn-yr-Eos farmhouse, built in the 1820s. The historical structures built or re-erected at the site since the museum's establishment in 1948 include an Iron Age settlement based on archaeological evidence, a medieval church from Llandeilo Talybont near Pontarddulais, a twentieth-century workers' institute from Blackwood in the south Wales valleys, an eighteenth-century Unitarian chapel from Drefach Felindre in Carmarthenshire, a post office from Blaenffos in Pembrokeshire, an eighteenth-century cockpit from Dinbych in north Wales, a tollgate from Aberystwyth, a nineteenth-century schoolhouse from Maestir near Llanbedr-Pont-Steffan, a mill from Cross Inn in Cardiganshire, a blacksmith's shop from Trefeglwys in Powys, a post-war pre-fabricated house from Gabalfa in Cardiff, a row of shops from Ogmore Vale in Glamorgan, a terrace of houses from Rhydycar in Merthyr Tudful and a variety of agricultural houses and buildings from all over Wales spanning the fifteenth to the nineteenth centuries. What constitutes the history of Wales at this site, the way it is presented and interpreted, has been the subject of considerable debate.[70] On one level, the parkland environment provides a context from which it is impossible to escape, and in which it is inevitable that the farmhouses and cottages speak of the rural past. Buildings reflecting the history of the industrial south have felt incongruous in their isolation, thought this is now being countered by the addition of several more urban buildings such as the Vulcan pub from the former New Town in Cardiff and a police station from Taff's Well, both to be situated close to Oakdale Workmen's Institute.

The museum's latest incarnation at the time of writing as 'National Museum of History' reinforces its more recent emphasis on telling the story of Wales as a geographical area from the earliest time possible up to the present. This development means that the museum is open to telling all the histories of 'Wales'. But how are the histories of Wales to be told in this place? What is this place *about*? What story does it tell through its collection emplaced in this particular location?

The museum site operates as a palimpsest in respect of the earl of Plymouth's castle, the associated farmhouse, Sain Ffagan village nearby and the ground itself – not only does it adjoin the site of the Battle of St Fagan's, an important battle in the 'English' Civil War, it also bears the remains of part of the medieval village of Sain Ffagan.[71] Situated around these historical traces are the buildings that comprise the museum collection – examples of detailed preservation work, undertaken with immense care and expertise. They also possess the aura of the original, moved 'stone by stone, brick by brick' and are constructed so as to present the building at the most fruitful historical moment in its history. No matter how authentic the representation of the original building, however, such *in situ* displays are never neutral, as Barbara Kirshenblatt-Gimblett explains:

> They are not a slice of life lifted from the everyday world and inserted into the museum gallery, though this is the rhetoric of the museum mode. On the contrary, those who construct the display also constitute the subject, even when they seem to do nothing more than relocate an entire house and its contents, brick by brick, board by board, chair by chair . . . . 'Wholes' are not given but constituted, and often they are hotly contested.[72]

Illusionistic and naturalistic museum display that places objects in reconstructed scenes in which the object previously 'lived' is predicated on the idea that the immersive scene will convey the meaning of the objects with greater clarity, authenticity or sense of truth. All such displays are closely associated with the educational and scientific imperatives of the late nineteenth-century museum, but also reference popular spectacles and attractions. The emphasis on holding attention and on framing the object or event was part of a new form of spectatorship, or 'panoramic perception', fostered by the stage designer's need to capture the visitor's attention in a world of increasing mobility, speed and fleeting impressions. This emphasis on authenticity, prevalent on the European theatre stage and adopted by the nineteenth-century museum, encouraged the development of what Christopher Baugh has called the theatre language of 'material realism', which changed fundamentally the role of the audience, the actor and the idea of representation.[73] If the audience was to become 'lost' in the act of spectatorship, the actor needed to recede into the stage as though enclosed in a room, and the representation of life on stage became 'closed off', both in terms of dramatic location and literally, in the representation of the locale through scenography. Developments in theatrical lighting were important in increasing a sense of 'looking in' on the dramatic action that does not break out of its environment, and in differentiating between the stage and auditorium by closing the audience off in darkness. The audience were transported, were expected to dwell on the scene and consider, even study, the implications of the drama for itself. This scenography facilitated the conception of Drama as being self-sustaining in its own world – a world apart – heightening the experience of what Peter Szondi refers to as the Drama being 'absolute', or 'conscious of nothing outside itself'.[74] The darkened auditorium and the focal point of the parlour or other naturalistic environment (though usually a room) in which the drama unfolded, to be 'viewed' from a vantage point where the viewer could not be seen, led to the privileging of sight above all other senses. All the functions of naturalistic scenography and acting technique strove to uphold this visible system, where the actor was embedded within the stage picture in a three-dimensional room, enacting a dramatic event that is a representation of reality. The *in situ* approach to museum display works in a similar way, so that the viewer 'sees' without being visible. While this is apparently a position of power, such an unseen gaze in theatre usually masks a political position in which the audience member is given very little choice in terms of what to feel or how to respond. Similarly, with the habitat diorama, we look in voyeuristically through an imaginary fourth wall and from an apparently empowered position, yet this is actually a passive stance, in which we are placed in the unassuming position of accepting the scene as it is, un-problematised and with no recourse to critically open up its mode of representation. The uncritical acceptance of history is facilitated by the voyeuristic stance of gazing on, but is unhinged and potentially problematised by a flexibility in the telling, which more fluid and open-ended portrayals are able to provide.

In his writings on the content of the museum, including the performance of culture, Peate clearly sought to foreground a specific notion of a 'past' Wales that the visitors would experience and inhabit as they were immersed in the landscape and buildings set into the site. This was not necessarily a closed model that bore no possibility of questioning or potential for change, for some of Peate's ideas for the performance of culture at the museum are inherently participatory. In considering how the museum might perform this function Peate turned to the Scandinavian model of the folk museum. Of the many that he had visited in 1946,[75] one in particular represented for Peate the pinnacle of the performance of folk culture; this was Skansen, in Stockholm, one of the earliest examples of the European folk museum. Established by Artur Hazelius (1833–1901), the museum is designed as a representation of the landscape, peoples and culture of Sweden, with buildings from different provinces, including farmhouses, shops, a church and chapel and craftsmen's workshops, re-erected at the site.[76] According to Peate, the root of Skansen's success lay in its immersive context, the fact that it contains 'no label or glass case' and enables 'a warm living picture' that is 'comforting' in its emphasis on the living and on continuity.[77] At Skansen the landscape is more than mimesis; it takes on a transformational quality through the performances within it, so that it becomes an encapsulation of Swedish people, land and culture, or in Peate's words, a 'home for national inspiration', binding the pleasures of the outdoors with learning and culture. Skansen was built as a site for performance, with a theatre for the production of Swedish plays and spaces for folk dances, festivals and conferences. The recreational aspect is reinforced by its location on the hill of Djurgården Island, once the deer-hunting ground of Swedish aristocracy, part of which was bought by Hazelius in order to build the museum. Next to it is Gröna Lund amusement park, part of a network of complexes that are loosely associated yet set apart. Skansen's relationship with popular culture is ambivalent; while it privileges folk customs and folk ways, contemporary communal events such as singing sessions with a well-known 'sing-along leader', first held in 1936, are annual highlights. It also reveals its relationship with the amusement park in its small games booths, its fairground and zoo, even though its animals are indigenous to Sweden. The museum hosts contemporary dances and concerts and live or recorded broadcasts for radio and television, as well as the traditional Swedish folk celebrations, and undertakes a role as a social space or forum where government agencies, businesses and special interest groups can put on short exhibitions.

In the movement towards museum as participatory place human engagement is paramount, and the museum guide, often costumed, is a key constituent in the performance, leading the interpretation and the experience overall. The human figure is central to the function of the museum as enactive cultural space, though paradoxically theatricality can often undermine the sense of immersion provided through the domestic setting. The costumed guide, by inadvertently establishing a distance between performer and audience, can make the visitor aware of her own gaze. This uncanny dichotomy was present from the very start of the folk museum tradition, when Hazelius used mannequins as well as people in costume as a theatrical device that was both immersive and alienating in his 'folk life pictures' of the 1870s, which revealed a dramatic moment in the 'story' of life, for instance a deathbed scene.[78] By 1891, when Skansen was founded, Hazelius was using performers in native dress, craftsmen and costumed guides. Today at Skansen, people in period costume assume the role of villagers displaying craft ways and interpreting historical artefacts and performances, though they are not 'characters'. Having moved away from a strictly authentic portrayal of Sweden, where the people dressed as Sámi were required to be Sámi, and the turf used had to be actual turf from the corresponding area of Sweden, Skansen now provides a more fluid stance towards what is means to be Swedish, encapsulated within a general sense of 'patriotic love' and social reform.[79] That museum visitors are able to locate themselves within the landscape of this imagined Sweden, populated by costumed interpreters, legitimises the claim to a national identity and character, even if it is entirely performative. However, Skansen as a whole is not an imitation of Sweden; it bears no resemblance to the country or its actual landscapes. It is a virtual world in which the culture and mythology of the nation is sustained through performative events that are flexible enough to allow for a broad range of interpretations of Swedish culture. Paradoxically, such interpretations are invariably contemporary understandings of history, mediated through perpetually new ways of 'seeing' history. Tony Bennett refers to this aspect when he states that the past referred to in the open-air folk museum, while 'existing in a frame which separates it from the present, is entirely the product of the present practices which organize and maintain that frame.'[80] The very existence of a reconstituted house is secured 'only through the forms in which "the past" is *publicly demarcated* and *represented* as such' (p. 130), resulting in a representation that inevitably references the present moment. If this is the case, then the immersive museum has found a way to self-consciously reference its own construction in the interpretations at Sain Ffagan, where signs of the present are occasionally referred to playfully. For instance, at Llandeilo Talybont church, set circa 1520, the remarkably detailed rood screen, carved anew by master carpenter and wood carver Ray Smith for the church's opening in 2007, has the carpenter's own face carved into it amongst the religious figures and symbols depicted, an entirely appropriate reference to the maker that draws attention to the process of interpretation.

These qualities of changeability, of filtering present understandings of the past through performance, of inviting unstable and mutable understandings of history through processes of participation, all point towards the open-air museum site as a performance space, one that is predicated on history as being invested in place.

Sain Ffagan and the performance of culture as *poiesis*

> Nes na'r hanesydd at y Gwir di-goll,
> Ydyw'r dramodydd, sydd yn gelwydd oll.
> R. WILLIAMS PARRY,
> 'GWAE AWDUR DYDDIADURON'[81]

In the interpretation of the museum as participatory the emphasis is not on how history is told as much as on the way in which we, the public, are implicated in its telling. This has been a core concern for Amgueddfa Cymru / National Museum Wales during the renovation of Sain Ffagan and the 'Making History' project, which has seen the museum work towards an entirely new iteration of the museum for its seventieth anniversary in 2018. This approach involves the collective memory of all the peoples of Wales in the construction of history. This is encapsulated, for instance, in the proposed new galleries called '*Cymru*' ('Wales is . . .') and '*Byw a Bod*' ('Life is . . .'), where a key concern is that 'Life is personal . . . not national.'[82] The attention to participation, the situating of culture as an enactive performance and the emphasis on personal interpretation enable a definition of Wales that is as inclusive as the community that decides to participate in its making. These aspects are not dissimilar to the principles present in Iorwerth Peate's conception of the folk museum, the significant difference being the basis on which we now consider and define 'Wales' and the recognition of cultural diversity as a constituent of its long history. In this process, culture is defined and redefined in a perpetual process of *poiesis*, a process in which the performance of culture is instrumental.

The performance of culture had always been at the forefront of the folk museum movement. Peate had advocated the performance of culture at Sain Ffagan from the museum's inception in 1948 through using craftspeople, dancers and musicians. In 1951, when the Welsh Committee of the Festival of Britain invited the National Museum to arrange a 'Festival of St Fagans' that was to include performances of music, drama, dancing and craft demonstrations, the idea was that such a programme would be permanently embedded into the provision of the folk museum.[83] The incorporation of such cultural performances was not fully implemented until much later, in 1960, when J. Geraint Jenkins, assistant keeper under Peate, took on a range of craftspeople including a miller, a blacksmith, a cooper, a saddler, a clog maker and a baker, and their public displays of these craft ways became the mainstay of the performance of folk culture at the museum.[84] Jenkins was also to establish the Calan Mai (May) Fair at Sain Ffagan, as well as musical events, a *cymanfa ganu* (concert of hymn singing), the performance of *anterliwtiau* (interludes) and Welsh plays, the Autumn Fair, including a thanksgiving service, and the traditional Christmas Fair. Other events included a day of traditional jazz and *Gŵyl y Cymoedd* (Festival of the Valleys), situated around Rhydycar Terrace from Merthyr Tudful.[85] In addition to the festivities and events, immersive interpretation techniques were introduced at Sain Ffagan in the 1980s, reflecting the increase in the use of performative practices in the museum sector more generally, and the introduction of live interpretation as an educational tool in the negotiation between event, artefact and place and the way they constitute the telling of history.[86]

The word 'interpretation' was first used in a heritage context by Freeman Tilden in *Interpreting Our Heritage* (1957), where he describes the communicative practice between visitors and rangers in the American National Park in terms of a 'provocation', rather than a means of instruction.[87] Tilden believed that the visitor should encounter 'a kind of elective education that is superior in many respects to that of the classroom' (p. 25), where the visitor 'meets the Thing Itself – whether it be a wonder of nature's work, or the actor or work of man', an act that attempts 'to reveal meaning and relationships' (p. 33). In Wales, live interpretation developed alongside the educational context in museums and the framework for theatre-in-education (T-i-E) supported by the Arts Council of Wales and local education authorities in the 1980s, which ensured a fully funded professional company in every Welsh county, usually serving theatre for young audiences (subsuming T-i-E into a broader remit) or the wider community, and many of them working with the museum sector on special educational programmes. Education departments within museums have historically led the way in the use of live interpretation, reflecting changes in pedagogical practice influenced by methodologies of applied drama. At Sain Ffagan, live interpretation was introduced by Walter Jones, head of the education department, who developed the Victorian classroom interpretation at Ysgol Maestir, a rural single-classroom school from Maestir near Llanbedr-Pont-Steffan, rebuilt at Sain Ffagan in the early 1980s and furnished in the style of 1900. In this role-playing exercise, which was largely improvised, schoolchildren sat in the Victorian classroom, and were 'taught' by a member of staff performing in role as Victorian schoolmaster. Since the early 1990s, in order to clarify the nature and dynamics of this immersive interpretation for the children involved, the museum has instigated training for schoolteachers to play the schoolmaster/mistress themselves, in what has since become the quintessential immersive museum experience for schoolchildren from south Wales. The live interpretation provision was developed further in the 2000s with activities such as 'Diwrnod Golchi Mamgu' or Grandma's washday, again specifically for schoolchildren and part of the education department's provision.[88] Other kinds of interpretive practices have involved the performance of traditional folk customs, and their associated artefacts, often on specific holidays, such as the Twelfth Night customs of *hela'r dryw* and the *Mari Lwyd*, practised across Wales up to the end of the nineteenth century and, in a few areas, up to the present day. *Hela'r dryw* (hunting the wren) is the tradition of carrying a wren in its 'wren-house' or tiny bier from door to door to the accompaniment of singing, the relics perhaps, of both a ceremonial hunt and an associated procession, though only one of the custom's ceremonies has survived. *Mari Lwyd* (grey mare/holy Mary) is a processional performance during which a horse's skull is carried by a band of men who lead the 'Mari' from door to door, engaging in an improvisational battle of wits loosely based on a dialogue in song between the party seeking entry and those inside trying to keep them out. In several examples of this tradition there are specific characters such as Leader, Sergeant, Merryman and Punch and Judy, along the lines of other folk performances involving mummery and animal disguise throughout the British Isles. These, when performed, are living interpretations of traditional customs, and examples of practices that highlight the museum's collections, especially in relation to artefacts that are only made fully meaningful within their performative context, such as the little 'wren-house' and the *Mari Lwyd* skull.[89]

University students studying live interpretation and theatre-in-museum as part of theatre and drama courses have done a significant amount of work at Amgueddfa Cymru as a whole, including the National Museum of the Welsh Woollen Industry in Drefach Felindre and the National Slate Museum in Llanberis. At Sain Ffagan, theatre students have performed in the majority of houses and buildings, including Hendre-wen barn, Oakdale Workmen's Institute, the cockpit, Maestir school and Pen-rhiw chapel.[90] One example, *Chwarae Mai / May Play* (2000), a play in ballad form that interpreted traditional May customs, including an enactment of the mock fight between winter and summer traditionally represented by wicker effigies, took place in processional form along the pathways on the castle side of the museum, close to the barn, and was performed by theatre students of Aberystwyth University and directed by Matthew Davies, then education officer, and myself.[91] As well as having the pedagogical aim of exploring the interpretation of May customs, the work was an experiment in museum performance in so far as it explored the parameters of audience attention and participation in the event. Visitors would witness the initial moment of performance, creating what Richard Schechner has referred to as a 'heated centre and a cool rim' around an event's eruption. During the performance, which was formed from units of action that took place at stopping points within a procession, the spectators needed to establish themselves in a circle formation in order to see what was happening. At this point some spectators would wander away and some would commit to staying with the performance until the 'known goal'[92] or planned event at the end of the procession. The project sought to examine the extent to which this was dependent on the investment in the performance itself, for instance, the meaning of the performance overall for the participants and their eagerness to sing along and be part of the procession. According to Clare Parry, *Chwarae Mai / May Play* worked through singing and processional movement to create a sense of unity . . . [that] could be seen to partially dissolve the distinction between audience and performer. Rather than interpreting individual artefacts or re-erected buildings the play contextualized the performers and the site of the museum within a particular temporal framework. For the duration of the performance the site of the exhibition was to be viewed through the lens of this framework. This provided an imaginative and broad interpretation of the social context of the exhibited collections of Welsh rural life.[93]

Some research projects that utilise the site have engaged with enactment directly as a methodology. One such project, 'The Experience of Worship', (2009–13), funded by the Arts and Humanities Research Council and the Economic and Social Research Council and led by Bangor University, set out to examine what it was like to worship in a late medieval cathedral and a parish church and used Llandeilo Talybont church at Sain Ffagan and Salisbury Cathedral in order to answer these questions directly through enactment. Participants took on the roles of medieval priests, religious assistants, musicians and lay people, and participated in a series of public enactments performing the rituals of the medieval church.[94] In all such examples the performance provides historical information through embodiment, or knowledge regarding the performance of culture itself.

In 1995, during Colin Ford's tenure as director of National Museums and Galleries of Wales (1992–8), the National Museum established a full-time resident theatre company called Anterliwt (Welsh for interlude), based at Sain Ffagan. Ford was previously director of the National Museum of Photography, Film and Television in Bradford when the resident museum theatre company, Action Replay, had been a cornerstone of the interpretation programme.[95] Anterliwt's performances included interpretations of the different houses at Sain Ffagan such as *Characters in Cottages* (1997) and *Castle Characters* (1998), promenades through the site, such as *Stepping Back* (1997), theatrical performances in specific buildings, such as *A Child's Christmas in Wales*, an adaptation of Dylan Thomas's book at Oakdale Workmen's Institute (1998), and *In Pursuit of a Suitable Suitor*, an interlude performed at Hendre-wen barn (1998), as well as dramatic pieces for the National Museum and Gallery in Cathays in Cardiff, which interpreted gallery portraiture or scientific exhibits for children, such as *The Famous Five and the Spiffing Footprint Mystery* (1997). At other

NMW sites examples included *A Century of Motoring in Wales* at the Welsh Industrial and Maritime Museum (1997), and *Lice, Loricas and Legionnairs* and *Boudicca* at the Roman Legionary Museum, Caerllion (1997). Anterliwt was prolific but the venture was short-lived, possibly because the concept of using theatrical performance as part of a broader interpretation programme was not as thoroughly embedded in the museum's infrastructure or curatorial policy as it was at Bradford, where a working theatre company was able to enliven and enhance the exhibition of a working television studio. Clare Parry has suggested that the introduction of the company did not sit well with the overall curatorial and conservational stance of the museum, and that in addition to being called a 'theatre company', a potential drawback within the museum context, group members were never perceived as true interpreters of the museum's collections and the company overall was viewed as an embellishment rather than a core part of the interpretation process.[96] This difficulty with perception might have been compounded by the fact that numerous theatre companies have performed at Sain Ffagan on an ad hoc basis, utilising the site as a backdrop. This is a site of performance after all, atmospheric and replete with familial associations that evoke a sense of the past. It is also a seductive theatrical site that holds an endless variety of performance possibilities due to the different time periods and its overall immersive nature. Companies such as Everyman Theatre, a popular community-based group, have used the site as a pastoral backdrop, often for staging Shakespeare in an open-air setting, the site providing a setting for the drama without direct reference to the site as place (or museum).

There are numerous companies and artists, however, whose work has been closely integrated into the site itself, such as Welsh theatre company Brith Gof's *Boris* (1985), performed at Hendre-wen, the seventeenth-century barn. This production, an adaptation of John Berger's short story about a shepherd driven to suicide, resided in the site with ease, and spoke about rural Welsh life and our relationship with it. The audience sat on straw bales along the side walls of the barn, a familiar set-up for many Welsh audiences, reflecting the *noson lawen* tradition of sketches, stand-up and song.[97] The performance referenced curatorial practices, such as the *in situ* display: 'the two large wooden doors opposing each other once facilitated winnowing. One end is dressed with furniture and ornaments as a rural kitchen, after the manner of museum practice here', and the production took mimetic display to its natural conclusion with the inclusion of farm animals: Boris 'talks to his horse, feeds his dog – a chainsaw belches fumes – sheep run into the barn during a thunderstorm – a shower of autumn leaves covers the hunched body of Boris.'[98] Director Mike Pearson remarks how the barn, as part of a formal collection, needed to remain unmarked, a common concern for museum performance, and yet it was robust enough to accommodate the animals, the hay and natural materials, and the comings and goings of the performers as they enacted a series of habitual tasks associated with the barn.[99] This is theatre performance as a set of compatible tasks, reflecting the habitual activities of the building.

In 1996, Eddie Ladd's production *Once Upon a Time in the West* was performed on an open field at Sain Ffagan in a performance that merged two discrete narratives, that of the Western film *Shane* (1953) and an account of the events surrounding a landslide on Ladd's aunt's farm in Llandudoch, Pembrokeshire, two years previously. That the piece was also played at Ladd's home farm in Cardiganshire as part of the tour gave the performance at Sain Ffagan a ghostly sense of repetition, which drew attention to the site as uncanny copy of the rural. This doubling was reflected in the performance itself, which according to critic Emyr Edwards presented 'the dichotomy of the romantic and the real, of escapism and the present, truth and lie, woven throughout the performance.'[100] Similarly, artists eager to reflect on the significance and meaning of place have produced site-responsive interventions at Sain Ffagan. In *shed * light* (2004), artist Marc Rees, in collaboration with Berlin architect Benedict Anderson, presented a multimedia installation in two parts, looking at 'the reconstruction of an individual's experience of space, place and identity through architectural design, building, film photography and sound installation.'[101] In the first installation, entitled 'Replica', a reconstruction of a dynamite shed from the Swansea Valley in south Wales was situated at Sain Ffagan. A copy of the site of the artist's first sexual encounter, the shed was covered both inside and out with specially designed flocked wallpaper referencing the ivy covering the original shed, but it also in its detail presented 'subtle male erotica [naked male bodies] that echoe[d] the rites of passage within the building's history.'[102] Making explicit connections between the mundane everyday building (the space) and the meaning and implications of a particular building in a specific location

4. A) Y Talwrn Ymladd Ceiliogod, the Cockpit, from the Hawk and
Buckle Inn, Dinbych, Sain Ffagan Amgueddfa Werin Cymru (with
kind permission of Amgueddfa Cymru/National Museum Wales)
Photo: Lisa Lewis.

for the artist's own personal experiences and the way it informed his
identity (the place), the piece articulated the implications of embodied
experience for the interpretation and presentation of historic buildings
as meaningful places. It also drew attention to the reconstruction of
the building as a cultural statement, and the identity politics inherent
in the choice of building and materials.

In one of the most playful installations, artist Bedwyr Williams presented *Tafarn yr Iorwerth Peate* (The Iorwerth Peate Tavern) in 2008,
as part of the museum's sixtieth anniversary celebrations.[103] Bearing a
deliberately provocative title in reference to Peate's teetotalism and his
staunch belief that there should not be a public house on the museum
site, the piece plays on the centrality and importance of the tavern to
the community in Welsh cultural history. *Tafarn yr Iorwerth Peate*
consisted of a miniature model of a pub called 'Tafarn yr Iorwerth
Peate' installed on the seventeenth-century cockpit stage, and was
publicised as 'the first time ever a pub was opened at the Museum',
which Williams insisted was needed in order to represent the lives of
the Welsh, with a playful nod to Peate's well-known abstinence. It also

B) 'Tafarn yr Iorwerth Peate', by Bedwyr Williams.
Photo: Bedwyr Williams.

C) 'Tafarn yr Iorwerth Peate' beer mat, by Bedwyr Williams.
Photo: Bedwyr Williams.

referenced the cockpit's site of origin as part of the outbuildings of the Hawk and Buckle Inn from Dinbych. During the week of its installation *Tafarn yr Iorwerth Peate* included an *ymryson y beirdd*, a poetic contest often referred to as *talwrn y beirdd* (the bards' cockpit, echoing the building's Welsh name, *y talwrn ymladd ceiliogod*), and entitled, even more playfully, *Trafferth mewn Talwrn* (trouble in a cockpit), a play on twelfth-century poet Dafydd ap Gwilym's *cywydd*, *Trafferth mewn Tafarn* (trouble in a tavern).[104] As Peate was also a poet, the installation had a particular resonance despite its irreverence, highlighting the interrelatedness of social and cultural practices, and perhaps, offering a critique of notions of Welshness that deny or seek to eradicate binding social customs.[105] Both installations, by Rees and Williams, referenced the meaning and implications of the historical buildings and the activities undertaken in them but did so in such a way that the space became a playful one, open to containing various and contesting interpretations and responses. These performative interventions also serve to heighten the contradictions at work in Sain Ffagan, which Rhiannon Mason has referred to as a 'text' that is 'open-ended and internally contradictory', in which 'it is possible to identify competing definitions of Welshness'.[106] Here we glimpse the possibility of Sain Ffagan as an open-ended narrative on Wales and Welsh identity. In this narrative process, performance and the performative are central, for they enable a discursive space in which to negotiate different and opposing meanings and significances – modes of operating that facilitate dialogic understandings. This is performance as *poiesis*, enabling 'the making and breaking' of cultural constructs in order to reflect on their composition and relevance in relation to contemporary identity questions.

TREFTADAETH: HERITAGE

3

Heritage is a slippery term, associated in an English context with government departments, lottery funding and an appropriation by stealth of the culture that is deemed to be of value. In this context, it is a word that denotes power. The 'heritage industry', damned by cultural commentators since the 1980s, has become such a significant sector that its causes are now difficult to discern, despite the burgeoning of a heritage discourse that has its roots in late nineteenth-century Europe and the rise of nationalism and liberal modernity. Following a trajectory slightly different from the English definition, though remaining in thrall to nineteenth-century ideals, the Welsh term *treftadaeth* (patrimony, birth right, signifying inheritance as well as heritage), has been unambiguously associated in Welsh culture with the formation of Welsh ideals of culture and tradition, and is inherently bound up in the mix of Nonconformity and linguistic nationalism that characterised nineteenth-century Wales. The earliest recorded uses of the term *treftadaeth* all occur within a religious context, which places it within a theological and patriarchal definition of inheritance and lineage, an inflection that has profoundly influenced its meaning.[1] It is only in the more recent growth of the heritage industry and its affiliation with tourism in the latter half of the twentieth century that we see the emergence of a more explicitly secular use of the word in a Welsh language-context. Contemporary *treftadaeth* is ephemeral but also firmly rooted in a sense of place, signifying activities and performances that are culturally emplaced. *Treftadaeth* continues to bear strong social (occasionally religious) connotations demonstrated by the way in which it is often prefixed by 'ein' (our): ein treftadeth. In all definitions of the word, the present has a duty to the past and there is an implicit assumption that processes associated with treftadaeth forge a sense of belonging and identity out of the past. The inferred sense of duty in treftadaeth, the suggestion of the need to pass on sets of knowledges that exist in and between members of a community, ensures that the word bears significant meaning in relation to perpetuating a personal and communal sense of identity. Through language, culture and knowledge, treftadaeth is transmitted (or not) from one generation to the next; it is a knowledge enacted in the present, and in a way that defines a community of people.

This explicit meaning of treftadaeth is to be found in Iorwerth Peate's writings on the establishment of a Folk Museum for Wales and contributes to the notion of the folk museum as an active construct in which people participate and where the people of a nation define and see themselves as treftadaeth. Peate's writings also reveal a strong tendency towards the participatory, albeit as an integral part of the process of performing culture in a specific way. Following Skansen's example, Peate sought to establish a responsive community space, where performers and participants come together to perform their traditional culture. Although preservation through participation in the folk museum suggests a strong cultural revivalism, the principle of interaction necessarily allows for diversity of opinions and for shifts and revisions, and it is this aspect that reveals the potential for the folk museum as an adaptable site in terms of changing portrayals of identity. Peate's definition of 'folk' as gwerin, or all people, would eventually result in multitudinous readings of what Sain Ffagan Amgueddfa Werin Cymru should be and culminated most recently in the museum as site of the history of all the peoples of Wales, reflecting the emphasis both on ordinary lives and on participatory interpretation in recent museum interpretation. The emphasis on ordinary life in the open-air museum or heritage site, which became more prevalent from the late 1970s onwards, has been attributed by Bella Dicks to a 'vernacular turn' in museum display, in which questions of identity, place and belonging abound.[2] These questions are deeply connected to an emphasis on local history and to what Sharon Macdonald refers to as telling the people's story – a way of providing agency for communal identity and of ensuring that multiple voices are heard.[3] In contemporary museum practice, this emphasis has caused a shift towards a participatory model, explored in Nina Simon's book *The Participatory Museum* (2010). The Museum of Art and History in Santa Cruz (of which Simon is executive director), provides the ultimate open and fluid community-based endeavour where the visitor is a participant in the creation of meaning and of the definition of history itself, through her collaboration in the processes of interpreting history and culture.[4]

It is in the heritage site, as opposed to the museum (though there is a significant overlap), that ideas of participation have gained traction. Usually situated on a reclaimed site, the heritage attraction is governed by a different set of rules regarding the nature of its interpretive and educational aims. This is because, in the context of Tony Bennett's exhibitionary complex, in which a differentiation is sought between the museum and other sites such as theatres and fairgrounds, the heritage encounter is defined as a primarily touristic leisure experience. Unlike the museum, the heritage site does not need to work very hard to declare its story, because the communal memory of what the site once was is often enough, and this has a strong role to play in its performance, which in turn supports the collective memory regarding its past. In this way, the heritage site is an emergent realm of memory, a place that has special significance for the group's remembrance, born suddenly from the ashes of a real environment within living memory.

The centrality of the bodily experience in the understanding of history and the emplacement of the self in relation to a/the past, is increasingly evident in the heritage 'experience' and the work that heritage sites do, though in the museum there continues to be a strong tension between 'heritage performance' and what is considered to be the museum's core activity, that of educating through its collections. This dichotomy of popularist or entertainment-led versus the educational is based on a fallacy, one that masks a power relationship between knowledge bearers and receivers, or what Laurajane Smith calls the 'authorised heritage discourse', the dominant way of understanding heritage in European public policy and practice. According to Smith, this way of understanding is institutionalised in cultural agencies and is based on 'the grand narratives of nation and class' on the one hand, and 'technical expertise and aesthetic judgement' on the other, and because its methodologies are associated with nation building, 'it . . . defines heritage as a "thing", which must be authenticated and preserved, unchanged for the future by heritage experts'.[5] Subsequently, the authorised heritage discourse operates in a way that obscures the work that heritage 'does' as a social and cultural practice. Smith's response, informed by critical discourse analysis, is to examine the work that the practices and performances of heritage do culturally and socially, and it is in this context that Smith can assert that heritage is a process, a thing done:

> As the subject of international treaties, conventions and charters, and the subject of national laws and policy programmes, heritage is often defined as a thing of value – something to be cherished, managed, conserved or curated. There is, however, no such *thing* as heritage. Rather, heritage is a cultural performance that occurs at, and with, heritage sites or museum exhibitions. It is a process of remembering and forgetting, and while particular 'things' or spaces may be used as tools in that remembering, it is not the things or places that are themselves 'heritage', it is the uses that these things are put to that make them 'heritage'. Heritage is a process or a performance, in which certain cultural and social meanings and values are identified, reaffirmed or rejected, and should not be, though it often is, conflated with sites or places. (p. 69)

In describing heritage as a cultural process, and one in which memory plays a central role, Smith is defining it as a movement predicated on active participation, where visitors engage with a form of cultural performance. Such open-ended or flexible thinking about the practices of heritage stands in direct opposition to the 'hegemonic discourse about heritage, which acts to constitute the way we think, talk and write' (p. 11) about it, an uncompromising stance that validates a set of practices and performances affecting both popular and authoritative views of heritage, undermining any alternative. Opening heritage up, or re-theorising it as performance 'rather than a "thing", place site or monument', and remaining alert to the processes involved in constituting such performance, broadens the conceptual understanding of heritage, and shows the cultural 'work' that heritage does in any society: 'The idea of heritage as performance . . . is based on the premise that all heritage is intangible, in so far that heritage is a moment or process of re/constructing cultural and social values and meanings.'[6] According to Smith heritage includes a range of activities, 'remembering, commemoration, communicating and passing on knowledges and memories', and the emotions, experiences and memories associated with these activities succeed in fostering identity, a sense of belonging and of community.[7] Furthermore, she locates performativity as an element arising out of the writing on remembrance, citing Gaynor Bagnall's position that visiting heritage sites is an experience of performance and reminiscence that assists in either affirming or rejecting the vision of history offered by the museum. Smith's views and analyses of the visitor forging heritage, and therefore identity, as an *act* or performance of remembering or commemoration, within the participatory context of the museum or heritage site, challenge the idea that the process of communication at such sites is one-directional and that visitors are nothing more than passive consumers. The view of the visitor as passive receptacle is a consequence of the museum's inherited purpose of educating (and civilising) the masses and results in a stance in which the spectator's agency is removed. Smith remarks in particular on what happens when the visitor steps outside the legitimised relationship of the authorised heritage discourse, only to face criticism from heritage professionals, which suggests that 'heritage performance' can be problematic for some within the museum and heritage sector specifically because it might provide an abundance of agency for the visitor, and by extension a freedom to interpret. It follows that one of the central issues in heritage is that all matters of personal memory, narrative and association can be obscured by the emphasis on the authorised discourse.

The critique of the folk museum in the 1980s is rooted in the critical assault on heritage that emerged in Britain at that time by historians focusing on the development of mass consumption and the marketing of attractions for tourists, which in their opinion reduced heritage to entertainment. There were frequent and weighty condemnations of heritage re-enactments as amateur, inauthentic, sanitised and escapist.[8] Cultural historian Patrick Wright, writing in 1985, associated the contemporary heritage obsession with a decline that can be traced back to the late nineteenth century and that advanced further following the Second World War, eventually turning Britain into a form of heritage theme park: 'This sense of history as entropic decline gathers momentum in the sharpening of the British crisis. National heritage is the backward glance which is taken from the edge of a vividly imagined abyss, and it accompanies a sense that history is foreclosed.'[9] In an echo of Nora's shift from *milieu* to *lieux de mémoire*, Wright tells of the specific form that the decline took in Britain, where historical consciousness had been dominant: 'History becomes, more urgently, the object of ceremonies of resonance and continuity when it seems actively to be threatened and opposed by an inferior present epoch – when, to put this differently, society is developing (or 'receding') in a way that cuts across the grain of traditional forms of security and self-understanding' (p. 166). Cultural historian Robert Hewison, writing in 1987, lamented the cultural decline of Britain as an inevitable consequence of the growing trend in heritage consumption. In his damning indictment, the heritage industry is defined as backward-looking, escapist and anti-innovation. Perceiving the rise in museum visiting, the popularity of open-air museums and of civil war re-enactments, along with the conservation agenda for the country house, as part of a retrograde and nostalgic drive, Hewison concludes that the movement is 'evidence of the persistent fantasy that it is possible to step back into the past.[10] In direct opposition to this critique of heritage, historian Raphael Samuel discusses the heritage industry as a medium in which the democratising stance of people's history is enabled.[11] Castigating the 'heritage baiters',[12] for their attacks on what he calls 'living history' Samuel perceives a polarisation of education and entertainment and 'an unspoken and unargued for assumption that pleasure is almost by definition mindless' (p. 271). While Wright and Hewison are concerned with the distortion and commodification of history as a form of late capitalism, for Samuel the heritage industry operates as a form of 'resurrectionism'[13] that opens history up to numerous people and that facilitates a telling of history 'from below'. Samuel defines the playing out of cultural and historical identity performances as a 'living history', and explains that it is an ubiquitous form, or rather a new incarnation of 'ancient forms of play'; he also defines historical re-enactment as 'one of the oldest of the mimetic arts' (p. 180). Citing the civic ceremony and procession in early modern Europe and the earlier Corpus Christi processions as performances in which re-enactment was central, he proceeds to describe the extent of the practice as a tool for social, communal and cultural cohesion and refers to its use by political and social groups, such as nineteenth-century friendly societies 'with their elaborate processions and floats', the importance of impersonating legendary historical figures for 'rituals of resistance and rebellion', its practice as an aristocratic folly and its widespread popularity in general (p. 180). Samuel locates two early re-enactment societies, The Sealed Knot, which focuses on the English Civil War, founded in 1968, and the Ermine Street Guard, the first Roman army group, founded in 1971, within the development of a new museology and the general culture of immediacy in 1960s Britain.[14] Acknowledging that the idea and practice of living history is highly problematical, even 'offensive' to the professional historian, in that it shows no respect for the historical document, plays 'snakes and ladders with the evidence' and treats the past as though it was 'an immediately accessible present', Samuel makes the case for it, explaining that its ambition is not at odds with traditional scholarly ideals. In elaborating on these ideas, he cites Michelet's 'resurrectionism', the concept of bringing the dead to life, which he considers pivotal in the nineteenth-century revolution in historical scholarship, and romantic realism, which values the idea of authenticity. Samuel reads living history as a form of making up for gaps in memory that attempts to improve on the original and goes beyond inference in deciphering the historic. Above all else, living history operates as a representative of the social history that 'enjoyed a recognized, if contested, place in the public sphere' (p. 197–8). This position is a reminder of the space for negotiation found in interpretations of history and a warning against the dogmatic realm of the authorised heritage discourse.

In an echo of Samuel's resurrectionism, Barbara Kirshenblatt-Gimblett refers to a particular form of heritage performance as 'resurrection theatre'.[15] In her analysis of the heritage site as a reworking of itself, for instance from closed mine to heritage site, as in the case of the Rhondda Heritage Park, place is imbued with a marked change in significance, one that allows the site to continue to exist and some of the people who worked there to continue to be in place, albeit with a drastic change in the parameters of daily working life, a shift that involves the presentation of the site as a performance of itself. The role of heritage in economic restructuring following industrial decline is expounded upon further by Bella Dicks in her work on the south Wales valleys, where she considers the social impact of the drastic change from mining community to 'heritage park'.[16] Certainly, the expansion of the heritage park correlates with the closure of the industrial sites that were once central to many of the communities in south Wales. J. Geraint Jenkins, curator of Sain Ffagan in the 1980s and early 1990s, comments on the sudden rise of history and heritage sites across Wales (50 sites before 1960, 45 more established between 1969 and 1976, and by 1992, the year of Jenkins's retirement, a total of 325 sites), 'from nautical to slate museums, from wool museum to coal mines, before we come to mention collections of objects such as love spoons and ploughs, milking and agricultural equipment'. Such a proliferation suggested to Jenkins that some Welsh traditions were being 'over-interpreted',[17] a significant statement from the first chair of the Society for the Interpretation of Britain's Heritage (which later became the Association for Heritage Interpretation). It is no coincidence that such a drastic rise in heritage institutions in Wales was to happen across the areas being decimated by the decline of heavy industry – Welsh communities in which identity questions were to become urgent following the destruction of their livelihoods. The impetus behind the industrial heritage site can be seen as a cultural necessity, a 'resurrection' of the site in a different form, one that now provides an entirely different commodity, that of the heritage experience. Such sites in Wales include the Rhondda Heritage Park in Porth, operated through Rhondda Cynon Taf county council, the National Slate Museum in Llanberis, north Wales, and Big Pit National Coal Museum in Blaenafon, south Wales, both Amgueddfa Cymru / National Museum Wales sites. As they operate under county council and museum their focus is broadly educational, though they all utilise elements such as live interpretation, an element of role-play and a sense of immersion. This is particularly true of Rhondda Heritage Park, which has more scope for play, given that it is a heritage attraction. While situated on the site of what was once a working mine, the attraction does not actually take us into it, though it appears to do so. Following a visit to the operational buildings above ground, where visitors are given their hard hats and torchlights, the simulation begins with the descent into the pit in a cage, a walk through a 'mine', which includes a simulated explosion, and a ride experience. The combination of performative components is a patchwork quilt of different experiences related to the history of the mine and of mining, its playfulness reined in by the authenticity provided by the guide, a former miner, who is central to the experience. Our memorialisation and understanding of the importance of this place to the community is carried by the guide, whose aura of the original puts us in touch with the reality of the site, even though we are aware of the shift from place of work to place of memory. In the change from closed industry to heritage site the common denominator is the site as place and the memories the place hold for the community itself. This shift also chimes with the romantic version of 'theatre of memory', which according to Samuel 'focused on the family circle and the individual self. Its landscapes of the mind or memory places were, as often as not . . . the childhood home. Romanticism built on time's ruins. Its idea of memory was premised on a sense of loss.'[18] The making of heritage out of that which has been lost, and in recollection of it, places the heritage site firmly within the romantic tendency to revere place as locus of memory. While Laurajane Smith argues that heritage itself should not be conflated with site, the concept of place is crucial to the way heritage works. In a reflection of the tension between place as a 'category of thought' and as a 'constructed reality',[19] Smith argues that a sense of place is an important aspect of heritage, as it enables the situating of people 'as a nation, community or individual in our 'place' in our cultural, social and physical world.' In this way, heritage is a device that communities can use to form and share identities that are represented through 'the power of place'.[20]

Sain Ffagan's shifting representations of place and the evolving English title from Folk Museum to National Museum of History, the critique that revolved around the nature of its collections, as well as developments in the museum's aims, can all be seen as a performance of heritage in which conflicting cultural and social identities are contested. Sain Ffagan has always emerged the better for its entanglements with heritage discourse, the museum able to assimilate and discuss the critiques presented to it. There are sites, however, that have failed to instigate change, due to an inability to acknowledge the idea of heritage as process. Celtica (1996–2006), situated in a former stately home near Machynlleth in mid-Wales, was to be a national centre for the study and interpretation of Celtic culture, with an explicit remit to educate and provide space for scholarly research. However, it operated first and foremost as a tourist attraction that presented Celtic history as a backstory to a definition of Welsh cultural distinctiveness. This ambivalence was partly to blame for its failure. The idea behind Celtica's exhibit design was brave: to hollow out the main hall of a stately home, Y Plas (donated to Machynlleth town by the marquess of Londonderry in 1948), and to construct a maze of circular sets inside it, atmospherically lit, and navigated in near darkness by the visitor, who would be led by the instructions received via an audio commentary on headsets. The meandering nature of the experience and the difference in exhibition techniques used meant that it was stimulating and surprising for the first-time visitor. The sets themselves were designed and constructed by eminent historical interpreter John Sunderland, who had been responsible for the design and construction of Jorvik Viking Centre in York. Even more so than Jorvik, in which the visitor travels through a reconstruction of Viking York complete with mannequins and 'smells', the experience at Celtica was fully immersive. Entering the experience on foot, and at their own pace, the visitor was tethered to the audio recording composed of spoken commentary, music and dramatic dialogue and eventually met a performer in a reconstruction of a 'Celtic' village. The journey included sections with film, interactive exhibits, special effects and *in situ* displays. Central to it all was the sense of subjective encounter, almost of being in a dream world, heightened by the audio headset experience, which inevitably isolated (and controlled) the visitor. The aesthetic was purposefully abstract and atmospheric, as John Sunderland explains: 'Celtica is not simply a reconstructive, walk-through history lesson, a parade of the past, but a subjective, emotive, and dynamic presentation which attempts to put visitors in contact with a sense of what it is to be Celtic.'[21] This aspect was an overriding part of the experience, necessary because it is actually difficult to claim a strong identity connection to the Celts once the historical information is presented. Different moments in the journey through the exhibit emphasised the mystical qualities of the Celts; the first sequence at *Y Pair* (the cauldron), provided background, before the visitor moved on to the origins gallery, which presented the culture and beliefs of the Celts. In the central reconstruction of a Celtic village around AD 85, the habitat diorama presented mannequins of Celtic people at work; one of them, in a surprising moment, moved – an actor portraying a young girl called Nia, who asks '*Ydych chi'n siarad Cymraeg?*' (Do you speak Welsh?). She introduced her family – Cadfab and Rhiannon, both warriors, and her brother Gwydion, who aspires to become a druid – and told of life in the village. Following on from this meeting, *Y Tŷ Crwn* (the Roundhouse) provided an opportunity to place the spotlight on a specific character in a diorama of human figures, each one telling of their past exploits and feats. The next section, in the magical forest, explored ideas about Celtic religion including *Annwn*, the underworld, and was followed by *Y Trobwll* (the whirlpool), a semi-circular seating arrangement around a circular screen into which the visitor peered to see the boy Gwydion shapeshift and look into the future. Behind the screen is the tree of life and above it a further screen that shows the face of the druid. Here Gwydion must solve a series of riddles that offer glimpses of the Celts' future. We were now in the realm of the hero's story, rather than in any representation of history, and at stake is our own identity. Having passed through the whirlpool Gwydion glimpses signs of contemporary Wales that are interpreted by him from a 'Celtic' viewpoint – flying dragons are airplanes; the miners are 'fallen heroes'; and language and culture continue. The emotional impact of this final section is heightened by the mythic structure and the investment we place in the central character. Following on from this, the merging of Celtic history with the identity issues raised by the heritage centre are compounded in a film of a choir of schoolchildren in traditional Welsh costume, singing folk singer Dafydd Iwan's anthem '*Ry'n ni yma o hyd*' (We're still here).

Celtica strove to make connections between the Celts and contemporary Welsh identity through motifs and tropes it borrowed from Celtic revivalism, as well as references to recent Welsh history of the time (the Eisteddfod, poetry, song). Early promotional material had stated the intention of focusing on projecting Wales to the world, but locating contemporary Welsh identity as a whole in relation to what is understood and known about Iron Age Britain is inherently problematical. Dismissing the difficulty of interpreting what Celtic culture is or means, Celtica unabashedly defined it as Welsh, in a highly subjective dramatisation. In addition to the complications involved in defining Celtic history, Celtica was also adversely affected by its blurring of the edges between history and fiction, the centre's use of dramatic material and theatrical replay coming at a time when these aspects were being problematised in the museum and heritage context. While the fact that Celtica's state-of-the-art technology was bound to date undoubtedly played a part in its closure, the apparent split between history and fiction within the heritage attraction itself was also a factor that contributed to the critique of the project as a whole.[22] This split continues to trouble the museum and heritage site.

Laurajane Smith's 'authorised heritage discourse', which has its emphasis on accuracy and the objectivity of history, portraying a national ideal from 'above', is a direct descendent in heritage terms of the split between fiction and scientific rationality in historical discourse. This split is analysed by historian Hayden White, who describes and pulls apart 'the fictions of factual representation'. White's deconstruction centres on the reliance of history on narrative, and the resemblance between the discourses of the historian and the imaginative writer, which are differentiated only by the opposing ideas of truth that we locate within these narratives.[23] This schism between imaginative act and scientific objectivity in history, promulgated by the authorised heritage discourse, ensures that memory's role is demoted, because its subjectivity and perceived fallibility are suspect. Both performance and memory in the museum context are highly problematized areas that continue to cut across authorised versions of historical method. Heritage, in its free form and fluent application of different methods, ideas and modes, upstages and upsets attempts to defend historical objectivity. Nowhere is this more apparent than in the fields of heritage performance known as living history and re-enactment.

Ail-chwarae Hanes, living history: making and breaking history through performance

> 'Doedd dim clociau / There were no clocks.'
> ENGRAVED ON A STONE ON THE PATHWAY
> UP TO CASTELL HENLLYS.[24]

Despite Raphael Samuel's analysis of the historical presence of re-enactment as a ritual enactment and his advocacy of contemporary 'living history' as a form of public sphere in which history is discussed and defined, its development in the museum and heritage site in Wales has been restrained. While in North America living history has sat alongside formal museum practice for a long time, it has not been as well received across the museum and heritage sector in the British Isles and has consequently lacked status and remained peripheral.[25] While American theatre and museum groups such as the Association for Living History, Farm and Agriculture Museums (ALHFAM), established in 1970, and the International Museum Theatre Alliance (IMTAL), established in 1990, have become instrumental in establishing a philosophy, terminology and methodology for living history, serving museums and practitioners of living history, the European branch of IMTAL was not set up until 1999.[26] At the same time, living history has a strong community following amongst heritage enthusiasts. Practice varies greatly and a general mistrust of the field and a splitting of living history participants into factions (considered professional or amateur), have hampered its acceptance. Very few sites in the British Isles use living history continuously as the mainstay of the

5. Stone situated on the walk from heritage centre to Castell Henllys,
site of a reconstructed Iron Age Fort, Meline, Crymych.
Photo: Lisa Lewis.

visitor experience. The only site to do so on a daily basis is Llancaiach
Fawr Manor, near Caerffili in south Wales, thought to be unique
because of its emphasis on interpreting in the first person.[27] That is,
it is renowned for upholding the device whereby the heritage visit
takes place as though within the historical period being interpreted, so
that interpreters interacting with visitors are unable to refer to history
beyond the date they inhabit within the interpretation, which almost

always means that they may not refer explicitly to contemporary life. While a representation of life at a specific time in history is also given at Castell Henllys (site of an Iron Age fort) in Pembrokeshire and at Cosmeston Medieval Village (site of a Norman settlement and set in 1350) in the Vale of Glamorgan, the communication between visitors and interpreters at these sites does not adhere to the conventions of strict mimetic representation and visitors may converse with inter-preters in a comparative capacity – drawing lines between now and then. Interestingly, Sain Ffagan has been widely perceived to be a living museum, despite the lack of performers in costume, and was upheld by directors of Colonial Williamsburg in the USA as the 'finest living museum in the world'.[28] Before proceeding to discuss Llancaiach Fawr in more depth I want to consider the context of the development of living history and its background in American interpretation and to provide an account of the living history experience at two sites by way of comparison, because they reveal the heritage site as performance of national history. These are Plimoth Plantation in Massachusetts and Colonial Williamsburg in Virginia, both widely seen as the chief representative sites of heritage interpretation and performance.

Attempts at establishing a genealogy of living history practices are numerous, reflecting a desire to find a foothold in the history of museum development. American Jay Anderson, author of one of the earliest studies on living history, *Time Machines: The World of Living History* (1984), offers three categories of living history: practices used in education, those related to research and those pertaining to rec-reation. Tracing the form back to Artur Hazelius's use of musicians, craftspeople and folk performances at Skansen in the late nineteenth century, Anderson perceives an evolution of the form along a line of increasing sophistication, reaching full-scale re-enactment in large-scale living history sites in the USA. This developmental line in living history, from simple to sophisticated, is rooted in an apparent association between Skansen and the American museum, through the shipping of six dioramas from Sweden to the Centennial Exhibition in Philadelphia in 1876. That these dioramas were much admired by Henry Ford and John D. Rockefeller, who went on to create Greenfield Village and Colonial Williamsburg respectively, supported the idea of the diorama's sphere of influence. The connection provides Anderson with a direct link between early techniques of museum display, for-mal displays, the diorama and, at the other end of the spectrum, the live techniques utilised by outdoor sites such as open-air museums,[29] the pinnacle of which, for Anderson, is Plimoth Plantation in Massachusetts. Plimoth Plantation is important to Anderson's evolutionary line as it represents the developmental narrative from static display and diorama evolving through to the use of actors performing the pilgrims. Barbara Kirshenblatt-Gimblett refers to Plimoth Plantation as a heritage site constructed to mark the 'site of origin' of modern (white) America due to the fact that Plymouth Rock, where the pilgrims are supposed to have landed, is 'mute' and 'incapable of conveying anything about "the pilgrim experience".[30] Thus, Plimoth Plantation becomes a performance site that bears the weight of the historical explication as well as a site of origin that satisfies the desire for authenticity. The network of 'authentic' sites – the seventeenth-century village itself, Hobbamock's Homesite (the site of Native Wampanoag interpretation), the reproduction ship *Mayflower II*, the Craft Center and the Plimoth Grist Mill, provides an inescapable sense of heritage in the region as a whole, marking it as the place where the pilgrim narrative begins. That 'Plimoth' is not built at the site of the original and excavated settlement (that lies in modern-day Plymouth) makes this heritage site a simulacrum, a copy of something that does not actually exist. The 'not original' status of the site allows a sense of place to emerge that facilitates and underpins the historical replay. Predicated on the idea of immersing the visitor in a working village that is perpetually in the 1620s, Plimoth Plantation appears as though in a continuous process of being built, and to facilitate this ploy buildings are taken down or removed in order to begin the process of building anew when the annual programme is repeated. In a kind of perpetually unfolding performance of *terra nullius*, the village is always new, continually in the process of becoming. Bearing no marks of the original, the site is not archaeological and is able to perform the function of an 'empty space' within which we come to understand the historical interrelationships of European pilgrims and native Wampanoag Indians, a view that does not wholly acknowledge the power relations implicit in the history of the land. Despite the theatricality that is the premise of Plimoth Plantation as site, the experience of verisimilitude in the pilgrim village is acute, and this is supported by a striking lack of overt theatricality by the performer-interpreters. Life, 'as it was' in the 1620s, according to the best research, is interpreted and re-presented to exacting mimetic standards; the seventeenth-century dress is meticulously researched and constructed, the actors talk in appropriate dialects, the animals kept are part of a rare breeding programme and are as close as could be to the animals the pilgrims brought with them. All such detail is a psychological device underpinning the illusion that the representation is as realistic as possible. The thousands of objects unearthed at the original site and the research into them, as well as the detailed analysis of ways of work and of craft, provide the authority that signals an authentic recreation. This sense of immersion, enabled by the exacting authenticity, ensures that it is possible to manage the imaginative leap of believing that you might truly be 'there', which in Plimoth Plantation, predicated as it is towards the pilgrim narrative of white Anglo-Saxon America, is the identity that you might feasibly walk in with.

The initial journey on foot into the village has the feel of visiting a religious community removed from society, though this impression is shattered when actor-interpreters begin to perform a narrative before a small group of visitors, one that is loosely-structured enough to appear of the moment but is essentially a key marker in the plot of the drama of Plimoth Plantation. Narratives refer to the loss of family members and crew during the sea voyage or the first year on land, denoted both in what the performers have to say and in terms of the familial interrelationships portrayed; they also reference ways of life, craft ways, laws and social customs. In these meetings, the visitor is expected to respond, to interject and to ask questions, as though in conversation. The fact that the performance is so immersive encourages such interaction, but often substantial sections of narrative, if delivered dramatically, are unable to support the general sense of everyday life that the performers work so hard to convey. That is, the performance charge is sometimes unavoidable and the performer's energy punctures the everyday quietude of the exchange. Outside such dramatic interactions, low-key everyday activities are happened upon by the visitor and the impression is one of life carrying on, regardless of who is watching. Indeed, the interpreters as pilgrims have certain tasks and errands that they must complete, many of them manual, and these take place irrespective of whether they are being watched or not. It is only later and outside the context of the performance that wider questions arise – are they eating or performing eating? Are they performing after we leave the house or are they just continuing to eat as themselves? In practice, there is a limit to the potential discussion. This constraint stems from the fact that pilgrim interpreters are caught within the seventeenth-century device; in deference to historical accuracy the horizon of expectations is not set beyond this date and thus interpreters are unable to engage in a conversation regarding events that took place at a later date. Such a strict take on historical interpretation is almost always overturned by the broader awareness of history. In stark contrast, representatives of the Wampanoag people, who are all American Indian interpreters though not necessarily Wampanoag, do not represent the imagined history. Situated on a separate site and wearing seventeenth-century dress, the Wampanoag interpreters converse in twenty-first century dialect, discussing freely outside the 1620s 'restriction'. They tell stories and sing in a contemporary rendering of American Indian heritage. For this reason, the Wampanoag site is the only context in which the pilgrim experience can be discussed outside the period constraint, making this site crucial to the overall understanding of the history. At the pilgrim village actor-interpreters portray a story that legitimises a particular heritage identity and emphasises the interrelationship between the pilgrims and the American Indians, honing in on the 'first thanksgiving' and the coming together of two different cultures in mutually beneficial co-operation. The unfortunate drawback in this is that, even though the Wampanoag people are represented as a constant presence, their story is never related fully other than in relation to that of the pilgrims. While the pilgrims are the 'others', the two shops inside the heritage centre, at the time of my visit, were designated 'main' and 'Native', betraying the narrative at play and raising questions about whose history is being presented and who the audience is. Similarly, the focus on the initial relationship between the emigrant European community and Native Americans in this particular area obscures the devastating narrative of oppression of the Native people – neither pilgrim nor Wampanoag interpretations refer beyond themselves to the hundreds of years of conflict between the colonisers and the Native peoples of the area, which is problematic given the celebratory tone of the 'initial meeting', portrayed at Plimoth as a key moment in America's history.

In contrast, Williamsburg, in Virginia, is both an actual town and an archaeological site in the process of being excavated, as well as being a partly reconstructed town, 'Colonial Williamsburg', the most developed heritage performance site in the West. It is a place haunted by its own history: at over 300 acres the historic area includes eighty-eight original eighteenth-century structures and hundreds of houses, shops and outbuildings reconstructed on their original foundations, some of which are open to the public, while others are private residences or offices. The actuality of Williamsburg as 'original' has been upheld as the main criterion since its inception, when John D. Rockefeller, figurehead and financial backer of the project, proclaimed authenticity to be his chief aim, an ambition that has prevailed in all matters relating to the rebuilding.[31] Its authenticity is crucial, as this is a key site for the history of the American Revolution and the formation of the United States. The notion of authenticity seems to have changed over time, however. Richard Handler and Eric Gable have suggested that it is possible to read the site as a developing narrative of trends and tendencies in the practice of heritage interpretation, as evidenced in their discussion of the arrival of 'road apples' (horse excrement), a signature artefact in living historical environments in the 1970s.[32] Handler and Gable examine the shift towards social history, specifically to Afro-Caribbean and Afro-American culture, which has taken place in Colonial Williamsburg's interpretation programme. Two strains of historical scholarship are identified by them, the first being a realist or objectivist slant in which historians consider themselves getting progressively closer to the real history, which is the basis of all interpretations. In this context, evidence is the primary factor upon which to base historical truth and re-enactment is a mimetic or progressive realism with accuracy its main aim. The second strain is that of the constructivist historian who advocates a model of presentation that comments on the lives and histories of subjects, highlighting the fact that all history is subject to change. This position recognises that there are significant blank spots in history based on the fact that surviving documentation often belonged to those who held power. Handler and Gable's conclusion is that Colonial Williamsburg cannot be living history, for the mimetic realism used 'destroys history' by ignoring or leaving out certain aspects of the past based on cultural values and 'deadens the historical sensibility of the public.' (p. 224). Emphasising the museum's construction in the present they state that 'Colonial Williamsburg, like any other museum site, is a present-day reality . . . It is not, nor can it be, the past brought to life. It is not, nor can it be "authentic"'' (p. 223). This seems self-evident, yet the seductiveness of the site itself pulls the visitor away from 'present-day reality' into a realm of collective memory (of the nation), where eighteenth-century ways of life in colonial Williamsburg are assumed to be a norm, a feeling supported by the commemorative stance of the heritage site as celebration of a crucial period in the formation of the United States. Devices emphasising the separateness of the colonial town govern the experience of visiting. Entrance to the historical site is via the heritage centre and across the 'bridge through time', on which a bronze timeline describes significant moments in world history between the present and the eighteenth century. The heritage centre is presented as a form of liminoid zone in which we prepare for entering the flux of eighteenth-century life. Here, visitors are instructed on what to expect and may hire eighteenth-century costume in order to heighten the immersion. Once within the heritage site, an introductory interpretation is given at the governor's palace, where a costumed interpreter introduces the differences between our own sensibilities and those of the colonial town, forewarning visitors that notions of appropriate behaviour and morality may be shattered. Within the town some buildings are contemporary community spaces, such as the tavern, market theatre and church, while others are family homes or administrative buildings. Historic buildings are complicated by their ambiguous status and their diverse roles; Bruton church, for instance, is both the actual parish church attended by the local populace and a heritage site; there is no costumed interpreter here on a daily basis, though there are occasionally interpretations such as sermons 'in costume'. Houses along the main street have a variety of interpreters in skilled craft and trade roles, such as a silver-smith, a tailor, a wigmaker, a bookbinder, a gardener etc.; there is a brickyard where a group of costumed interpreters are engaged in making bricks from a clay pit in which visitors can stomp barefoot. Tavern interpreters become storytelling hosts as we eat in eighteenth-century inns and actor-interpreters interpret performance styles of the time by delivering speeches (from *Othello* and excerpts from French farces) on a wooden trolley stage situated in a clearing where the first English-speaking theatre in the Americas once stood.[33] Individual thematic interpretations are offered in specific houses at given times. At Randolph House, in an immersive visit of over an hour, an African-American interpreter divulges the experience of slavery in colonial Williamsburg through the lens of this particular household. Here, visitors are given cards describing an inhabitant of the house (mine was that of a five-year-old child of slaves) and are asked to think on this person as we are guided through the house, the interpretation designed to elicit our considered responses in relation to the identities allocated. Across the entire site, the intricate inter-pretation programme is designed to reflect a layered experience of the historic place in all its complexity. It is a reflection on the mean-ings and interpretation of place as it figures in the collective memory of a nation, referred to as 'Becoming American'. Here, interpreters follow a narrative structure, with each year's storyline a theme within an overarching interpretive programme that constructs a narrative around the idea of the founding of the American nation. Thematic strands, including religious freedom, family, respectability (ways of life, manners, fashion etc.), the acquisition of land, revolution and slavery, are mediated through various forms of interpretation, with different strands coming to the fore at specific times and in diverse locations, all of which fuse to tell the story of how America was 'founded' and the nation it is today. In most interpretations visitors and interpreters discuss history freely, but there are also opportunities for the visitors' dramatic absorption into the town itself. In the immersive performance *Revolutionary City!*, for instance, an episodic account of the revolutionary cause presented through dramatic vignettes in various locations through the town, the visitor partici-pates in highly charged interventions, voicing opinions, rallying the revolutionaries, shouting at the British redcoats, booing Cornwallis, each mediation instigated and supported by the interactions of inter-preters placed within the crowd. Here, interpreters are characters, and the visitor a participant. Participation is at its height at the end of each day at Colonial Williamsburg with the march of the fife and drum band towards the green, where visitors can take part in the field display by marching in a 'visitors' army'. Though this seems to be a celebratory display of military might – Washington gallops in on horseback, cannon are fired and American patriotism is performed with gusto by the crowd; characters commenting from the sidelines at the same time effectively undercut such performances of power. These are female and African-American interpreters in character questioning the proceedings, often undermining the pageantry of colonial revolution with their own statements of experience from female and black, enslaved, points of view, shared with small pockets of the audience. While the pomp and ceremony of military procession takes place a white female interpreter sits next to a middle-aged man under a tree and asks him if he is married, sparking a conversation on eighteenth-century ideas about marriage, the role of women, family and respectability. Close by, a black male interpreter dressed as an eighteenth-century gardener stands behind a crowd of onlookers, charging them to consider the fact that he is not allowed to play his own drums, like those he would have played 'at home', prompting thoughts on race and slavery in the colonial context and in relation to the contemporary celebration of the birth of America happening in front of us. This political and social juxtaposition subverts the completeness of the representational frame, destabilising the narrative from the inside. While disrupting the bravado of hundreds of patriotic Americans in this way seems an alarming prospect, these interpreters' thwarting of the pageantry is only partial, and is legitimised by their costumes. We have already been warned that it might be difficult, that views may collide. But the views that are being attacked are not necessarily our views of eighteenth-century society; they are twenty-first century ideals regarding the American nation, problematised by the questioning of those who purport to speak to us from another time. In this way, Colonial Williamsburg achieves a delicate balancing act; it supports the memory of the nation through commemorative bodily practices and ritual enactments such as the parade and its representation of the American ideals of freedom and tolerance, but also recognises the difficulty of accepting history as closed, its interpretations acknowledging the fact that issues of race, intolerance and inequality continue to trouble the present. In this way, the museum's questioning of the past and how it is formed comes into dialogue with the enacted ritualisation of communal memory, and problematises it. Colonial Williamsburg's performance of the nation 'becoming' itself is a feat of narrative presentation through performance. It is a complex, multi-layered and intricate interpretation programme that places the narrative of 'becoming American' on uncertain ground through a variety of conflicting and contradictory elements. It problematises the notion of liberty and equality seemingly enshrined in the general performance world encountered, and it is the contradictory, episodic and fractious nature of some of the performances that enable this understanding.

The view of interpretation or living history as a form that references its own process of making history has increasingly been adopted by theorists who have been eager to problematise it as a simple reconstruction of historical events. Theatre historian Scott Magelssen points out that history itself can no longer be considered as a reconstruction of past events based on empirical analysis alone:

> As Michel Foucault reminds us, the language of origins is silent. Therefore, since the original event is irrecoverable, the function of the historian is to create the event anew in the present, each time it is enunciated. The idea that history can be 'brought to life' though combining research and performance needs to be rethought. If living history museums are not making windows into *real* past moments, what *is* being produced?[34]

Magelssen situates the problematics of living history within nineteenth-century notions of time and space, in which accuracy and authenticity are central to the representation. Realism portrays an all-encompassing and yet enclosed world, one that it presents both dramatically and theatrically, and that operates to evoke an empathetic response. In this sense, it is the most persuasive of all theatrical forms. In a Welsh context Phil Smith writes of the theatricality of the heritage site as a '"late" mimetics'[35] that has a problematical nature stemming from the fact that it hides itself: 'Realism, even when conscientiously done, tends to *mask* the site, not only in the sense of obscuring it, but also in making it subservient to the immediate conditions of its re-presentation' (p. 165). Smith discusses his work as writer for Theatr Clwyd Outreach, *Gwŷr y Goron / All The King's Men*, a play set in Wales during the 'English' Civil War, performed at Chirk Castle in 1992. He describes the naturalistic studio-sized scenes written for the castle spaces, which were utilised 'like substitute theatres'. Realising that such realistic representation drew attention to nothing but itself, Smith regrets the fact that there was no reference to the site as place or recognition of the dissonance between castle and the self-contained performance: 'material traces of the Castle surfaced through the blizzard of image and character at moments of contradiction, when seventeenth-century costume rubbed up against modern signage and explanatory texts for visitors' (p. 165). The script was composed of 'hyper-fabricated' fragments based on historiographical research, which resulted in concealing the site 'in order to sustain its own "logic"' (p. 165). Based on this experience, Smith describes the ideal possibility of interpretation as an open-ended performance, 'not simply a performed exegesis of the given, expert 'meaning' of a site, but rather the open, explicit, performative *making* of that meaning' (p. 168). In heritage performance there is a need to emphasise the possibilities of performance as a means to advance an understanding of the way in which history, memory or heritage is constructed. This raises a question regarding the use of realism, a performance form primarily associated with the late nineteenth century and why it should continue to be the interpretive frame in early twenty-first century museum and heritage sites. What does its use tell about the ways in which we want to relate the past? Theatre in the West has moved through other forms and conventions and the idea of representation has been put into crisis by the increase in non- or anti-representational forms of art and the problematising of the process of interpretation itself. Why does the museum insist on realistic settings when the main theatrical movements of twentieth-century European theatre reacted against the naturalistic representation so forcefully? What does it say about the politics of museum performance that it adheres to the principles of mimetic representation so long after its demise in the theatre?

Magelssen puts forward a recalibration of the terms of living history that might finally free it from the shackles of representational theatre. Rejecting the stance advocated by Jay Anderson, that living history museums are to be understood in terms of a progressive evolutionary narrative nearing perfection in relation to authenticity or mimesis, Magelssen suggests a different mode of understanding time and history based on Gilles Deleuze and Félix Guattari's philosophy of immanence, in which immanence is defined as a plane that already includes life and death (as opposed to perceiving death as beyond life, or transcendent). This philosophy negates the possibility of development (or Hegelian dialectic), as there is only one plane – a network of forces, particles, relations, affects and becomings. In this context, 'history is not to be "undone" by digging along an imaginary timeline into the past'; rather, the past is conceived as a 'plane that contains all possibilities', and thus, 'history is found each time it is articulated in the abundance of the present'.[36] As the past does not exist outside the present, but in the here and now, it follows that there are no chains of cause and effect; rather, events happen 'at spatial "junctures" within the field'.[37] Here, Magelssen is defining living history as an art that imitates life, though 'its stagings of the past go beyond any lived event', and this is how living history sites operate as 'monuments that collect a variety of sensations in the present, which, in alignment, give a sense of the past, even though they are not *of* the past' (p. 55). In adopting this philosophy Magelssen allows the focus to rest on *creating* history in the present. This provides a space for heritage practitioners to dwell on the way in which performance, as *poiesis*, mediates identity and community in relation to history and discloses the interstices between history and personal agency in such a way as to absolve heritage performance of the need to represent history under the guise of the authorised heritage discourse. In this way, heritage performance could be the most radical and unorthodox retelling of history, but one in which the impossible problem of telling it as it happened is fully acknowledged. This is not about accuracy; rather, 'it is about the praxis of performance itself, which offers an agency and authenticity outside the discursive boundaries produced and policed by academics.'[38]

This view of heritage performance as a process involving an open performative *making* of meaning, or *poiesis*, is exemplified by one particular site in Wales, which is unique as the sole full-time interpretive heritage centre situated in a historical site and using live interpretation intensively and in an immersive way.[39] Llancaiach Fawr Manor provides an open and self-conscious construction of history, one that engages the visitors more fully the more they are willing to participate. Restored to how it might have been in 1645, when it was the home of Colonel Edward Prichard, Llancaiach Fawr Manor enables an interpretation of social history during the 'English' Civil War and provides an interpretation of Wales's involvement in it. As with Plimoth Plantation, an entire year is replayed at Llancaiach Fawr, which allows for the interpretation of particular customs relating to the seasons. Consequently, different kinds of activities take precedence at certain times of year in an annual calendar of events, underpinned by the more constant everyday activities of the regular characters in costume, the servants. This means that everyday aspects of seventeenth-century life in this part of south Wales are portrayed on a daily basis, but against the backdrop of the Civil War and its effects on the people living in Llancaiach, an example of the political periphery. The year of interpretation is set as 1645, as this is when Charles I visited Llancaiach Fawr, prior to which Colonel Edward Prichard, the master of the house, had been appointed as commissioner of array to the king, responsible for raising funds and soldiers from Glamorgan. Following the king's visit, the Prichard family, along with other members of the Glamorgan gentry,

6. Interpreters at a 'court session', Llancaiach Fawr Manor.
Photo: Llancaiach Fawr Manor.

switched their allegiance and began to support Parliament, Edward
Prichard eventually defending Cardiff castle against the Royalists. It
is a multifaceted story, representing several dimensions of the Civil
War and the way it affected the lives of the people in one house in a
remote part of Glamorgan.

On entering the manor, the visitor becomes implicated in the performance immediately. The immersive device is that the manor is a safe haven for people seeking refuge who enter bearing a letter of recommendation from Bussy Mansel, brother-in-law of Colonel Edward Prichard of the manor 'written at Britton Ferry in this troubled year of our Lord 1645' (the letter is handed to visitors when they buy their tickets). Because we are visitors to a house whose master is absent, 'the servants of the owner offer a warm welcome'[40] and discussions with them take on an unassuming aspect, which gives them licence to divulge the habitual goings on and to tell us about the life of the family. This keys us in to the interpretation and provides us with a role as a member of the household, albeit a rather passive one, which is not incongruous with the premise on which we enter. The frame of play is immersive first-person mode (the Llancaiach website provides detailed biographical material on each servant), although interpreters explain much within the historical context, entirely at ease with breaking the parameters of the timeframe in a self-consciously playful way if necessary. While the interpreters do not perform characters, there is an inevitable reading of the performers in role as particular personalities with their own traits and foibles, which adds to the theatricality of the visit. This recognition of the theatrical frame itself does not detract from but rather accentuates the play involved in the interpretation, and in a very different way from Plimoth Plantation it provides an engaging hook, so that the visitor becomes involved in understanding the experience as both play and interpretation. While the visitors wander through the manor house apparently at will they are guided by performers who have clear roles within the household hierarchy, such as music master or chambermaid, which gives the interpreter a particular social world to convey. Heritage detractors might criticise the lack of everyday life: there is no rotting food, no sign of messy life, only the moving tableau of an *in situ* performance. This assumes that the performance is built on the premise of a mimetic picture, which is not exactly what this interpretation is, predicated as it is on an understanding based on participation: asking questions, talking and chatting, taking part in the making of seventeenth-century craft ways etc. This participatory practice tells us as much about our own interpretation of history and how we want to engage with it as it does about history itself. This is how Llancaiach Fawr delivers an experience of imagined history based on fact (history as we think it might have happened) that provides a valuable insight into our thoughts, ideas and interpretation of the history of the time. Such interpretations are often successful because the performative frame begins with the visitor's own frame of reference and there is no point in highlighting historical discrepancies or chasing anachronisms since the play does not conform to a total immersion in the past. How could it? Some have referred to the discrepancy between the language spoken during the visit and the language that would have been spoken at the time.[41] While the gentry would have undergone a process of anglicisation, the servants would mostly have been Welsh-speaking, but while there are Welsh-speaking interpreters at Llancaiach, the interpretation is mostly in a form of seventeenth-century English. In this way, certain fundamental aspects of social life are foregone in order to convey history by bending it towards the experience of the visitors, who are inevitably mostly English-speaking. In this case the past is not a foreign country – it is the visitors' country, and mediated through communicative means and devices that have currency for them, a characteristic of the creative proclivity of heritage in making place meaningful for the context in which it is to be projected and understood. While Llancaiach could feasibly provide a Welsh-speaking experience for a Welsh-speaking audience, an immersion in Welsh for those who do not speak it would prohibit the most basic communicative practices upon which this form of interpretation is based. What this means in terms of collective memory is difficult and problematic, since the way in which the past is mediated here is partly projected according to the visitor's current linguistic understanding, and the interlinguistic tensions of Welsh and English during the seventeenth century, and the social and class implications of this for the particular locality, cannot be tackled directly. This is the point at which the cultural and historical expertise must confront and challenge the flexible experience of heritage performance, in which affect is a powerful tool, and indicate its limitations.

The affective turn in the humanities and social sciences, which provides a framework for understanding spheres of experience outside the paradigm of representation, where affect and emotion mediate the process of belonging, is echoed in Lauren Berlant's analysis of 'the politics of intimacy'. In her view, there is no longer a public sphere in the traditional sense, but rather an 'intimate public sphere', where nationality is reduced to a question of feelings and traumas.[42] If this is the case, living history, which sits on the fence between an attempt to learn from the past and a desire to know what it felt like, is its pre-eminent performance form, facilitating a construction of nationness from a series of empathetic gestures. When the frame is broken in live interpretation and participants step 'out of time' to compare or to discuss the present context, the emphasis is on affective comparison. This can result in the skewing of history so that it is only meaningful in terms of the individual's identity within the group. Taken to its extreme, this form of empathetic interpretation results in a performance in which the visitor immerses herself as participant, and in which the complex of relationships between memory, place and the people performing are synthesised one with the other. When all participants are equally immersed, it presents a mode of mediating history for oneself and the community in an embodied form, literally, through re-enactment. As a social structure re-enactment is not easily deconstructed, such is its emphasis on participation and experiential involvement, so that notions of audience, performer and event are not easily divisible. In essence, it is not a representational form, despite the fact that it is predicated on mimesis, and is generally not performed in order to represent a historical event to someone else, despite its roots in commemorative events that purport to represent what once happened. Perhaps re-enactment, which seems to be extremely involved in processes of identity formation and communal remembering, is able to provide insights into the reasons for the emphasis on empathy and embodiment in the performances of the museum and heritage site.

Re-enactment

Re-enactment, a performance that consciously retraces the steps of an event in history, such as a battle, from the supposed point of view of a participant in the original event, though often incorporating a broad understanding of the crowd movement and strategies involved, is one of the most problematised areas in the performance of history. As a form, it has been criticised for what is perceived to be its simplistic function as bolsterer of national pride, or as a superficial leisure activity for those who enjoy role play. Re-enactment is perceived to be the realm of the enthusiast, the fan and the hobbyist, its participants frequently patronised in scholarly writing, though there are many expert re-enactors, including academics and museum professionals. The spectrum of activity that comes under the broad umbrella of re-enactment is vast, and there is overlap with many of the activities involved in professional curatorial or archaeological practice, such as experimental archaeology. Re-enactments can involve heightened or dramatic simulations, for example of life in military camp and battle preparation, or they may be more mundane and include general ways of life for a particular people in a certain period. One of the most recurrent themes in re-enactment, particularly battle re-enactment, is the way in which it relates to a particular place and manifests a need to replay or somehow be placed in contact with what has happened there before.[43] Mike Crang has argued that re-enactors are usually engaged in negotiating the meaning of what has happened in the site in which they perform and that the performance is a way of exploring the implications of what happened in terms of their own heritage.[44] The notion of enacting history in order to have a bearing on its meaning for one's own heritage entails a consideration of heritage as something that is re-defined according to our specific situation. This is far removed from the idea of heritage as an objective history that cannot be changed or tampered with. Reflecting on the preoccupation with bringing the past closer to the present, Peter Burke describes the use of 'active techniques of familiarization or . . . 'approximation' (on the model of *rapprochement*),'[45] of which re-enactment, such as that performed at anniversaries and centenary remembrances, battle re-enactments and re-trodden pilgrimages, is an extreme example.

Of all the forms of re-enactment, discussion most frequently returns to that of battle re-enactment, such is its prevalence, popularity and hold. This is not surprising, as it centres on the relationship between performance, place and memory and invites an understanding of the complex way in which these aspects interact and coalesce, sometimes problematically, in the memorialisation of war. It is also the most commonly frequented form of re-enactment, suggesting that the activity is as important as a communal activity for the spectators as for those embodying the historical participants, and may be significant as an instigator of collective memory for both parties. Collective memory plays a significant role in relation to national military history and processes of identifying with the nation more generally. Commemoration of the war dead is the national remembrance form *par excellence*, where memory finds expression through bodily practices. Remembrance of the dead brings with it specific ceremonial rituals which are associated with memory and the process of remembering, and they are emotive.

The laying of wreaths, for instance, a core part of the remembrance service, ritualises the act of attending to the graves of the dead in a symbolic set of gestures representing national grief, while its gravity is reinforced by the participation of figureheads representing the group.

Commemorative practices associated with the war dead and battle re-enactments seem to share a common impetus that is associated with remembrance, but also with standing in place of the deceased. Theatre scholar Leigh Clemons suggests that battle re-enactors 'view their representations of history not as performance but as embodiment', during which they conduct 'impressions' rather than perform 'characters', and that in this way they are able to 'sidestep the major ideological arguments that surrounded the war in question'.[46] That the re-enactment is often repeated reveals a desire for communion with the historic event and the predecessors who participated in it, as though its repetition were a form of sympathetic or imitative magic. This order of re-enactment is a ritual type of remembrance that has the external trappings of pretence, because its mimetic aspects and the historically accurate detail in clothing, food and other material effects involved are significant signposts towards the depth of experience. As objects approaching relics, rather than conduits for play, these authentic objects of material culture operate in a talismanic way, encouraging an empathetic response that is, in turn, a doorway to the experience sought. The experience is not representational; rather, it is forged from a sense of communion with what is believed to have happened to people in a particular place, and what is continuing to happen to them now. This sense of continuity is important to the re-enactor and to the audience in terms of their identity. Clemons also makes the association with ritual, describing the re-enactment as occupying a liminal space and 'functioning as a rite of passage from enacted present into re-enacted past' (pp. 10–11). During the re-enactment, even though the audience are not necessarily participating in role play at first hand, the overall context and sense of community at the event ensure that all are focused on the same emotional goal. This is very similar to what is achieved through remembrance, or at a memorial service. Rather than simply men or women playing soldiers, involved in 'historical hooliganism on Bank Holiday weekends',[47] battle re-enactors are involved in a form of memorialisation more complex than mere role play and are, for the most part, deeply aware of the implications of re-enacting past battles. Similarly, notions of time involved in re-enactment seem to be more complex than simply representational time. Clemons analyses the slippery timeframe of the battle re-enactment and its significance to participants and explains that, while re-enactments are events that reference a specific battle or period in time, they 'cannot be considered battle simulations . . . as there is a historical event to which they refer'; at the same time, she concedes that 'they are not specifically historical because they are reoccurring in present times, causing a rupture between the signifier and the signified'.[48] Here, re-enactment and the history it purports to enact are trapped together in an 'oscillating process' that 'bounces around in an in-between space whose function is dependent upon how it is observed: as history, as performance, or as education' (pp. 10–11). This oscillation reflects the liminoid state of being in between that is a condition of theatrical performance. Battle re-enactment seems to channel strongly the distinctiveness of theatre as representation of life. In actual hand-to-hand battle death is close by and the event is not for repetition, despite the long history of strategic battle analysis that utilised a form of embodiment and the theatricality of the battlefield, which frequently has 'audiences' watching from afar. For the participants in battle re-enactment, the event is about repetition in order to remember an extreme occurrence that bears social and cultural meaning for those who identify with it and claim it as an important identity-marker. In this process, role play and immersion work to re-create a sense of being with the fallen. Clearly, this is problematic for those who deem such identification contentious in terms of historical accuracy, though this standpoint ignores the deep connections participants feel with their history and what that history means for who they are. Participants' responses to questions regarding the activity suggest that they are fully aware of this fact. Rebecca Schneider, who attended many American Civil War re-enactments between 1998 and 2006, asked the re-enactors: 'why fight?'. The response discloses their belief that they are doing more than remembering a past; the past seems to be on-going and 'negotiated through a shifting affiliation with the past *as* the present'.[49] Within this notion that the past is not over, or that there is interdependence between events of the past, the present and the future, Schneider detects an understanding of 'ongoingness' in which, she says, '"remains" might be understood not solely as object or document material, but also as the immaterial labor of bodies engaged in and with that incomplete past: bodies striking poses, making gestures, voicing calls, reading words, singing songs, or standing witness', and events might be constituted as an interaction 'with traces of *acts* as history: carrying a replica nineteenth-century musket on a historic battlefield, uttering the "phonic materiality" of a cry to arms, or engaging in surgical amputation practices of the 1860s' (pp. 33–5). Schneider observed participants 'putting themselves *in the place of* the past, re-enacting that past by *posing as if* they were, indeed, soldiers and civilians of the 1860s' (p. 9), and became interested in the effort made by many battle reenactors to 'achieve a radically rigorous mimesis many of them feel can trip the transitivity of time' (p. 10), as though exact repetition constitutes some kind of touching of time, as the enactment itself provides what documentary evidence alone cannot: the live experience. Here, concerns of verisimilitude and authenticity are eclipsed by the need to experience the moment, which accesses a different way of experiencing the past. Schneider reveals that in this context, mimesis, rather than being the antithesis of 'some discreet authenticity', is 'a powerful tool for intra-temporal negotiation, even (perhaps) interaction . . . of one time with another time' (pp. 30–1). Suggesting that there is a sense in which performance is considered to be beyond the now or, at least, not merely 'live', particularly for those taking part, Schneider acknowledges that the affective elements that emanate from what she refers to as 'cross-temporal slippage', when 'it can occasionally feel "as if" the halfway dead came halfway to meet the halfway living, halfway' (p. 14), are commonplace in theatre, art and ritual, though not usually in the realm of history or historiography. Here, the performance is a self-consciously replayed event, undertaken in complete awareness of the fact that it is part of an indefinitely incomplete rendering, and yet a recalling of an original event that has considerable meaning for participants. Schneider posits that this play with time and the suggestion that it brings participants closer to history is inherently problematical in the Western world:

> To trouble linear temporality – to suggest that time may be touched, crossed, visited or revisited, that time is transitive and flexible, that time may recur in time, that time is not one – never only one – is to court the ancient (and tired) Western anxiety over ideality and originality. The threat of theatricality is still the threat of the imposter status of the copy, the double, the mimetic, the second, the surrogate, the feminine, or the queer. Detractors say: The then is *then*, the now is *now*, the dead

are dead, lost; we cannot go back, we can only, in the spasms of our misguided traumatic remainders, lurch forward (backward and forward being the only imaginable directions). To some who ridicule the activities of reenactors as naïve, the faith that linear time is the one *true* time couples with an investment in the contingency offered by the linear temporal model to reassure that any *true* temporal return or overlap would be impossible because *different*. (p. 30)

We can read points of contact here with the concept of *cwmwl tystion* in Welsh culture, and the sense of inhabiting a 'cloud of witnesses – witnesses in the mind, witnesses from the past' that are also witnesses to who we are as people.[50] Tracing this kind of awareness or thinking in Welsh re-enactment practices is far from easy however, and it is not possible to say with any certainty that practitioners experience or seek to feel such an embodied awareness.

The range of re-enactment practices of the numerous groups based in Wales are extremely varied. Some groups concentrate on their period of history in isolation, with a focus on historical precision in day-to-day life, tending to concentrate on living history rather than on specific events, such as battles. Others specialise in battle re-enactment and a range of associated practices, such as camp life, medical re-enactment, and battle strategy. Groups engage in a wide range of activities, from participating in film and television battle scenes to educating the public. Welsh museums call on experienced re-enactment groups such as the Sealed Knot, whose members interpret and re-enact the English Civil War, to provide specific interpretive events; some museum sites require human movement, as their spatial configuration signifies social relationships so distinctly that if the site is not populated, a fundamental part of the interpretation is lost. The National Roman Legion Museum (Amgueddfa Cymru) in Caerllion, for instance, depends on re-enactment groups from all over Europe to animate the Roman amphitheatre. Other large-scale re-enactment gatherings, such as Fortress Wales, held in Margam Castle grounds, have brought numerous societies together for a variety of activities and events, in a festival of living history where groups re-enact battles, events and behaviours from different periods in history, often side by side.[51] Despite the anachronistic juxtapositions – a group of Victorian re-enactors drink tea sedately around a table, while Second World War battle re-enactors stage a large-scale battle event on the

7. Interpretation of the Roman Amphitheatre, National
Roman Legion Museum, Caerllion (with kind permission
of Amgueddfa Cymru / National Museum Wales).
Photo: Lisa Lewis.

field before them – they all sustain a deep sense of ritualised activity characterised by stillness and a strong sense of deliberation. Such concentrated embodiment draws attention to their own focus and activity as re-enactors, suggesting, in this example, that the performance is perhaps more meaningful to them than it might be for the onlookers. Some seem lost in their actions, and there is a feeling that the onlookers might be intruding. Detractors criticise the implicit theatricality of battle re-enactment, where the live body is a potential site of error and misappropriation, and emotional involvement seems to trump the analysis of 'what really happened'. This critique assumes that the performance is intended to communicate outside itself, to those observing. This is not always the case in the subjective sphere of living history immersion such as battle re-enactment, where much of the emphasis is on the individual's own identity. What constitutes this identity is open to conjecture, and whether the re-enactment events or the nature of the re-enactors' practice facilitate a sense of nationness that is specifically Welsh, for example, is difficult to grasp. From one point of view, the personal nature of re-enactment is such that it is impossible to detect its aim. There is a certain inevitability in the association between military history, commemoration and the idea of nationness, though none of the battle re-enactments I have witnessed in Wales engage in a jingoistic patriotism, nor do they side with one camp more than the other, preferring instead to be part of the flux of history. Indeed, the majority of re-enactors seem happy to represent and to perform on either side of the battle, strongly suggesting that participating in the event and understanding something about a generic past is more important in terms of engendering memory than empathetically emplacing oneself with a certain tribe. Similarly, most Welsh re-enactment societies do not reveal a direct correlation between the nature of the re-enactment and the area in which the re-enactors are based, making it difficult to establish a relationship between the historical period or identity set re-enacted and a contemporary sense of identity. While there have been several Welsh groups that concentrate on Iron Age re-enactment, such as Silures, other Iron Age 'Celtic' groups are based elsewhere, such as Brigantia, based in Hampshire (the Brigantes were a tribe that inhabited a large area of what is now the north of England). In re-enactment, place is not a primary factor in terms of authenticity and may be re-created.

Choosing to dwell on a very specific aspect of Welsh history will often disclose the deep historical ties between Wales and England, bringing the complexity of history into sharp focus, and this has implications for questions of identity. For instance, Meibion y Ddraig / Sons of the Dragon, who specialise in medieval archery, see the history of their chosen re-enactment reach its peak in the battle of Agincourt. Similarly, Cardiff Castle Garrison, a medieval re-enactment society, set their period of re-enactment between 1350 and 1370, during the reign of Edward III, and participate in events such as Llantrisant's Beating of the Bounds, held every seven years to commemorate the townspeople's participation in the Battle of Crécy in 1346, and the subsequent charter allowing the people to become freemen. In these examples, Welsh identity, if present at all, is performed within the broad embrace of British history. The Freemen of Gwent, for instance, a medieval re-enactment group concentrating on the Hundred Years War (1337–1453), from the early years up to the battle of Agincourt in 1415, also portray life during the reign of Edward III, and their descriptive literature dwells on 'the kingdom of England', with Welsh characters or events portrayed as satellite aspects, which may be an attempt to approximate to the view held at the time (most of the characters portrayed by the group being Norman lords). This view also reflects Monmouthshire's historically ambivalent status on the borderland between Wales and England. Other groups dwell on the intercultural nature of their chosen people and times, such as the Blaeddau Du, a Viking re-enactment group who concentrate on the Hiberno-Norse / Welsh in south Wales *c.*850–1100, investigating 'what it would have been like for Viking / Welsh traders' at this time, or the Montgomery Levy, concentrating on the life of a company of foot-soldiers on the Welsh Marches during the Wars of the Roses.[52] The preponderance of groups in Wales focusing on complex identity questions related to diversity and transcultural exchange suggest that these issues are relevant or at least of interest to them, and that there is a correlation, perhaps, between these identity questions, especially the interrelationship of the Welsh and the English, with the groups' own identities. Re-enactment groups are generally not politically motivated, however, and are more interested in the experience of the play of history; as a consequence they tend to focus on historical accuracy with a sense of commemoration. What is chosen as the historical field in question and the way in which the history is constructed reveals much about cultural and identity aspirations. Those re-enacting the Second World War in particular tend to have a strong hold on identity questions and their relationship with memory. This is partly because they re-enact what continues to be within recent memory, but it is also related to their attempt to understand the impact of a historical event on their particular community. The 'Welsh Tommies 39–45' group, for instance, represent the Welsh in a range of battalions during the Second World War, with the aim 'to keep alive the memories of the men and women who served . . . and to educate the general public on the issued kit, weapons, food and everything else about the regular tommy soldier in the "poor bloody infantry"'. While there is an emphasis on educating through display, using blank firing weapons to provide insight into the experience, they are adamant that 'we will never truly know what these brave men actually went through.'[53] There is no suggestion that this is based on any sense of adventure, patriotism or pageantry; rather, it is wholly commemorative and based on a shared identity, in which ideas of belonging are shared and strengthened through the re-enactment itself. The form through which this commemorative re-enactment takes place is frequently remarkably non-dramatic, with the spectacle of the soldiers themselves the only attempt at theatricality.

In a re-enactment at Cardiff Castle in 2012, entitled 'The Fight for Canada! 1812–1815', organised by Firing Line: Cardiff Castle Museum of the Welsh Soldier,[54] the notion at work is that in replaying a set of positions or gestures as an approximation of what might have taken place in the context of battle, the re-enactor is positing a relationship with the past, and stages this relationship in such a way that she seems to be stepping in to its traces as a form of commemorative performance. The bicentennial celebration includes a war-games re-enactment (with miniature soldier figures), living history camps and a large-scale performance/re-enactment of the storming of Fort Detroit performed by various re-enactment groups. In the main battle re-enactment, which is performed with little theatricality, regiments are seen marching towards the fort – there is no dramatic storming – conveying the idea that a strategic understanding is preferable to a mimetic representation of the men as charging soldiers. The battle re-enactor often stands with blank face, a body amongst the throng of other soldiers. The lack of drama supports the impression that this is a kind of *tableau vivant*, executed with energy enough to facilitate the bare tasks required in battle, such as firing and marching. The stop-start nature of positioning miniature toy soldiers is replicated here in the form of historical interpretation. The lack of characterisation is perhaps in deference to the soldier as integral member of an army, where individuality recedes, and the task in hand, the battle itself, becomes the main focus. But it is also inevitably dehumanising in its portrayal of history, as men become no more than bodies, the main dramatic focus being the battle and whether it was lost or won. While there is a level on which this 'not-acting',[55] task-based re-enactment is considered to be authentic, as though too much human agency might tamper with the audience's ability to read the actions carried out as mere actions, it does not assist with interpreting the personal context of battle. The popular, hobbyist nature of re-enactment facilitates this detachment, so that audiences do not witness battle re-enactment as theatre, drama, or historical museum interpretation, but something else altogether. While the voice-over dramatisation heard over the sound system at Cardiff Castle creates tension and suspense in the narrativisation of the battle, the embodied practice of the re-enactor presents a different sense of commemoration, that of ritualised and pared-down action.[56]

Social anthropologist Paul Connerton argues that recollection works in two distinct areas of social activity, in commemorative ceremonies and in bodily practices. Focusing on non-inscribed cultural practices Connerton analyses the way in which traditions are constituted through embodied ritual performances, and the past 'kept in mind' by 'a habitual memory sedimented in the body'.[57] Investigating how group memory is conveyed and sustained, Connerton looks at the way in which recollection and bodies come together to form cultural traditions other than those that are inscribed, and gathers that 'the past and recollected knowledge of the past . . . are conveyed and sustained by (more or less) ritual performances' (p. 4). Similarly, social memory is to be found in commemorative ceremonies, which 'prove to be commemorative only in so far as they are performative', and the performative is constituted through habit, and habit, in turn, is directly connected with the body. In this context, re-enactment is linked to incorporation as bodily practice, and it is a vital mode of collective social memory.[58] In re-enactment as a form of collective social memory participants engage in learnt bodily practices (e.g. formal battle drills for the soldier, or the cooking of food in a particular way for the camp-dweller), and these are learnt anew by the individual, or re-learnt as part of social memory, perhaps embodied in order to be passed down, or in order for the re-enactor to align herself with an experience of the past which is associated with her own life. This has performance implications that go beyond that of the mimetic, for re-enactors often place themselves in a position where the replay of physical actions puts them in contact with the past, as though the social memory, performed in an embodied way, binds the cultural and social implications of the past to who we are now. Schneider refers to historical re-enactors positioning their bodies consciously and deliberately in such a way that they may access 'a fleshy or pulsing kind of trace they deem accessible in a pose, or gesture, or set of acts'.[59] Inhabiting this trace, when it recurs, may constitute a replay of what is both then and now:

> If a pose or a gesture or a 'move' recurs across time, what pulse of multiple time might a pose or a move or gesture contain? Can a trace take the form of a *living* foot – or only the form of a footprint? Can a gesture, such as a pointing index finger, itself be a remain in the form of an indexical action that haunts (or remains) via live repetition? . . . To what degree is a live act *then* as well as *now*? Might a live act even 'document' a precedent live act, rendering it, in some way, ongoing, even preserved? An action repeated again and again and again, however fractured or

partial or incomplete, has a kind of staying power – persists through time – and even, in sense, serves as a fleshy kind of 'document' of its own recurrence. (p. 37)

While certain branches of historical analysis might baulk at the suggestion of such discomforting replay, the critique of re-enactment as historical fact is arguably misguided, for re-enactment as performance of social memory is closer in many ways to commemorative rituals and has more in common with forms of representation found in ritual performance, such as mask-wearing in order to literally re-present the ancestors who have disappeared. Representing the spirits of the dead in ancient ritual acts often entailed 'becoming' the ancestors portrayed by the masks for the duration of the ritual. Similarly, re-enactment may not be about historical mimicry for the purposes of interpreting history alone, but rather an embodied performance driven by communal and social memory requirements and the way in which they are structured socially through performance. This is not to say that participants in historical re-enactment might not gain knowledge and understanding of history; the imaginative act involved in immersive performance of this kind often enables a comparative and deeper understanding of certain social and cultural affects, the traces of which are incorporated in the moment of performance. This understanding and awareness of history is a consequence of performative activity driven by communal memory, and there is a sense in which such activity can be a restorative act.

This capacity of enactment to engender restoration following the failures or traumas of history is a quality also present in theatre. Freddie Rokem elaborates on the way in which theatre participates in debates regarding representations of the past, by creating 'an awareness of the complex interaction between the destructiveness and the failures of history, on the one hand, and the efforts to create a viable and meaningful work of art, trying to confront these painful failures, on the other.'[60] That is, an awareness of the duality between life and the attempt to structure an artwork that deals with it, is potentially transformational. Crucially, for Rokem, this duality is intensified by the theatrical experience itself, by the presence of the actors for instance, who perform history by 'relying on different kinds of theatrical energies' (p. 3). Rokem examines the strategies employed by theatre through which certain events and figures from the past, which are at the heart of the national consciousness of certain places, have been "'resurrected" in the *here* and *now* of theatrical performances', and in the creative endeavours of performers, playwrights, directors and designers (p. 2). This powerful concatenation between the participants, to which we could also add the audience, all striving towards a transformative experience through theatrical performance, could also be applied as a model in order to understand the desire to access our sense of a shared and binding past that is a core function of re-enactment. The denigration of living history as no more than hobbyist play is unfortunate, as it neglects the powerful agency of living history as a performance that mediates communal memory.

GŴYL: FESTIVAL

4

Caer ein gwarchod rhag tlodi – ac anwaith,
A'n gwahanrwydd ynddi:
Ein heniaith yw ei meini,
A'r Cof yw ei cherrig hi.
ALAN LLWYD, 'YR EISTEDDFOD.'[1]

B enedict Anderson's idea of the nation as an 'imagined community'
is often considered pivotal to the concept of nation as an entity
perpetuated by cultural performances that both compose and bolster its central myths. Anderson emphasises the conscious aspects of
collective identity, the perceptions or ideas of ourselves as belonging
to the same group of people. This idea of a consciously perpetuated
imaginary might only be useful up to a point. I argue that it is the social
act of performance that advocates and sustains the communal endeavour of imagining in this way and, in fact, that performance as a social
structure embodies the imaginary. In this chapter, I want to show that
the National Eisteddfod, one of the largest cultural festivals in Europe,
is of central importance in the imaginative act that sustains collective identity, although it is not immediately apparent how this works.
According to the sociologist Jürgen Straub collective identity is composed of a hidden knowledge, and this knowledge provides a structure
of ideas, feelings, desires and acts to the members of a social group.
In this context, national identity may be an 'unconscious structure',

and the nation a variable formation.[2] Perhaps the nature of the imaginative act is not as immediately detectable or even as conscious an act as Anderson suggests. Analysing specific cultural performances as manifestations of an imaginative act might bring us closer to an understanding of the way in which such performances function in relation to collective identity formation and memory, especially as they come together to construct a sense of nationness.

Eisteddfod: people, memory, and place

The Welsh noun *gŵyl*, signifying holiday, festival or feast, stems from the Latin *vigilia* (wakefulness, watch), from *vigil* (awake). This is an apt description of Eisteddfod Genedlaethol Cymru, the National Eisteddfod of Wales, a festival that has played a crucial role in cultural revivalism in Wales and continues to serve as a defining performance of culture for people interested and invested in Welsh culture and language.[3] The Eisteddfod is not officially called a festival by title, which is perhaps a sign of its veracity. According to cultural anthropologist Beverly J. Stoeltje true festivals are rarely described as such, 'employing instead a name related to the stated purposes or core symbols of the event'.[4] In this case the noun *eisteddfod*, derived from the verb *eistedd* (to sit), signifies a place to sit together or the act of sitting together and makes reference to the assembly of bards engaged in performing and competing over a 'session'. The word describes both the spatial and the temporal aspects of the event. An eisteddfod, of which there are several kinds, is an emplaced gathering, where participants come together to take part in a situated performance that is both broad in its provision and complex in terms of the combination of relationships that constitute it. Stoeltje elaborates on the characteristics that are generally displayed in most festivals as social activities or performances rooted in group life and describes their primary function as providing an opportunity for religious devotion or individual performance, as well as 'the expression of group identity through . . . memorialization', 'the performance of highly valued skills and talents', and 'the articulation of a group's heritage'.[5] An eisteddfod serves these functions directly and they are mediated *through* performance, as well as being constituted *as* performance.

The *englyn* quoted at the beginning of this chapter refers to the eisteddfod as a defence – a 'fort', protecting against a form of destitution, and also as the place where our 'difference' is located, a fort constructed of 'our language' and of 'Memory' (capitalised in the Welsh). This is a direct reference to W. J. Gruffydd's statement in 1937, that the National Eisteddfod is '*y gaer fechan olaf sydd gennym*' (the last little fort that we possess), which detractors were attempting to steal away, 'furious towards us for attempting to defend it'. This is a reference to the commotion around attempts to ensure the sustained use of Welsh as the official language during National Eisteddfod ceremonies, which since the advent of the modern National Eisteddfod in 1861 had shown a degree of equivocation regarding the use of English in competition and performance.[6] Between 1940 and 1950 the National Eisteddfod was on uncertain ground as a festival, and in particular as one that celebrated the Welsh language.[7] This was partly due to the difficulties in sustaining such a large-scale festival during the period of war, but mainly because of the opposition to the idea of a Welsh-language rule by many people, both Welsh-speaking and non-Welsh speaking, along with the pressure of outside influences considered to be central to the Eisteddfod's status (sponsors, and people of note such as MPs, council leaders and members of the royal family, who were unable to deliver public speeches in Welsh from the Eisteddfod stage). There was also the residual sense that the Eisteddfod was a performance of Welsh civility for the outside world, one that ratified a feeling of self-worth in a broader British context. That it has overcome such crises of confidence is testament to the tenacity of those attempting to establish the centrality of Welsh to the whole operation, as both creative endeavour and social event, but it also points to the coming of age of a festival in the truest sense: of being a fully functioning and mature festival that expresses and delivers on its main function, that of celebrating a community's culture with an emphasis on the emergent that is deeply meaningful to the participants themselves. The Eisteddfod, now inherently connected to the Welsh language, is referred to by Jan Morris as 'an effervescent affirmation of its survival'.[8] Such poetic language serves to emphasise what is at stake and the depth of conviction involved in an activity that is such a symbolic statement of Welsh nationness.

Despite the seriousness of the endeavour, the depth of feeling involved and the semi-ritualistic nature of ceremonial performances (in particular the Gorsedd of the Bards), the National Eisteddfod (hereafter, Eisteddfod) is essentially an opportunity to *play* culture. According to Stoeltje, the focus on the play of culture in festival is a result of the dissociation of festival and religion following Protestantism, in which the festival is set apart from religious ritual and moved into a secular realm, a consequence of which is the licence to play. It is this play of culture that provides a framework within which culture and identity can be mediated and re-invented: 'like play and creativity, festival explores and experiments with meaning, in contrast to ritual, which attempts to control meaning'.[9] The nature of the experiment with meaning in the Eisteddfod is varied and operates across a spectrum of activities, though it might be described, in essence, as an attempt to emplace or create within the community memories formed from an interplay between contemporary cultural practices and conceptions of traditional customs. In this way, the Eisteddfod facilitates the re-invention of tradition, enabling a performance of relevance while keeping a foothold in the past. The festival experiments with the relationship between identity, place and memory, forging new connections based on old ones and establishing a web of relationships between forms of memory – individual, collective, and generational. The Eisteddfod looks both backwards and forwards in its commemorative nature and its innovation. It appears to have perfected the marriage of tradition – the Chairing of the Bard, the practice of poetry in strict metre, and contemporaneity – in popular fringe events and gigs, and the evolving nature of competitions. This is necessary, for part of its function is to appeal and hold on to all constituents, though memory and tradition delineate and drive the nature of the event in terms of its qualities of time and space.

Even though it looks back towards 'a tradition', the modern-day Eisteddfod was actually formed in the 1860s, at a time when modern Wales was undergoing radical changes brought about by the agricultural and industrial revolutions. Issues that profoundly affect the formation of social and cultural identity, such as political and economic change, changes to the landscape of work through industry and population booms, economic deprivation, substantial demographic shifts, as well as increased political awareness and mobilisation, were the contributory factors to the social context out of which the modern Eisteddfod rose. Many of these profound social changes provided an almost insurmountable challenge to Welsh language and culture up to the 1840s and several factors and events associated with these changes accelerated the breakdown of an already weakened sense of

Welsh identity. One event was to prove particularly devastating; this was the publication of the *Reports of the Commissioners of Inquiry into the State of Education in Wales*, the so-called 'Blue Books'[10] of 1847, in which the prejudices of class are revealed in each statement of condemnation of the Welsh people and the Welsh language: 'It is a language of old-fashioned agriculture, of theology, and of simple rustic life, while all the world about him is English.'[11] The modern National Eisteddfod was formed less than twenty years after the publication of the reports and arose out of a concern to encourage and promote an interest in the Welsh language and its literature. By 1868, however, the Eisteddfod was distanced from contemporary concerns, which was clear from its literary output, as Hywel Teifi Edwards notes:

> It is the work of writers who knew that their language had entered a new and rapidly accelerating stage of rejection, who knew that they were not taken seriously as they were not expected to contribute much of value to the elevation of a small, bereft nation frantic with longing for a commendable place in the English imperial sun. At a time when Wales was undergoing tremendous cultural changes, when 'the stuff of poetry' lay thick on all sides, Welsh poets by and large remained within the compound of a 'patriotically' conceived past and a suitably imagined Christian eternity. Modern 'tempest-torn' Wales was best avoided.[12]

According to Edwards, a poetry that was relevant to the lives of the majority who attended the Eisteddfod failed to materialise, due to a loss of confidence that he attributes to the publication of the Blue Books. The systematic attempt to rid Wales of its own identity was resisted, but the attack on the Welsh people's sense of worth had a destructive effect and the National Eisteddfod became a performative venture designed to forge a new respect for a forward-looking nation: '[the Eisteddfod] would play its part in projecting an image of a progressive people whose particular culture was no longer "a thing of the past", dominated by perverse bards whose druidic posturing invited Fleet Street ridicule' (p. 23). As might be expected, the literary output and creative endeavour 'found itself trapped . . . in the counter-attack against the "Blue Books". It would essentially help to promote the image of a God-fearing, Queen-loving, Empire-supporting, self-improving, moral, earnest and wholesomely patriotic people whose National Eisteddfod annually displayed their worth' (p. 26). Thus, in an era dedicated to spectacle and exhibition, the Eisteddfod fed into prevalent representations of empire, almost as a form of colonial exhibition in itself, one perpetuated by the Welsh people and in particular the members of a growing middle class. The Eisteddfod main stage, Y Pafiliwn (the Pavilion), the commonplace title for the exhibitionary stage in Victorian expositions, as well as many other eisteddfodic traditions, reflect the theatricality of the Victorian exhibitionary complex and Wales's eagerness to be part of it. This is further exemplified in Wales's role in the international exhibition where the Eisteddfod came to represent Welsh culture in its totality. For instance, in Eisteddfod Ffair y Byd (the World Fair's Eisteddfod), held in White City as part of the Columbian Exposition in Chicago in 1893, the voice of the Welsh in Chicago was heard and acknowledged as the voice of goodness and loyalty.[13]

People
Victor Turner's definition of the particular form of social relationships in which a deep communal bond is formed – *communitas* – has several different forms. In 'ideological communitas', for instance, the primary mode of experiencing is being together, which is intensified in either 'liminal' or 'liminoid' states. Liminality, the aspect of ritual during which the participant experiences the ambiguous stage of being in between different identity stages, was an idea established by Arnold van Gennep in 1906 to describe rituals in small society groups.[14] Victor Turner developed the concept further in 1967 to include the effects of liminality on the individual participant.[15] For Turner, in contexts where liminality is defined as a time and place of withdrawal from normal modes of social action, it can be considered as a potential place and time of transformation, based on the questioning of specific cultural values of the society in which it takes place. As liminal rituals are rare in industrial societies Turner used the term liminoid to refer to analogous secular phenomena such as theatre. Liminoid experiences share many of the same characteristics as liminal experiences but involve a personal, individual resolution of crisis, as well as a break from society, and an element of play.[16] The Eisteddfod displays elements of both liminal and liminoid modes, though its primary mode is liminoid. It is neither explicitly religious nor a fully-fledged pastime, sitting between activities associated with duty and belief on the one hand, and cultural activities more associated with games and art on the other. Members

of the Gorsedd of bards, while dressed 'as' druids performing initiation ceremonies, have in reality a purely functional role as participants in the cultural arena. That they are some of the most eminent artists and literary giants makes their participation particularly significant, and on one level, who the members of the Gorsedd are is more important than what they do. For participants in events, the competitors especially, the process is overshadowed by an awareness of being on certain thresholds of experience and for some competitions, such as the chairing of the bard, the ceremony itself represents a rite of passage for the individual concerned and entry into the symbolic order of the Gorsedd.

In keeping with its mythic function, the Eisteddfod has been endlessly reinvented or revived. The first known Eisteddfod dates from 1176 and it appears across the fabric of Welsh history as a recurrent performance event,[17] but the representation of the Eisteddfod as a great unbroken tradition, and especially its relationship to the Gorsedd of the bards, is one of the brilliant machinations of the genius Iolo Morganwg (Edward Williams, 1747–1826), structured in order to fuel certain cultural aspirations.[18] The Eisteddfod was not a deliberate invention but it became a conscious performative gesture, amongst many others, which by its re-establishment as a modern festival sought to promote certain perceptions of Welshness. Part of a broader sweep of myth-making which grew out of the particular circumstances of Welsh life at the time, the Eisteddfod was established as 'a set of practices' of the kind described by Hobsbawm in the context of the invention of tradition as being 'normally governed by overtly or tacitly accepted rules and of a ritual or symbolic nature, which seek to inculcate certain values and norms of behaviour by repetition, which automatically implies continuity with the past.'[19] Crucially, according to Hobsbawm, such practices 'normally attempt to establish continuity with a suitable historic past' (p. 1), and are to be expected more frequently when

> A rapid transformation of society weakens or destroys the social patterns for which 'old' traditions had been designed, producing new ones to which they were not applicable, or when such old traditions and their institutional carriers and promulgators no longer prove sufficiently adaptable and flexible, or are otherwise eliminated: in short, when there are sufficiently large and rapid changes on the demand or the supply side. (pp. 4–5)

There were plenty of large-scale changes in terms of both supply and demand in nineteenth-century Wales, reflecting the myriad changes which took place in many countries; indeed, the invention of tradition formed part of a general romantic revival encompassing the whole of Western Europe.[20] The impulse took hold in Wales, however, in a way that saw latent cultural performances, which were understood to possess some vital form of performative agency, become isolated enactments forming part of a revived structure of traditions. The revival of the Eisteddfod and its amalgamation with Iolo Morganwg's partially fictional 'Gorsedd of the Bards of the Island of Britain', a conscious throwback to the ancient druidic tradition, was part of the process of the romantic mythologising of Wales. Iolo's Gorsedd 'met' on 21 June 1792 on Primrose Hill, London, a site chosen because Iolo believed it was the epicentre of the Brythonic world in ancient Britain. The word *gorsedd*, literally throne, refers to a mound of earth, a cairn or hillock, but through Iolo's imaginative and performative use it came to mean a gathering of poets. According to Ceri W. Lewis, the word *gorsedd* changed or shifted in meaning to reflect Iolo's thinking at a given time. Iolo had seen in the Welsh Laws, for instance, that the name was sometimes used in reference to a court of law held in the open air, and so took the word to refer to an outdoor assembly of poets; later in his life, however, the word took on specific druidic significance.[21] There is no detailed description of this first Gorsedd, but it is said that twelve stones were placed in a circle, with another serving as a central lodestone. The ceremony began with the placing of a sword on the lodestone, followed by a reading by Iolo of his English poem 'Ode on the Mythology of the Ancient British Bards', which praises the goddess Freedom and calls for an end to slavery.[22] Although the first truly national Eisteddfod was held in Llangollen in 1858, decades after Iolo's death, the Gorsedd performance at Carmarthen in 1819 was the first iteration of the merger of Eisteddfod and Gorsedd.[23] The event was not without precedent. Historically, the Welsh poets had taken a central role in the machinations of identity and had served the princes, and subsequently the Welsh *uchelwyr*,[24] as keepers of cultural memory (of names, genealogies and traditions). Iolo's conception of the Gorsedd was true to this, but was also of its time. In 1792, the year of the fall of the Bastille, Iolo's hope was that the Gorsedd would lead the Welsh towards the kind of 'freedom' (also the Eisteddfod's motto – *Rhyddid*) brought about by the French revolution.[25] In his declaration on the rediscovery of the ancient Druidic tradition he makes clear that he was presenting to the nation a vision of the forgotten past. Gwyn A. Williams describes it as a national movement: 'through his new creation, the Gorsedd of Bards of the Isle of Britain, he offered the Welsh people a democratic movement for intellectuals, a guild of commemorators of the nation that would restore the memory of our glorious past and use this history to re-create a free nation in Wales.'[26] There appears to be no intention of declaring this constructed ritual as new. According to Iolo, this was an ancient druidic ritual that had remained virtually unchanged for two thousand years, which had survived in the hills of Glamorgan. Furthermore, Iolo declared himself and Edward Evans of Aberdare, to be 'the last of the druidic bards', a fact that fuelled the necessity of making the ceremony public. By the time of the Eisteddfod in Carmarthen in 1819, held by the Welsh society Cymdeithas Cymreigyddion Dyfed, Iolo was invited to hold the Gorsedd ceremony as part of the festival's proceedings and subsequently designed the costume, the ritual and the properties involved in its performance. By 1850 the Gorsedd had been established as a regular component of the Eisteddfod's event structure and has been central to its performative functions since, both in terms of ritual efficacy and pageantry. The ritualistic dimension also brought to the Eisteddfod a theatricality that is absent in the competitions performed on stage, an aspect which is discussed by Anwen Jones in her exploration of the relationship between National Eisteddfod and national theatre.[27]

The emphasis on ceremonial rites, including rites of passage and of initiation, proved a powerful gesture, though the Gorsedd rituals are never conceived of or practised as a religious ceremony in any sense. The spatial configuration, the circle of twelve stones and the central loadstone, has resonances with ancient monuments and theories regarding the ritual purposes they served. Stones are placed in specific settings to represent the points of the compass, with one stone facing 'the eye of the sun' when it rises on the longest day of the summer, another facing the sun on the shortest day of the winter.[28] This is *play*, using specific props in order to sustain a culturally significant liminoid experience. Today, replica stones are placed on the Eisteddfod site, unless there is a pre-existing Gorsedd stone circle in the locality, and this has made the self-consciously ritualistic Gorsedd more central to the main event, removing some of its discrete mystery.[29] It is now framed as one performative event amongst several different forms. Gorsedd ceremonies include the proclamation, a year in advance, of the *bro* (region) that will host the Eisteddfod, as well as the low-key initiation ceremonies that welcome new members during the Eisteddfod week. Though not religious, these ceremonies are nonetheless ritualistic in structure and have a ceremonial authority. That this is invented matters not; the reversal of the secular and the sacred is commonplace in festival structures, and slippages between them, such as the Gorsedd hymn (sung to a deity), and the proclamations '*Y Gwir yn Erbyn y Byd*' (The Truth against the World) and '*Gwaedd Uwch Adwaedd*' (Voice against resounding voice), which form part of official ceremonies, only serve to highlight this ambivalence. The bardic symbol made up by Iolo, a span of three lines (/ | \), accentuates the cryptic, almost mystical nature of his invention, and is described by him as follows: 'And God vocalizing his name said / | \, and with the word all the world sprang into being, singing in ecstasy of joy / | \ and repeating the name of the Deity.'[30] Despite the ritualistic touches, these ceremonies are intended to frame the chief cultural activity at the heart of the Eisteddfod, the main competitions: the Crown, awarded for writing poetry in free verse, the Chair, given to the winning poet who has composed in *cynghanedd* (a strict metre), the Prose Medal, as well as the Daniel Owen Memorial Prize, awarded to the best novel, the Literature Medal, and the Drama Medal. During the ceremonies, held in the Pafiliwn, members of the Gorsedd sit in tiers across the wide stage, arranged according to the colour of their robes, with white for the highest designation, the Order of Druids, followed by blue for the Order of Bards and green for the Order of Ovates. The Archdruid, the Recorder, the Herald, the Swordbearer and other officiators sit in the front row facing the audience. The collective understanding and the claim on centuries of culture that the Gorsedd represents provides meaning and context. Therefore, despite its fabricated beginnings and overt mysticism, the ceremonial performance itself carries the deeply significant implications of the award to the poet, because the participants are invested in it and believe it to be symbolic of the continuation of culture. Each ceremony includes the delivery of the adjudication by experts who are eminent poets and past winners. The announcement of the winner by his or her *nom de plume* is a charged moment, because no one knows who the winner is apart from a small circle of people, including the victor. Facing the audience, the Archdruid calls on the bard by his or her pseudonym, asking that he/she rise to their feet on the sounding of the trumpet fanfare, a moment of high theatricality and suspense heightened by roaming spotlights. The winning poet stands and is revealed, enrobed and led to the stage in a procession. This liminoid moment, when the bard stands between the audience and the Gorsedd, is made all the more significant by the participation of the audience in the unsheathing and resheathing of the sword held aloft above the poet's head. As the victor stands in front of the chair, facing the audience, the sword is held aloft and the Archdruid, unsheathing it halfway, asks the congregation:

Y Gwir yn erbyn y Byd, A oes Heddwch? (The Truth against the World, Is there Peace?)

To which the audience answers, *Heddwch!* (Peace!), and the sword is resheathed. A second time and a third, the Archdruid unsheaths the sword and asks,

Calon wrth Galon, A oes Heddwch? (Heart to Heart, Is there Peace?)
and
Gwaedd uwch Adwaedd, A oes Heddwch? (Voice against resounding voice, Is there Peace?)

Each time, the audience responds with declarations of peace and the sword is resheathed. Finally, the Archdruid declares in *cynghanedd*, '*Eistedded y bardd yn hedd yr Eisteddfod*' (let the poet be seated in the peace of the Eisteddfod). The dialogue is a symbolic declaration of acceptance. In this moment of initiation, one of the audience is accepted into the Gorsedd in acknowledgement of their achievement, representing their initiation into the community of cultural experts. The initiation is also a performance where behaviour related to cultural identity is continuously (annually) enacted in order to sustain a sense of shared collective memory and a deepening awareness of a particular form of nationness. The phrase 'the truth against the world' places the ritual in the realm of the world at large, elevating its implications beyond the cultural. The cultural, as performed here, has ramifications for our role in society and this initiation ceremony, like most others, is laden with performative utterances and symbolic moments that have meaning beyond the moment of their performance. Anwen Jones has suggested that by participating in the Gorsedd ceremonials individuals trade in their real identities for a new role and status in a virtual society, which suggests that this cultural performance has the capacity for transformation on both an individual and a communal level.[31] This is possibly related to what Stoeltje refers to as a festival's capacity to resolve 'social conflicts and concerns rooted in social relationships and/or survival issues',[32] that is, of confronting a set of concerns and at the same time enacting their resolution within a symbolic frame. The Eisteddfod is essentially structured around a competition, but by locating the victory within such a ritualised frame the ceremony is elevated to the status of communal ritual that represents the perpetuation of culture and therefore safeguards who we are. The deep disappointment when there is *'neb yn deilwng'* (no one worthy), strongly suggests that this is the case, for it is more than mere competition that is at stake. Providing a set of ritualised and framed behaviours, which express and to an extent resolve 'survival issues', involves recognition on some level of what is at stake. This happens in the Eisteddfod in relation to ideas of cultural duty towards tradition and tradition-bearing, even though the methods invented to carry tradition are relatively new. In this way, the Eisteddfod is a crucial performance that operates as a holding frame for deeply meaningful cultural customs that otherwise might not be sustained so comprehensively. Notions of what is traditional are built up from years of repeated behaviour and gain traction from the fact that this behaviour is embodied in the self and in others.

Memory
The Eisteddfod also provides a frame of reference for the way in which culture is remembered. People may refer to an event as pertaining to the year of a particular Eisteddfod, but more than this, the Eisteddfod itself forms part of the way in which social remembering connects people in larger group identities. Memory is culturally mediated and the process of remembering is dependent on a number of cultural devices that are negotiated in social settings. The Eisteddfod is a conduit for a range of Welsh cultural activities, from writing and different art forms to social and political activity, to come into contact with each other through performances undertaken in close proximity and in rapid succession, thereby quickening a sense of identity. Whether we relate to the Eisteddfod as a longstanding tradition or one that is more modern in its making, it continues to operate as a tradition that assembles connections between the generations and represents a

continuity of practice, particularly in relation to artistic forms such as poetry and, more recently, the novel, visual art and drama. That which constitutes tradition is located in the relationship between knowledge and repetitive practice, and because traditional knowledge is often embodied, based in the body's repetition of certain patterns and behaviours, the sense of the past that it creates is one of belonging via a set of shared behaviours over time. Tradition here is not an unthinking and unwitting continuation held to dogmatically, but rather a process of imbuing a certain set of customs with value, a value that relates to the way in which the community has used such customs in the past. Operating in this way, the Eisteddfod is a holding place for a network of activities, from the informal – meeting people, chatting, drinking – to the highly structured ritual of the competitions. All such activities are permeated with a strong sense of memory and recollection, for example recalling a win by a specific poet or artist, meeting old friends, or remembering one's own life refracted through the lens of numerous eisteddfodau. Memory is also instigated by the district in which the Eisteddfod Maes, or field, is emplaced each year, as the festival usually returns to an area in which it has previously been located and has left traces, such as the stone circles in several towns and villages that are relics of previous Eisteddfodau. The Maes itself becomes a sort of palimpsest of local cultural history; the area, if not the patch of land itself, is referenced in the annual title given to the festival and it is always, inevitably, laden with cultural references. For instance, in 2012 the National Eisteddfod in the Vale of Glamorgan was 'Iolo's Eisteddfod' in reference to the proximity to Iolo Morganwg's home village of Flemingston; in 2013, in Denbighshire, it was 'Twm's', in reference to Twm o'r Nant, the eighteenth-century writer of dramatic interludes. In this way, the Eisteddfod becomes imprinted on and into local culture, to be remembered and recalled as part of the experience of place and it draws the locality and the community into it, recognising their specific culture as part of its performance.

Symbolic processes are at the heart of festival and emerge in relation to time. Stoeltje defines these processes as 'the manipulation of temporal reality' and 'transformation'.[33] The temporal reality of the festival incorporates at least two dimensions of time. Principles of periodicity and rhythm define the experience, reflecting the seasonal repetition. Not much is made of the fact that the Eisteddfod takes place during the first full week of August, nor are cosmological and seasonal elements immediately apparent in the Eisteddfod as secular festival, though the Gorsedd ceremonies heighten this latent aspect, with their emphasis on elements of summer ritual practices in the offerings to the bard, such as the horn of plenty, and the flower bouquet given by women in symbolic roles (virgin/mother), as well as the flower dance performed by young children, redolent with references to the summer solstice.[34] This ritual 'lite', performed for the first time at the National Eisteddfod at Machynlleth in 1937, seems to have no clearly discernible significance other than its celebratory and romantic tone, but if we look beyond the general Celtic Twilight feel of the performance, we see that it is in fact a carefully scripted pageant and that its author probably believed in its function as performance, because it fulfilled a symbolic role in a country so deficient in theatricality. Written by Albert Evans-Jones (Cynan, 1895–1970, Recorder of the Gorsedd from 1935 and Archdruid in 1950–4 and 1963–6), who had no belief in the ancient druidism of the Gorsedd, the carefully structured ceremony encapsulates the binding of the people of a region to the culture and its perpetuation through the performance of a symbolic rite.[35]

The second dimension of temporality in festival is more complex and involves a degree of cultural dissonance, where ideas of tradition and change collide and new ideas are thrown forward, their effect impacting on established formal structures of festival. This is a paradoxical quality, as Stoeltje explains, 'meaning in festival derives from experience; thus festival emphasizes the past. Yet festival happens in the present and for the present, directed towards the future. Thus the new and different are legitimate dimensions of festival, contributing to its vitality.'[36] Recent concessions and additions, such as the selling of alcohol on the field, the visual aesthetics and planning of the Maes by professional designers, as well as the increase in simultaneous translation facilities, all point to and reflect gradual social shifts and have contributed to the Eisteddfod's currency as a contemporary cultural festival. The principle of transformation, through which 'principles of reversal, repetition, juxtaposition, condensation, and excess flourish' (p. 268) to encourage a situation and behaviour that is extradaily, or different from the everyday, is predicated on various forms of participation in a wide variety of performances. This transformation incorporates more than the change in behaviour brought about through holiday/vacation activity, and includes participation in a highly structured performance, either officially, through what is performed on stage, or in the celebratory festivities that surround events, such as eating and drinking. The Gorsedd, in whose ceremonies the established order is reversed, also represents a process of transformation or inversion. Membership of the Gorsedd represents an alternative social order based on merit, and here the concept of competition is crucial to the way social order is altered. The competition is not only an alternative social order, it is also associated with notions of revitalisation and transformation and visitors to the Eisteddfod become actively engaged as both audience and participants. This engagement is underpinned by the structuring of activities on the Maes. Part market square, loosely structured and informal, and part highly controlled production in the competitions and ceremonies at specific performance venues, the Eisteddfod actively engages participants on different levels and in a public context. Stoeltje elaborates on the active mode of festival as an intervention requiring or expecting a response,

> What is spoken, acted, or displayed in festival – public or private – anticipates a response, social or supernatural. This active mode, then, makes demands on participants, requiring their attention. And this concentration of attention heightens consciousness, creating an intersection of individual performance and social reflexivity. (pp. 262–3)

The Maes instigates the 'active mode' in its participants. It is a stage, a designated site for a major shift from the frames of everyday life. The fact that the National Eisteddfod occurs over a week during which much of the population of Welsh-speaking Wales moves to it involves a substantial change from daily life, and an investment. It represents a shift away from routine and towards structured events that permit heightened moments of cultural expression, which Stoeltje refers to as 'frames that foster the transformative, reciprocal, and reflexive dimensions of social life' (p. 263). Such is the importance of the reflexive dimension that it is shared beyond the site itself by those who may not be able to make the pilgrimage to the Eisteddfod itself, via televised competitions and light entertainment programmes (*Y Babell Lên*, *Talwrn y Beirdd*), which are crucial to the wider understanding and awareness of the festival.[37] Broadcasting provides another window on the Eisteddfod, with the BBC, via S4C, the Welsh-language channel, providing almost perpetual coverage of the main competition events, so that the extra-daily structure of festival permeates home life, beyond the festival grounds.[38] Stoeltje also elaborates on how the festival's intent and purpose is communicated in the broadest sense, making the experience meaningful in different ways: 'the message of festival concerns the shared experience of the group and multiple interpretations of that experience'. This aspect is not only enacted in the cultural content but 'dominates the rhetoric as well as the action of an event clearly defined as "ours"'.[39] In this context, the representation of the Eisteddfod through broadcasting is not only a presentation of the locality of national culture, but an essential function within the collective memory of a nation, supported here by the Welsh media. However, the remoteness of television (or radio) is unable to provide direct engagement in public shows of familiarity, those moments of personal social engagement of which the Eisteddfod is composed, an aspect commented upon in *Y Cymro*, the Welsh newspaper, in 1940, following the National Eisteddfod at Aberpennar, the first to be broadcast on radio.[40] In the flesh, the Maes is a place to traverse and catch up with friends, acquaintances and family members, and at the same time it is a venue for encountering new experiences together, testing the waters, allowing new variables, new artworks, new politics and performances to be witnessed. Not all Eisteddfod activity takes place in the fleeting mode of the festival, however, and many of its traces constitute cultural artefacts that will be revered for years to come. Though the vehicle is an ephemeral event, the cultural production becomes part of the cultural canon. In literature, this is accomplished primarily through the publication of prizewinning works and specifically the volume of compositions and adjudications, *Cyfansoddiadau a Beirniadaethau*, during the Eisteddfod week. This is not only a record of the week's competition results; it is also pedagogical in its inclusion of key competition adjudications and responsible for the transposition of the festival into archive, encapsulating the wealth of creative practice and expertise that is invested in the Eisteddfod and its legacy. Much has been made of the foundational and mythic qualities that the Eisteddfod engenders in relation to tradition, but it is in actuality a site that is made meaningful in various ways that are defined by its participants; it can be, in fact, a highly experimental place, a place of possibilities, where habitual behaviours may be suspended.[41] This balancing act makes the Eisteddfod the primary site for the renewal of Welsh-language culture, poised between the strictures of tradition and those moments where there has been a shaking of the foundations.

Such a stance is negotiated at the Eisteddfod by virtue of its ephemeral and performative nature, which enables the repetition of traditional forms while at the same time encouraging new and diverse cultural responses that may conflict with notions of tradition. The concept of place itself in the Eisteddfod is composed of such contradictions.

Place
The Eisteddfod site is usually separated from the world outside by a perimeter fence and several gateways. On the inside, the Maes is everything. While it is hardly ever situated outside a rural context, as it needs a considerable amount of space for the Maes and adjacent fields for parking and camping, the Eisteddfod is inevitably never far from a town or city. Even so, the rurality feels total and the Maes, in its isolation, can often seem remote. The significance of this is debatable; the sense of rural return might be a fitting idealisation of a retreat to Welsh-speaking Wales, though at the same time there have been voices articulating the idea of holding an Eisteddfod in a city centre (it has taken place on suburban outskirts and in city parks).[42] The Maes shares some of the spatial forms of the agricultural fairs, which are also significant events in the Welsh calendar.

Part of its modern history has included the debate on whether to fix the Eisteddfod in one location, for its planning and execution is a complex undertaking. Alternating north and south each year, its coming to a specific *bro* or square mile is officially proclaimed a year in advance. In organisational terms, it is a two-year community project supported by the local populace, as well as the local authority concerned, in a monumental fundraising effort facilitated by the Eisteddfod Act of 1959 and the Welsh Assembly Government. Despite the logistical complexity of the roving Maes and the recurrent attractiveness of a static Eisteddfod, the idea of one fixed site has been resisted, for much would be lost, not least the benefits of the festival's peripatetic nature and the cultural implications of forging memories in different locations, a crucial function of its celebratory and itinerant nature. Fixing its location would also damage both its transitory nature and its reach, aspects that are imperative to some of the festival qualities the Eisteddfod continues to retain. Holding it in stasis would also negate the complex web of cultural creation and local support that sustains not only the event itself but also the experience of collective memory. The travelling nature of the festival binds us to it in a perpetual enactment of hope for the regeneration of a particular community, but this is not specifically about gain, either financial or even cultural, it is about the bonds of communal performance and their importance for sustaining the memory of the group. This is a critical function of the Eisteddfod, which Hywel Teifi Edwards describes as a means of instilling and focusing on 'an awareness of language and literature as humanizing forces which no society can neglect with impunity'.[43] Situating the National Eisteddfod in one location would limit its significance as a social event that has direct consequences for the local community involved, for its effect is far more than that of a social gathering. The Eisteddfod creates a social space, which extends beyond the reach of the week's events into the wider community; indeed, it is the community's 'invitation' to host an Eisteddfod and the long period of community preparation that sustains the focus on the 'humanizing forces' referred to by Edwards. The role of the local community is directly reflected in the ritual representation of *communitas* associated with the chief competitions; the chaired bard is presented with a *Blodeuged*, a large bouquet of regional flowers, given to him by a local girl; an older woman presents him or her with the *Corn Hirlas* (the horn of plenty), a symbolic performance of the bond between the *bro* and the wider community (or nation) that is also a reflection of shared cultural concerns. The communal effort to stage the Eisteddfod by the local population and the attempt by the rest of Wales to participate – either directly, by being there, or through merely watching from afar – creates a reciprocal, communal knot, the value of which is equal to if not greater than the immediate value of the event as a cultural competition. At its heart, the Eisteddfod is a cultural performance that reaches out in time and has a distinct presence before, during, and after the event, in what is often characterised as a cultural reawakening or linguistic renaissance for a specific locality. It is actually far more significant than this: it is a complex, portable microcosm of a national culture that is able to magnify the social and cultural bonds for the community in which it resides, as well as the bonds of those who participate. In this respect, the Eisteddfod is a multidimensional event, and one that also represents many different spaces.

In his work 'On Other Spaces', Michel Foucault elaborates on sites that have 'the curious property of being in relation with all the other sites, but in such a way as to suspect, neutralize, or invert the set of relations that they happen to designate, mirror or reflect'.[44] These spaces, which are associated with all others though standing in opposition or contradiction to them, are of two types, the utopia and the heterotopia. The utopias, 'fundamentally unreal spaces', are sites that have a general relation or analogy with the real space of society and may present society in a perfected or a subverted form (3).The heterotopias, on the other hand, are

> Places that do exist and that are formed in the very founding of society – which are something like counter-sites, a kind of effectively enacted utopia in which the real sites, all the other sites that can be found within the culture, are simultaneously represented, contested, and inverted. Places of this kind are outside of all places, even though it may be possible to indicate their location in reality. Because these places are absolutely different from all the sites that they reflect and speak about, I shall call them, by way of contrast to utopias, heterotopias. (3–4)

In discussing the nature of heterotopias Foucault asks what meaning they may have, and in reading such spaces as '[a] simultaneously mythic and real contestation of the space in which we live', arrives at what he calls a 'heterotopology', an ordering or classification, arranged according to a set of principles. A key principle is that the heterotopia can hold within itself – in an actual space – several sites that are incompatible with each other, as in theatre, which 'brings onto the rectangle of the stage, one after the other, a whole series of places that are foreign to one another' (6). Similarly, the Eisteddfod provides a representation of all Welsh life in one place; on the Maes all of Welsh-speaking Wales, and more, is represented, and each society, institution or group has a stake in its own performance of Welshness, and in how it contributes to the overall performance of nationness. More than a calculated commercial spin, the presence of major institutions speaks of their need to declare their participation. Thus, most of the political parties share terraces with the Electoral Commission and Cymdeithas yr Iaith (the Welsh Language Society), Coed Cadw (the Woodland Trust in Wales), the Campaign for Nuclear Disarmament, the Society of Friends, the police services, the fire service, the University of Wales Press and the Red Cross, as well as with universities and trade unions, learned societies, publishing houses, charities, trusts and religious denominations. These are interspersed with stalls selling books, music, jewellery and crafts and all manner of clothes.

Heterotopias are also temporal and are 'most often linked to slices in time – which is to say that they open on to what might be termed, for the sake of symmetry, heterochronies. The heterotopia begins to function at full capacity when men arrive at a sort of absolute break with their traditional time' (6). The Eisteddfod represents a commitment to being 'out of time' for days at a time, despite the fact that it is seemingly part of a long tradition. It also has a presence all year, from early childhood onwards, for the Welsh-medium school year has its own eisteddfodic structure, as do many villages and towns. Urdd Gobaith Cymru, the Wales-wide youth society, supports the superstructure of a national youth eisteddfod, underpinned by county, area and school eisteddfodau, whose competition stages have a bearing on the school year.[45] Rural villages and localities, Young Farmers Clubs and other associations, as well as post-industrial communities such as the south Wales valleys, all have their own eisteddfod traditions and customs. Hundreds of eisteddfodau are held all over Wales each year, from the intimate village event to the largest and most complex festivals, such as the Llangollen International Musical Eisteddfod and the National Eisteddfod itself. Together, they permeate the calendar with a particular eisteddfodic pattern, which becomes denser towards Whitsun week (the Urdd National Eisteddfod) and the first week of August (the National Eisteddfod). Thus, although the eisteddfod is an ephemeral event, it has a solid calendrical structure. Foucault situates places associated with 'time in its most fleeting, transitory, precarious aspect ... time in the mode of the festival', in opposition to certain perpetual heterotopias linked to 'indefinitely accumulating time', such as museums and libraries. His primary example of a site that is linked to the fleetingness of time is the fairground.[46] While the Eisteddfod is not a fairground it has the fleetingness of a market or town square gathering, or a busy street, and possesses the temporary qualities of a performance venue, leisure activity and exhibitionary space. It is a place that comes into being through social interaction, through the participants' engagement. It is played into existence, as is evident from the performance competitions, the sport, the ritual, the socials rites and customs, and the protests, which may involve law-breaking; each is a normative part of the performance on the annually designated patch of land. To take part in such a transformational space and time, the participant will enter either via competition or as a dweller on the Maes.

Heterotopias also have a function in relation to all space, and this function takes on one of two extreme positions:

Either their role is to create a space of illusion that exposes every real space, all the sites inside of which human life is partitioned, as still more illusory … Or else, on the contrary, their role is to create a space that is other, another real space, as perfect, as meticulous, as well arranged as ours is messy, ill constructed, and jumbled. This latter type would be the heterotopias, not of illusion, but of compensation. (8)

The space of compensation has a particular significance for most Welsh people, whether they are the 20 per cent of the population of Wales who speak Welsh, those for whom Welsh is residual, those whose children speak the language, or others who support it. The Eisteddfod's language rule, which designates Welsh as the official language of all competitions, was enacted for the first time at the Caerffili National Eisteddfod in 1950, though it had been established as early as 1937 in the historic Machynlleth Eisteddfod, during which the Eisteddfod Society and the Gorsedd of the Bards were merged as one body, becoming the Eisteddfod Council.[47] Debates regarding the relevance of the language rule have occurred at regular intervals, reflecting different positions on bilingualism and the perceived status of the Welsh language at a given time. The rule is a stance, and in order to understand how fundamental this stance is to the forging of the contemporary Eisteddfod and its impact on Welsh society, we need only recall the historical context in which the modern Eisteddfod arose.

In order to bolster this space of compensation, the Eisteddfod has as many spaces of performance as could be imagined, a combination of satellite performance spaces that draw on a range of cultural practices and a variety of spatial configurations. These are usually gathered around the Pafiliwn, the natural focal point and main performance venue for ceremonies such as the chairing and the crowning. Despite being the epicentre of most competitions and performances, including *y gymanfa ganu* (a religious singing service), the school pageants and evening concerts, the Pafiliwn is the least theatrical of stages, an impersonal performance space distant from the audience and dependent on microphones. The audience are seated at a variety of angles, configured to face the widest of empty stages, which is the ultimate destination for thousands of competitors. It is a prestigious performance space, on which there is intense focus because the stakes are high. The performance on the Pafiliwn mainstage is the final round of competition. Hundreds will compete in prelim heats held elsewhere in order to '*cael*

"*Llwyfan*'' (literally, 'get "Stage"'). Final-round competitors will not only perform to the Pafiliwn audience, they will simultaneously be heard over loudspeakers across the Maes, and their performance, potentially, will be broadcast to the nation. Competitions include monologues, interludes and sketches, all manner of singing competitions, solo, duets and choral, *cerdd dant* harmonies and unaccompanied folk songs, as well as oratory and recitation, *cydadrodd*, various forms of dance and instrumental performances, both individual and orchestral.[48] So broad is the stage that a single figure is dwarfed by the surrounding space, though held by the intense reciprocal gaze between audience and performer, for all performances here are played out towards the audience, almost as a direct address. The immediacy of this transaction masks its complexity as communication, for all performers are held up for comparison against the memory of previous competitors and winners and there are distinct performance techniques and expectations at work.

Not all eyes are on the Pafiliwn, as the Eisteddfod also includes an array of non-performed competitions involving essays, translations, visual arts and dramatic writing. These fields have their place on the Maes, which also houses Y Babell Lên (the literature tent), Pabell y Cymdeithasau (the societies' tent), and Y Pafiliwn Gwyddoniaeth a Thechnoleg (the science and technology pavilion). There is an area for eating, an essential component of festival rather downplayed at the Eisteddfod, which becomes an informal space for evening performances on open-air stages. Since the 1990s the Maes is no longer singular; bands play at Maes B, a venue for Welsh-language popular music, while Maes C is an informal performance area, providing an eclectic programme of theatre, music and poetry and Maes D, the Welsh learners' area. Small-scale performances and aesthetic events such as experimental theatre practices take place at Y Lle Celf (the visual art space) or on the Maes, and minimalist theatre productions at Theatr y Maes (the theatre of the maes) and more recently at the Cwt Drama (drama shed) of Theatr Genedlaethol Cymru, the national theatre of Wales. Yet despite its dimensions as a large contemporary festival, the Eisteddfod retains the feel of a community or village festival; crossing the field one is comforted, for this world is Welsh-speaking. The Eisteddfod world becomes itself through staging not difference exactly, but a version of Welshness – an almost total version of Welshness for the Welsh speaker – and the festival goer's immersion and participation in this world is absolute. The Eisteddfod is not delivered for an external audience, or at least it does not appear to be; we are the participants and the audience and the competitors. In a marked difference from most other folklife festivals and a definite departure from the historical aim of performing Welsh culture and civilisation for a larger neighbour (an important part of past Eisteddfodau),[49] this festival is open to anyone who cares to participate. Social structures of participation enable an understanding of what the Eisteddfod is and how it operates, although in such a community venture there are many alternative ways of participating and this is crucial to ensuring that its purpose remains relevant to all members of the group. As a festival, it has adapted in order to ensure this sense of currency and relevance, as most festivals do, in order to achieve the highest degree of participation and integration. Its peripatetic nature also ensures maximum geographical coverage and participation by diverse communities.

What makes the performances held at the Eisteddfod so central to the performance of Welsh identity? Apart from the value of the art forms themselves, the Eisteddfod is in need of constant renewal and this in turn places emphasis on the need for cultural and social engagement of the highest degree. Although it produces artefacts of significant meaning, the primary function of the Eisteddfod is the awarding, the becoming of the bard, and the public recognition. A projection of 'all of Wales' is represented on the Maes, to bear witness to the performance, and national identity is reinforced in different ways for different Eisteddfod-goers, facilitating 'regeneration through the rearrangement of structures'.[50] A consequence of such regeneration in festival is that identity is strengthened and social issues, including conflicts, can be articulated. This recalibration through festival does not only happen with regard to specific cultural, social or political beliefs, but operates in relation to the entire social life of the participants, and in this way the Eisteddfod is a cultural nexus where all the pressures of social life are expressed. Stoeltje remarks upon this when she explains the dynamics of the festival's communal nature: 'because the festival brings the group together and communicates about the society itself and the role of the individual within it, every effort to change or to constrain social life will be expressed in some specific relationship to festival' (p. 263). Though it may not appear to be the most radical site of cultural transformation, the Eisteddfod's deep binding of place with cultural performances associated with memory truly enables an enactment or articulation of contemporary culture, from all manner of political dissent on the Maes to the regeneration of cultural meaning in the competitions and ceremonial events. Its itinerant nature and the lack of permanent site sustain its cultural vitality, ensuring that the festival site and the festival structure retain a dangerous unpredictability, socially, politically and culturally. In this sense, the Eisteddfod operates a performance that works towards construction (*poiesis*), which concentrates on the capacity to make, or to enable becoming. This aspect influences and enables the stance of performance as *kinesis*, 'as a decentring agency of movement, struggle, disruption, and centrifugal force', or performative actions bound up with defining nationness that cut across the pedagogical, the master discourses of nationhood, enabling a move from 'cultural *invention* to *intervention*'.[51] This, in turn, binds the Eisteddfod to the public imagination, where it is understood to be a performative site and locus for both personal and collective memory that relates the present circumstances to the past.

Performing Wales in America's Front Garden

In 2009 the Smithsonian Folklife Festival, possibly the largest festival of its kind in the world, included a curatorial programme entitled 'Wales Smithsonian Cymru', that was exhibited, or performed, on stalls and stages across the National Mall, 'America's front garden', at the heart of Washington DC. This section of writing explores the way in which the festival constructed a performance of 'Wales', how we might understand such a performance in relation to ideas of people, memory and place and how these notions were mediated for an audience on the other side of the world.

The Smithsonian Folklife Festival (hereafter Festival), was instigated in the context of unprecedented social changes and the programme recognises this drastic shift by celebrating and exploring cultures that face challenges arising from globalisation. The Festival's role in safeguarding culture is put into context by Daniel E. Sheehy, Festival director in 2009, who describes the social changes that have taken place in the twentieth century as 'a tsunami of unchecked global intrusion via commerce and the media', which overwhelmed 'cultural self-determination . . . displacing the local with the foreign'. He elaborates on the fact that this has happened in such a short time span, which has meant that 'entire languages, musical traditions, and other expressive cultural systems were abandoned in favour of cultural trappings invented by others' or 'foreign' to indigenous culture.[52] The Festival does not tell this story directly; rather, it perpetuates the exploration of what Sheehy calls the 'process of cultural evolution from the other side of the equation', encouraging an exploration of 'creativity, resilience, and fortitude of people, institutions and cultures that follow their own path amid a torrent of contrarian voices' (p. 8). It is against this canvas that the Wales programme was designed in order to explore the tensions between cultural self-determination and the foreign or new and to understand how 'the Welsh people successfully integrate both the tradition and the change that are part of their cultural heritage' (p. 8). This emphasis removed the possibility of portraying a form of native revivalism and focused instead on questioning how a community of people has dealt with significant social and cultural shifts encapsulated by the juxtaposition of Welsh, 'one of the most ancient languages in the world, spoken by one-fifth of the country's three million inhabitants', and the fact that Wales 'can lay claim to the nineteenth-century mantle of being "the first industrialized nation".' Subsequently, the main aim underlying the exhibit was to explore how 'the Welsh managed to navigate the turbulent waters of continuity and change to shepherd an economically and culturally sustainable society into the future' (p. 8). Wales was presented in this context as a small nation and minority culture existing against the odds, and the Festival's performance was constructed according to what might best represent the fortitude and inventiveness of the Welsh people. As the Wales Smithsonian Cymru exhibit was jointly curated by the Smithsonian and a curatorial group from Wales, with the backing of the Welsh Assembly Government, Wales was presented as a historic country with a wealth of traditional crafts and culture and at the same time a people emerging from a post-industrial landscape ready to embrace new and divergent ways of living:

> Wales (Cymru in Welsh) is a dynamic and resilient nation. The industrious and resourceful nature of its people provides a firm platform from which to present its rich culture and heritage. *Wales Smithsonian Cymru* will celebrate language, literature, and the spoken word, present crafts and occupational skills, share music and cooking, and evoke the spirit that powered the industrial revolution and is now championing sustainable solutions. The program will explore how age-old

knowledge, skills, and materials continue to be refashioned, recycled, and reinvented to meet modern demands and to continue to connect Wales to the world.[53]

The way in which the Festival presents its exploratory exhibition is related to its background as 'a living cultural exhibition outside museum walls',[54] in which visitors interact with the people whose culture is on display and who embody the culture in question. Festival programmes are curated specifically to facilitate such an exchange. Established in 1967, the Festival is renowned for breaking new ground in its conception of the Museum as fluid and participatory site. In order to understand its impact, we only need to consider the significance of its location on the National Mall in the capital city of the United States, 'America's greatest urban park', the site of the most important of national memorials and home to the largest museum complex in the world.[55] Bordered by elm trees, the Mall runs the two and a quarter miles from the Capitol building to the Potomac River, lined either side with the national Smithsonian museums, which seem to declare by their very architecture an authoritative view of history and culture (with the notable exceptions of the National Museum of the American Indian, opened in 2004, and the National Museum of African American History and Culture, opened in 2016, whose architectures are strikingly different). The Festival is all the more remarkable because of its symbolic location sandwiched in between the nation's museums, places that Foucault refers to as heterotopias of 'indefinitely accumulating time'. The Folklife Festival declares itself as different, even opposed, to the authoritative position of the Museum. The Festival's flexible and changeable nature is related, in part, to its roots in the Fourth of July celebrations inaugurated under President Thomas Jefferson, which included a festival on land adjacent to the White House, 'the President's park', and is in this way a version of Foucault's specific heterotopia linked 'to time at its most fleeting, transitory, precarious aspect, to time in the mode of the festival'.[56] The development of the Mall as national park stems from the historical importance of the place as a symbol of government, the people and the nation as a whole. According to Richard Kurin, former director of the Center for Folklife and Cultural Heritage, the place is a 'physical symbol of the tie between Congress and the White House . . . a symbol of rural-urban utopian union . . . a setting for public life'.[57]

The open spaces that the Festival inhabits, between museums on the Mall and around the Reflecting Pool, between the Washington Monument and the Lincoln Memorial, are of symbolic importance; these are the memorial sites for the American government, its presidents and its war dead. However, the natural corollary to its situatedness at the heart of US government is the fact that the Festival also has an element of the radical, of counter-culture, directly related to the history of the Mall as site of protest and dissent. Since the 1963 March on Washington that culminated in Martin Luther King's speech, the site has become a place for staging public demonstrations and protests set apart from victory celebrations, presidential inaugurations, Independence Day celebrations and concerts. The Festival taps into the energy of the demonstration and the protest song, but as a museum product it also represents the institutions that structure civic society. This dichotomy is part of its appeal.

The Festival's fluidity and adaptability is also rooted in its pedagogical rationale and in founder S. Dillon Ripley's advocacy of 'open education' – of the museum as a space of exploration. Realising that founding an exploratory site necessitated a more informal learning environment, and one that depended on freedom of movement, Ripley states that the Festival's aim is to 'take things out of their glass cases and connect them to real life'.[58] In doing so, museum curators do not control the experience in the same way as in static displays, because at the Festival participating subjects speak for themselves and often problematise any attempt to frame their performance with authority. Historian William S. Walker describes this structure as 'the festival's polyvocal nature and its de-centralized format', enabling 'cultural practitioners to express their individual ideas and opinions'.[59] Thus, the Festival enshrines some of the feelings of political and cultural dissent demonstrated in this site since the 1960s, instigating performances that are as contradictory as they are varied, and representative of different opinions and belief systems. Embodying the democratic ideal at the centre of the American constitution, the Festival takes place in an in-between space, a liminoid zone, which is full of potential. The symbolism is clear to Festival participants and visitors, who are not only performing in the midst of iconic historical buildings and memorials, but do so during the two weeks straddling the Fourth of July. At the same time, this is not an explicitly patriotic pageant but rather a festival that embodies an American ideal, celebrating the diverse cultures at the centre of its civic and national identity.

The Festival heralded a new era for the Smithsonian, characterised by a new approach to the performance of culture made possible by attuning the physical space of the exhibit to that of a festival, as William S. Walker explains:

> If the monumental barriers between museums on the Mall had limited the efforts of the previous generation of curators to decrease segregation, perhaps the solution was to step outside the museums. There, in the open air of the Mall, new combinations could be made and unmade and new possibilities explored without the strictures of museum buildings. By creating a temporary outdoor exhibition, Ripley and the festival's organizers were able to challenge the lines that had developed in the Smithsonian's physical geography. (p. 93)

Within the themed Festival programme, several interweaving, smaller, intimate events happen simultaneously, reflecting the importance of engaging with all of culture; there is no bolstering of one kind of performance of culture more than another, no linearity, and the focus in practice is on the performers and presenters, who are often from the same cultural context, concentrating on their own interpretation of their own culture. This structure facilitates an informal meeting of people – of visiting stalls and discussing with exhibitor practitioners, of listening and asking questions at the Festival stages where practitioners discuss their performative traditions, side by side with formal and informal cultural performances. The Festival has a daily schedule offering visitors their chance to immerse themselves as they wish and to chart their own experiential journey; this immersion is predicated on participation and underpinned by the use of live interpretation. According to Richard Kurin: 'the festival pioneered the research-based use of living performances and demonstrations', which was 'consistent with a larger trend in the museum world at the time – the use of "living history" as a presentational or interpretive technique'.[60] A similar programme of interpretation was adopted by the National Park Services, which in 1973 began working closely with the Smithsonian. Live interpretation meant informing an audience through inviting people to 'perform, demonstrate, and expound upon aspects of a tradition' (p. 122). For Kurin, the main difference between live interpretation and living history is that, in the latter case, performances 'were acted or re-enacted by present-day persona', whereas 'the festival emphasised authenticity – the presence and unscripted participation of the living people who were active and exemplary practitioners of the represented communities of traditions' (p. 122). This emphasis on authenticity provides the Festival with authority in terms of representation: 'The festival was powerful because the people were real participants in the represented cultures – not actors.' (p. 122).

Considering its experimental roots, it is not surprising that, initially, the Festival met with scepticism from curators at the Smithsonian museums, who saw it as duplication of work for many departments within the institution and even suggested that the intellectual content and purpose of the Festival was sub-standard. This critical stance by museum curators reflected in part their unease with the radical approach to exhibiting adopted by the Festival organisers. According to William S. Walker, 'ceding interpretive authority to non-professionals appeared to them [the curators] to be an abrogation of the Smithsonian's responsibility to increase and diffuse knowledge' (p. 111). The emphasis was not merely on the authenticity of the 'non-professional' cultural practitioner, however. In many ways Festival organisers had conceived of a structure of interpretation where authority did not lie with the 'non-professional' alone, but in the performance of culture itself, in the relationship between the cultural performer and the member of the public, facilitated in part by the work of the Festival presenters there to bridge the discussion. In essence, the Festival dwells on the processes implicit in the performance of culture for all participants and asks them to respond reflectively and discursively to the performance that is taking place. As Walker points out, the curators' unease may have also been a response to the unconventional and radical stance adopted by Festival staff, that of applied folklore, a field that originated in the treatment of traditional and popular folk material as a medium for cultural, social and political change, and blurred scholarly and political considerations (p. 111). As with the folk museum movement generally, the Festival has not been without its problems. According to Kurin, the breadth of its categories – 'education and entertainment, scholarship and service, the authentic and the constructed, collaboration and contemplation' – leads to occasional misunderstandings, with some scholars going so far as to say that the Festival applies discredited forms of cultural display, while others critique what is in their view a downgrading of the way the museum ought to function.[61] For instance, living cultural displays are always inherently problematical, and it is possible to find within them reflections of nineteenth-century forms of imperial exhibitionism in their most extreme forms, the kind of 'intercultural performance' elaborated on by Coco Fusco in her list of historical examples of the tradition of displaying living people.[62]

The emphasis on providing context at the Festival, however, ensures the creation of appropriate frames that mediate an understanding about cultural transmission and remove cultural stereotypes.[63] Kurin explains how this has evolved over 'decades of cultural research and discussions about representation', in addition to a change in stance in terms of curatorial vision based on collaboration and community advocacy:

> There have been shifts in authoritative voice; collaboration in self-representation, treatment of contemporary contexts, and the forms of discourse have significantly changed, thanks in large part to the efforts of a generation of cultural workers who have labored at the intersection of scholarship, cultural community advocacy, and public education. Large-scale cultural displays are situated in a public world in which various parties have a stake. Politicians, advocacy groups, rebels, and scholars may use these forms to forward their own agendas, and have become very sophisticated in doing so, as is readily apparent in various case studies of Festival programs.[64]

The idea that the most effective way to present communities is by re-creating social gatherings, weddings, feasts and other holiday celebrations reflects concerns in anthropology and folklore that maintain the idea that contextualisation of cultural practices is essential for an understanding of culture. For this reason, the Wales Smithsonian Cymru exhibit had several platforms for the presentation and performance of Welsh life and culture, serving as a window on Welsh culture in context, which drew on the situational frames of the culture in its home situation, referred to as 'induced natural context'.[65]

Visitors to the Festival – approximately 1.5 million visitors converge on the Mall over a ten-day period – roam freely around such stages, dipping in and out of the cultural performances on offer. There are no formal entrances or exits and there is a sense of fluidity of

movement, of throngs gathered to view storytellers and performers in makeshift performance tents, of small circle gatherings and
laid-back 'narrative stages' for conversing on all manner of topics,
from significant cultural practices to the 'square mile' and the habits of everyday life. Three themes are chosen annually, and in 2009
the Wales Smithsonian Cymru programme was nestled in between
'Giving Voice: The Power of Words in African American Culture', on
the Capitol side, and Las Américas: Un Mundo Musical on the other.
Each programme is similar to a curated exhibition at one of the museums and has its own dedicated space on the open fields of the Mall
(approximately two football fields for a large-scale programme), as
well as stages, dedicated signage and boundaries. But these are simply
demarcations between thematic areas; access is free to all and anyone
can wander in. The Festival is described by the Smithsonian as 'a rite
of cultural democracy', a way of witnessing 'exemplary practitioners
of diverse, authentic, living traditions – both old and new', with the
overall aim of 'preserving' by enabling the practitioners and the public to interact in order to 'begin to understand cultural differences
and similarities'.[66] Smithsonian curators immerse themselves in the
culture in question in order to find contemporary living traditions of
folk life, either continuous or redefined and adapted over time; they
identify and recruit cultural practitioners and work with local eth-
nomusicologists, anthropologists and organisations. The most basic
requirement for inclusion is that cultural practices are authentic, with
no folk troupes or revivalist performers. The curators must also be
able to intuit the power relations implicit in the reification of culture
in distinct traditional forms.

The cultural performances at the Festival range from storytelling
and singing to cooking, or explaining the process of working on wood
or other materials. Many of these activities are everyday tasks, but they
are elevated to a performance here precisely because they are framed
as such before an audience of onlookers. The process of interaction
has three modes; it might involve watching 'tradition bearers' as they
perform, it might be discursive, or it might be participatory for visitors as they take part in song, dance, storytelling, and language lessons.
Spatial configurations vary according to the nature of the activity; we
may sit in a storytelling circle or around a kitchen table, a flexibility that serves the informality of many of the performances. This is
a particular characteristic of the Folklife Festival, for although it is

8. Poet Gillian Clarke performs at the Storytelling Circle, Wales
Smithsonian Cymru at the Smithsonian Folklife Festival, 2009.
Photo: Lisa Lewis.

a large-scale cultural performance, it is inherently non-theatrical. This
unassuming quality is underpinned by the way in which the cultural
performance is framed and mediated. Two main forms of contribution
construct the performance witnessed by Festival visitors, that provided by 'participants' (the cultural practitioners) and that facilitated
by 'presenters'. 'Participants' perform their tasks, whether traditional
craft or art forms, while the 'presenters' are the cultural interpreters or
mediators, and the bridge between the participant and the audience-
member. The Festival puts a premium on the artist's perspective, while
presenters are there to support the artist, by asking questions and
framing the discussion.

Barbara Kirschenblatt-Gimblett, who worked at the Folklife
Festival during the 1970s, describes a curatorial problem implicit in
it, which involves the selection of participants and the facilitation
of the performance of their traditions in ways that lead visitors to a
deeper understanding of the culture in question. This is a problem
that hinges on the idea of the authenticity of folklore, a consequence
of which is that folk festival performances tend to be artefacts or

canonical representations. According to Kirschenblatt-Gimblett, there is a paradoxical trap, in that unknown traditions may be presented at folklife festivals as performances that conform to the idea of the 'traditional'. Similarly, there are pitfalls related to 'aestheticizing "folklore"', for 'no matter what is gained by the all-inclusive definition of folklore as the arts of everyday life – we are in danger of depoliticizing what we present by valorizing an aesthetics of marginalization'.[67] This is an interesting point when considering the 2009 programme of three 'minority' cultures represented by oratory (African-American), music (Latino/a), and sustainable culture (Welsh). These thematic programmes, in terms of their content and performances, did not seem to be depoliticised or disconnected from wider social and political concerns, but perhaps that is my own understanding as a Welsh Festival participant, a point of view that makes it difficult to distance myself from the social and political context of my own performance of culture. Kirschenblatt-Gimblett also points out that there are problems inherent in the festivalisation of culture, stemming from 'the promise of visual penetration; access to the back region of people's lives, the life world of others as our playground; and the view that people are most themselves when at play and that festivals are the quintessence of a region and its people', which could lead to the perception that we are actually seeing the culture at play, an effect she refers to as the 'illusion of cultural transparency' (p. 62). In contrast to the Eisteddfod's festival characteristics as inclusive performance for 'us', a self-determining community of participants, the Folklife Festival operates as a performance for others, and because these performances are designed for a particular kind of exchange, they represent numerous functions and develop multiple meanings. Robert Cantwell critiques this recontextualisation of folklife in festival performances:

> The power and authority of folklore consists precisely in the fact that, because it arises where power has lapsed, retreated, or failed, it lies outside all authority and power. Far from a kind of anomaly or residuum, folklore is one of the cultural resources of modern bourgeois civilization, which tirelessly produces it, consumes it, and produces it again.[68]

Presenting folklore as a cultural product framed and eventually consumed in an endless circle, Cantwell claims that the spectacle 'far from legitimizing it [folklore] or empowering it, may like the spectacle everywhere uproot and dispel it' (p. 214). Placing the invention of folklife within the broader cultural context of modernity, Cantwell defines it as arising from the romantic tradition as a response to modernity. Defining Rinzler's initial experiments on the Mall as reflections of idealised cottage crafts that belonged to 'the romantic socialist tradition' (p. 215), Cantwell associates the concept of a vanished world, implicit in this conception of folklore, with a kind of psychosocial regression – with the world of childhood or the security of the mother's breast. He also makes the claim that folk revivalism is bound up with social class, and folklore structured by influential people and institutions that gain power through its performance in a 'mandarin cultural construction' (p. 235). At the same time, Cantwell is aware that folklife more broadly is related to 'the long and complex pastoral dream founded in Western civilization's primary myths' (p. xv). With an awareness of the deep-seated and complex factors behind its creation, he does not repudiate the invention of folklife but rather participates in it with an awareness of the existence of a vernacular culture, calling it the 'unmediated substance' of what eventually becomes 'folklife' (p. xv). This provides a key to opening up some of the paradoxes of the Folklife Festival experience and helps to explain the fact that the restaging of cultural performances at the Festival elevates them in such a way that they sometimes lose their improvisational and ad hoc nature, the hallmarks of their authenticity. In being aware of this, we can forgive the unnaturalness of the framing devices at play and their capacity to remove the performance from its natural context. What we gain from this process is space for cultural advocacy and in a situation in which we benefit from knowledge and understanding based on personal experience. In this way, the Festival is able to provide a framework in which to consider the individual or the minority experience within the context of broader community. Aware of the critiques that may be aimed at the Folklife Festival, the Smithsonian is clear that 'by enabling culture bearers to speak from the "bully pulpit" of the National Mall, the Festival disseminates alternative forms of aesthetics, history, and culture' and that all cultural content meets 'Smithsonian standards of authenticity, cultural significance, and excellence', their very placement in a museum context reifying their value to all, including themselves. Kurin gets to the point regarding the concern with 'otherness' and cultural standards:

Some worry that 'lesser others' will be embarrassed in public or exploited for their 'otherness' in front of Festival crowds. Sometimes there is good cause to worry. But sometimes it is the worriers themselves who are most embarrassed, and who either from their own shame, romanticism, or paternalism would prefer to talk for those 'others.' From my point of view, the problem is not in giving people, all sorts of people who have something cultural to say, the center stage. The issue is the quantity and quality of mediation – how to effectively provide them the ways by which people can speak for themselves. We have found that people who come to the Festival are pretty skilled in self-representation, or get to be so quite quickly.[69]

My own relationship with the Festival began in 2008, when I attended as a visiting scholar from the University of Glamorgan's Centre for Media and Culture in Small Nations.[70] I attended again in 2009, this time contributing as a Festival presenter at the Wales Smithsonian Cymru programme, which provided an insight into curatorial practices and the workings of the Festival as performance. The idea of hosting a guest nation programme with an integral theme, that of sustainability, was a new approach that enabled the use of thematic strands as a device for linking different forms of cultural practices, regions and skills. Four distinct aspects of sustainability relating to traditional culture in Wales were chosen as umbrella concepts for this process of relating people, objects and practices across the programme: 1) keeping the best of traditional practices; 2) recycling in the broadest sense; 3) thinking globally, acting locally; and 4) planning for a sustainable future. A wide range of practices relating to these four areas was documented as part of the curatorial process, including music and dance, storytelling, farming and mining, building arts, industrial heritage, outdoor pursuits, maritime arts, textiles, ceramics, wood crafts, cooking, gardening, and traditional medicine. Such fieldwork took several years, and was chiefly undertaken by the lead curator, Dr Betty Belanus, of the Smithsonian's Department of Folklife and Cultural Heritage. Smithsonian curators work through a form of gentle cultural osmosis, where communication is paramount, and all attempts at representation and inclusion (or exclusion) are dealt with in a spirit of openness. In the same way that you can be startled by someone's perceptions of who you are, so the 2009 Festival was an eye-opener to the way in which 'we' are perceived. It was also a mass

collaborative representation, multifaceted, peopled by different characters and participants, different kinds of presenters and entirely different
viewpoints on Wales. There was no attempt to represent a total picture
of Wales; instead, five broad themes were presented through the activities performed: 'Heritage Meets Innovation'; 'Language and Arts in
Action'; 'Reimagining Home and Community'; 'Wales and the World';
and 'Working and Playing Outdoors'. A range of pavilions related to
any one or more of these themes and they included 'The Outdoors',
'Along the Water', 'Plants and Medicine', 'Energy', 'Woodwork', 'Musical
Instruments', 'Clog making', 'Creating Books', 'Ceramics and Basketry',
'Sport', 'Animation and Welsh Media', 'Welsh Roots', 'Wales and the
World', 'Taste of Wales', 'Around the Table' and 'Language'. The main
performance areas included 'The Welsh Dragon', a large pavilion-like
open tent, and 'The Rugby Club', while more impromptu and improvisational storytelling events took place in the 'Storytelling Circle'. The
'narrative stage', where the mediator is based, is really a breather from
the more formal performances and in 2009 it was where participants
came together to discuss their working methods or any aspect of
their 'Welsh' lives, before an audience. It is casual and the audience is
invited to ask questions and discuss. For me, presenting some of the
sessions on 'Y Filltir Sgwâr / The Square Mile' narrative stage involved
facilitating discussions between artists and public in relation to ideas
of home. For instance, a discussion on 'the Valleys' included a panel
comprising the general secretary of the National Union of Miners,
a member of the Hennessys, a well-known folk group from Cardiff,
and a science teacher from the south Wales valleys, while visual artist
Carwyn Evans, poet Gillian Clarke and singer-songwriter Gwyneth
Glyn contributed to the discussion on 'the Country and the City'. The
Festival seemed to take its shape gradually, evolving as it progressed
in the exchange between performer, presenter and member of the
public. Surprisingly, the Festival retained such unpredictability despite
the fixed timetable. It was a process of performing that allowed breaks
for discursive intervals. It was also an event that invited interpretation
and reflection on new perspectives. Welsh artists sharing the stage for
the first time found points of contact in their work and this added to
the transformative aspect of the Festival.

The 2009 Festival was also the first time a participating nation
had been responsible for the way in which they were represented
visually, with the Wales site designed by blacksmith and installation

artist, Angharad Pearce Jones. The main design elements evoked the landscape and artistic achievements of Wales and included the central walkway installation along the southern side of the Mall, where a wooden fence became *crawiau* (a slate fence), which in turn became an iron loop-top fence, then estate fencing, followed by rugby posts rising from dry stone walls to become entrances placed next to stiles, a kissing gate, and so on, in an unfolding collage of Welsh fences and enclosures. The effect desired, according to the artist, was of filling the Mall with the textures of Wales as a metaphor for how we use walls and fences as borders to protect or defend our culture, the gates and stiles representing ways into the culture for those willing to enter. The installation invited participation and included a long tract of dry stone wall, with opportunities for visitors to take part in building it. The Festival banners by artist Mary Lloyd Jones displayed visual depictions of links between Wales and America; geometric elements reflected traditional Welsh patchwork quilt designs, connecting them with the American tradition, and zigzags and wavy lines referenced prehistoric carvings on stones in Wales and motifs found in American Indian patterns. Using Jones's evocative paintings suggested that the programme itself was to be interpreted, or at least that there were no easily identifiable signs or stereotypes displayed here. Some of the most iconic names or artefacts were turned on their heads, echoing the transformation possible through adaptation; the longest place name in Wales, Llanfairpwllgwyngyllgogerychwyrndrobwllllantysiliogogogoch, was wrapped around the drinks stall, becoming 'the bar with the longest name in Washington DC.'

Welsh performers had a strong desire to collaborate with the visitors and each other, and the programme provided many spaces for interaction and creative participation. Gai Toms, Welsh singer-songwriter and environmentalist, accompanied the storyteller David Ambrose in an impromptu storytelling performance to the accompaniment of slate percussion at the slate tent. Andy Stuart of Coed Cymru constructed a sustainable *tŷ unnos* on the Mall (though over two nights rather than one).[71] Visual artist Carwyn Evans presented his photographs on the memory of 'home' for immigrants from Eastern Europe working in an abattoir in a West Wales town, the huge portraits capturing the workers and their families, eyes closed, in the process of remembering home. Textile artist Christine Mills had visitors creating letters from her 'alphabet of the fields', comprised of pitch marks and

9. Accompanied storytelling performance at the Slate Tent
with storyteller David Ambrose and musician Gai Toms,
Wales Smithsonian Cymru at the Smithsonian Folklife Festival, 2009.
Photo: Lisa Lewis.

letters of the Welsh alphabet imprinted onto felted wool. Ceramicist
Lowri Davies's exquisite porcelain was exhibited on corrugated plastic
Welsh dressers. Karl Chattington from Aberdare built a coracle from
scratch in the traditional way over the duration of the Festival, and
its testing out on the waters of the oval basin at the end of two weeks
summed up the experimental nature of the Festival as well as the concept at the heart of the event, that of sustainability and reinvention.
The comprehensive performance of culture as process, rather than
predetermined and closed structure, placed the 'culture bearers' in
a position where culture was perceived anew, or askance, as though
being out of place provided a context in which there was a quickening
of our understanding of our own culture. This, coupled with the visitors' desire to get a sense or a feel of the culture through food, through
the shape of the Welsh language in their mouths, through experiencing
stories and listening to poetry, through dancing and music, placed the
Welsh artist in unfamiliar territory, though one which was also familiar. This uncanny state of being at home abroad, and of performing
ourselves, yet not to each other, is encapsulated in the concept of the

mirror as placeless place, which Foucault elaborates on as a potential mixed or joint experience between utopia and heterotopia,

> The mirror is, after all, a utopia, since it is a placeless place. In the mirror, I see myself there where I am not, in an unreal, virtual space that opens up behind the surface; I am over there, there were I am not, a sort of shadow that gives my own visibility to myself, that enables me to see myself where I am absent: such is the utopia of the mirror. But it is also a heterotopia in so far as the mirror does exist in reality, where it exerts a sort of counteraction on the position that I occupy. From the standpoint of the mirror I discover my absence from the place where I am since I see myself over there. Starting from this gaze that is, as it were, directed toward me, from the ground of this virtual space that is the other side of the glass, I come back toward myself; I begin again to direct my eyes toward myself and to reconstitute myself there where I am.[72]

We saw ourselves reflected on the Mall, in that place where 'we are not', and this point of recognition where, as Foucault says, 'I come back towards myself' entails a redirection of my sight 'toward myself . . . to reconstitute myself there where I am' (4). Fundamentally, the Folklife Festival enacts a moment of cultural exchange between peoples, but it is also a moment of reflecting back on oneself and reconstituting the self in relation to others. This happens across the body of cultural participants at the same time. It has been suggested that the social space of the Mall and the Festival possesses a 'sanctified' status, and this, as well as the notion that the Mall belongs to all, that it is 'home', facilitates a liminoid state, which according to Kurin 'enables people to cross boundaries they usually wouldn't cross'.[73] It also encourages a sense of heightened agency: 'when people speak on the Mall at the festival, they often feel that they are doing so with a power they do not ordinarily possess. I think people listen in somewhat the same way' (p. 130). From a Welsh perspective, one of the great successes of the Folklife Festival was that it brought together artists who had never collaborated at home in Wales and, ironically, it is possible that after two weeks in Washington DC more Americans knew of the Welsh performers than do people in Wales, a consequence of the Festival's scale. This is also a result of its fluid nature as event and the fact that its performances are subject to change in a moment, their meanings adaptable and their interpretations open-ended. Collaboration within the moment of performance cannot be pre-planned or controlled. Kurin refers to this aspect and explains that cultural imagery is provided with a frame through which it is recontextualised, enabling the cultural performances to 'disrupt the complacent, linear flow of history' (p. 132), because the representation of culture can challenge accepted ideas of social life. We might imagine that collective memory might not operate in the usual way here, as both Festival participants and visitors are on unfamiliar territory, as we are not 'at home' and, above all, because the nature of the exchange is such that there is no possibility of shared understanding based on memory. This is not the case, however. The Festival has the ability to provide the circumstances in which cultural memory is instigated and unlocked. Cantwell refers to the cultural sign 'reemerging from obscurity into a new social present, so utterly uncoupled from its original world as to constitute something entirely novel and strange, meaningful only in a new order of signs equally strange and new'.[74] In reformulating cultural meanings in relation to that which re-emerges in festival, we are implicated in a process of collective memory, and 'the more deeply hidden the old order of meaning, the more powerful and persistent is our passion to interpret the isolated material sign – a turbulent, urgent desire to remember what we know we know' (p. 228). This reflects the process of revelation in performance as *poiesis*, the threshold occasion where something moves away from itself to become something other, and that is capable of producing collective understanding. This desire to remember in a collective act is shared by both artists and visitors to the Folklife Festival, so that the performance they engage in accesses this facet of shared understanding, and is a consequence of the investment in the performance of culture as shared experience, rather than merely transaction or exchange. In this way, the culture in question is able to exceed the confines of its own specific social context, and become meaningful to a broader audience through the binding and transformational nature of its performance.

THEATRE PLACES

5

According to David Wiles, the history of Western performance space in the twentieth century is characterised by the rise and fall of the 'empty space'.[1] Theatre director Peter Brook's dictum that we can take any space and call it 'empty' is problematised by Wiles in the contemporary theatre context (since the end of the twentieth century), where the idea of a blank or neutral space is neither suitable nor relevant. While the premise of neutral space has facilitated seemingly objective theatrical representation, contemporary theatre performance has problematised the concept of representation in theatre, and performance itself has become a site of multiple and contested meanings. Accompanying this shift there has been a movement towards performances that occur outside the conventional theatre space, referred to by Hans-Thies Lehmann as 'possibilities described as *site specific theatre*', where sites are '*cast in* a *new light* through theatre'. In elaborating on this Lehmann describes the way in which spatial dynamics emphasise the interdependence of relationships between performers and spectators:

> When a factory floor, an electric power station or a junkyard is being performed in, a new 'aesthetic gaze' is cast onto them. The space presents itself. It becomes a co-player without having a definite significance. It is not dressed up but made visible. The spectators, too, however, are co-players in such a situation. What is namely staged through site specific theatre is also a level of *commonality* between performers and spectators. All of them are *guests of the same place*: they

are all strangers in the world of a factory, of an electric power station, or of an assembly hangar.[2]

In speaking of the site as a 'co-player', or one layer within a network of elements with potential meaning, Lehmann is defining the performance as composed of the interrelationship between the space and the event, constituted of performers and spectators. This perception of site as a constituent of contemporary theatre performance owes much to the site-specific as legacy of the art exhibit, where the artwork needs to be perceived and understood on the basis of the context in which it is constituted in place or 'made' (the term 'made' referring to the way the process of art-making is considered to be a relative process of meaning-making between artefact, artist, public and site). This political stance, which acknowledges the power relations in an artwork as implicit in its making, became relevant in Wales in the 1980s, in a social and political context in which it seemed as though the world as we knew it and the meaning of community were being dismantled. I would argue that this conception of performance as interrelationship of space, performers and spectators also resonated with historical, social patterns of performance-making in Wales that were not reflected in its mainstream theatre, which following the disappearance of the indigenous Anterliwt[3] form in the early nineteenth century had been mainly dominated in an official and therefore professional capacity by an 'imported model'.[4]

The perception of space as a social construct defined by social relations is the central tenet of French philosopher Henri Lefebvre's work on space. According to Lefebvre, not only is social space a social product, it 'also serves as a tool of thought and of action . . . a means of control, and hence of domination, of power'. Yet it cannot be dominated completely by those in power, for 'it escapes in part from those who would make use of it.'[5] That space embodies social relationships is clearly evident in theatre. But if, as performance theorist Richard Schechner states, 'theatre spaces are the maps of the cultures where they exist', what do Welsh theatre spaces signify?[6] Which social relationships do they disclose and what are the relationships of power and domination that they display? Answering these questions entails a consideration of the complexity of theatrical spaces across Wales, from formal theatre buildings to village halls and chapel vestries, and an acknowledgement that many of the various forms in which theatre has operated here are distinct cultural forms that bear no relation to contemporary British auditorium-based provision. At the same time, the effects of the mainstream British provision are widespread and to be found in towns and cities across Wales that have historically been provided with theatre structures and practices that might have no immediate currency in the communities in which they have been placed. Theatre spaces inevitably reflect the cross-cultural dealings of people over time, assimilating the identity politics that develop in relation to cultural shifts and changes; they are often vehicles for sharing and debating the ways in which people wish to be represented within their communities and to the wider world and they are often spaces where certain power relationships are played out. In certain historical circumstances the processes of cultural assimilation involve eradicating and replacing signs of cultural differentiation, either deliberately or unknowingly. As a social structure, theatre can be a passive reflection of hegemonic forms, though it may equally be a site of contestation, a place in which the subject faces her identity. In twentieth-century Wales, for the most part, theatre became involved in forms of cultural interpellation, where the theatre we were provided with became the theatre we desired. In this process, the performance of culture begins to reflect the desire to be the same as the Other we long to be. Subsequently, theatre becomes a vehicle for a form of unrecognised imperial complicity, even when its popular veneer suggests it is benign. On the other hand, theatre can reflect and articulate clearly the wider social and cultural problems faced by specific people and it is in this context that the rise of performance outside the theatre building in the late twentieth century is significant.

Historically, the establishment of large, professional theatre companies and their resident buildings, a staple of the English repertory system, has never had its equivalent in Wales. Commercial theatre culture reached Wales in the late nineteenth century, its establishment warranted by significant population booms through urbanisation and the activities of a growing middle class. The majority of Victorian and Edwardian theatre buildings were built in Welsh tourist destinations of the time, and usually at the end of a railway line running laterally between England and Wales. Following the Second World War many English repertory companies toured in Wales, playing to substantial audiences, and a concerted effort was made to widen Wales's theatrical horizons through the benevolence of the newly formed Arts Council of

Great Britain. Roger Owen has written of the attempt by Arts Council officers, directing policy from London for 'the theatre-less areas', to establish a professional company and associated theatre building in the large industrial town of Swansea in 1949.[7] That the venture failed, despite an exceptionally accomplished network of amateur companies in this community and a strong dramatic tradition, reveals something about the difficulty of emplacing large-scale formal theatre structures in areas where the audience is committed to distinct patterns of attendance. It is not until the late 1960s that we see the emergence of several sustained and state-funded attempts to stabilise professional activities and the emergence of university theatres and community arts centres in towns such as Cardiff, Swansea, Aberystwyth and Bangor. Alongside this movement towards an assimilated theatre, the twentieth century saw a strong and prolonged effort to establish a Welsh theatrical tradition in the formal guise of a national theatre, underpinned by a dramatic canon.[8] The attempt to define a canon assumes a process of retrieval that begins with the study of extant texts, though attempts to create dramatic traditions rooted in the study of the text, however laudable, often obliterate traditions located in somatic and social practices, which all performative traditions inevitably tend to be, whether they are associated with literary renaissances and identifiable with a dramatic archive or not.

When theatre-making became a prominent social activity in Wales from the 1880s it did not appear out of nowhere. It emerged against the backdrop of popular performance traditions that had receded due to the prevalence of chapel-going as a communal activity following the Methodist revival in Wales, a social movement that gradually, and for a period of time, allowed no space for competing performances. In addition to the Anterliwt, Welsh drama in textual form can be traced back to the Middle Ages and a few surviving texts.[9] Other performance forms closely associated with the same social performance context as the Anterliwt, such as ballad-singing, took place at fairs, markets and special events, and other processional performances such as the Mari Lwyd, continued as rural folk customs.[10] The overwhelmingly proactive *mudiad drama* (dramatic movement) established towards the end of the nineteenth century was to step out of this background. Ioan Williams establishes the year 1880 as the starting point of the *mudiad drama*, a socio-cultural movement that embedded itself into Welsh communities the length and breadth of Wales.[11] Though first and foremost a dramatic movement, it was not a cultural resurgence through literary means; the movement was motivated by a psychosocial need to articulate questions relating to changes in cultural and religious identity. The central drive was that of theatre as a functioning social activity and its primary objective was communal. Dramatists were compelled to articulate the internalised conflicts of the Welsh-speaking communities in a way that was familiar to them, by resurrecting theatrical endeavour as a social movement that had been rendered obsolete by certain social changes, including the manoeuvres of the religious revival in Wales, and yet was sufficiently embedded in the social consciousness for it to be accessed with some fervour. That this movement initially operated within a Nonconformist context, through chapel companies and performances in chapel vestries and village halls, is not accidental, for the movement was bound up in the theological, social and moral aspirations of the Nonconformist community. Williams argues that the history of Welsh drama between 1850 and 1900 reflects a creative response to the increasing tensions felt by Welsh communities as a result of the gradual changeover from Calvinism to humanism. The centrality of the dramatic movement to industrial south Wales following the large influx of population brought about by in-migration to the industrial centres is significant, and the prevalence of Welsh language playwrights operating there in both Welsh and English is a measure of how close the theatrical activity was to the spring of change.

Repeated efforts to establish a national theatre were always to find footholds, albeit temporary ones. Such attempts included one by Lord Howard de Walden in 1911–14, another in 1927 with the establishment of a National Welsh Playhouse, the attempts by the Theatr Dewi Sant Trust and the Welsh Committee of the Arts Council of Great Britain between 1959 and 1967 and the formation of Theatr Genedlaethol Cymru in 1964–82, followed by Cwmni Theatr Cymru in 1982–4.[12] Every endeavour failed, although the impetus to form a national company never waned. Irrespective of whether the national theatre attempts were successful or not, the campaigns out of which they emerged provided a pivotal movement from which scores of other theatre companies, activities and projects ensued. Out of the demise of the national theatre company Cwmni Theatr Cymru[13] in 1984, for instance, came an explosion of theatrical activity which was also partly a response to the political events of 1979, when the disappointment at the failure of the campaign for devolution in Wales and the victory under Margaret Thatcher of the Conservative Party, whose policies were historically alien to the political sensibilities and traditions of Wales, provided the fraught conditions under which artistic reflection often escalates. The scale of the culture shock that followed this political situation cannot be underestimated, as historian Gwyn A. Williams points out:

> They [the Conservatives] swept with such force through non-industrial Wales in particular, that they obliterated landmarks which had been familiar for generations. . . . Moreover, the elimination of Welsh peculiarities and a powerful simplification strongly suggested an integration into Britain more total than anything yet experienced. One Welsh TV political correspondent wondered aloud whether he ought to resign. Welsh politics had ceased to exist. Wales had finally disappeared into Britain.[14]

This was a time of intense introspection and of articulating identity politics through the medium of theatre and other arts forms, particularly so in relation to the Welsh language. In 1982, the campaign for a Welsh-language channel came to a head with the establishment of the Welsh fourth channel, S4C, Sianel Pedwar Cymru (channel four Wales), launched the day before Channel 4, which provided a specific arena for performing nationness.[15] In addition to the new theatre companies founded out of the ashes of Cwmni Theatr Cymru, several more that were already well established came to the fore to form the theatrical landscape at the end of the twentieth century, such as Dalier Sylw, Theatrig and Brith Gof.[16] The mobilisation of culture at this time had a distinctly political edge. Roger Owen points out, that from 1979 onwards, the role of Welsh politics and culture was seemingly reversed as the politics of Wales appeared closer to a ritualised discourse, estranged from the real world, and subsequently it was not through political but rather by cultural means that Welsh-speaking Wales represented itself to the world. Theatre was operating as a social forum where social identity could be mediated.[17] Of all the companies that flourished at the end of the twentieth century Brith Gof, whose work embedded questions of memory and place so deeply into its construction, was to become one of the most notable theatre enterprises in and from Wales.

In his introduction to *A Short History of Western Performance Space* (2003) David Wiles quotes Mike Pearson, commenting in 1998 when he was director of Brith Gof, on the awkwardness and irrelevance of locating the auditorium as the centre point for theatre,

> I can no longer sit passively in the dark watching a hole in the wall, pretending that the auditorium is a neutral vessel of representation. It is a spatial machine that distances us from the spectacle and that allies subsidy, theatre orthodoxy and political conservatism, under the disguise of nobility of purpose, in a way that literally keeps us in our place.[18]

Pearson has proposed (and has practised) a poetics of performance that occurs outside the confines of the theatre building, or that at least reconfigures the architecture within which theatre can operate. This process has mostly taken place beyond the confines of the theatre as an institution, in such a way as to 'fold[s] together place, performance and public'.[19] That Wiles has chosen Pearson's statement to open his book, which then goes on to provide a history of Western performance space, is telling. Locating the history of performance space within the context of a broader discussion of the history of space, Wiles conceives of theatre as a network of performance relationships in space and shifts the focus of the event from that of activity watched to a thing made and defined through the interrelationships between spectators, between performers, between spectators and performers, and between all the different possible points in this chain of connections. This is a significant shift away from the Cartesian sense of 'gazing on' objectively in a subject/object split, which according to Wiles has created a longstanding tradition of passive observation by the watcher and active performance by the actor/event being watched.[20] Pearson clearly demarcates performance as an event composed of networks of relationships between performers, between performers and spectators, and between the spectators themselves. This charged network of relationships is the fundamental basis for a definition of performance as aesthetic event and is a foundational network that may be configured anywhere; it is not dependent on specific theatrical architecture and is not bound by ideas concerning traditional theatrical structures, such as the proscenium arch stage or studio theatre. In situating its work outside the auditorium Brith Gof was to alter the fabric of theatre in Wales at the end of the twentieth century.

Brith Gof: place and *poiesis*

Brith Gof was established by Mike Pearson and Lis Hughes Jones in 1981, in the university town of Aberystwyth, following their split from the experimental Cardiff Laboratory Theatre.[21] Initially based at Y Sgubor (the Barn), an old foundry converted into a community centre and creative hothouse, the company was prolific, and rose to become the main representative of late twentieth-century Welsh theatre both at home and internationally.[22] The Welsh word *brithgof*, literally 'speckled memory', meaning a faint recollection, is used in Welsh conversation in a similar way to the English idiom 'it rings a bell'. The fact that the word is split into *'brith'* and *'gof'* in the company's name only serves to emphasise the meaning of the words, and their interrelationship. The name is a fitting descriptor of the company's conventions and principles for making theatre – the partial and the fractured were at the core of their performance-making and hybridisation became a hallmark of the work. The layering of contrary and juxtaposing elements in the overall performance score contributed to a theatrical experience that was not predicated on illusion or completion of narrative, and the audience came to the work from different angles, aspects and points of view. This was performance that did not explicate or describe for a passive audience, but rather worked through evocation, providing a holding environment for the unfolding of histories and memories in collaboration with the spectators themselves. Because of this collaborative and fluid aspect of the performance the process of archiving and delineating the company's performance history is truly discursive and has been an ongoing project.[23]

Early performance work appeared to be an aesthetic project rather than overtly political theatre and this initial work was in the same vein as that of a series of small-scale theatre companies that had an impact on the European theatre scene and beyond from the 1960s onwards, such as Jerzy Grotowski's Teatr Laboratorium 13 Rzędów, and Eugenio Barba's Odin Teatret. Brith Gof's early performances, which were small and self-contained, consciously played with notions of the social and the communal; the Welsh audience engaged deeply with the work as artwork because it reflected social relationships they were familiar with from other forms of performance, such as the chapel or the Eisteddfod. Writing in 1985, Pearson explained that performing in a variety of social contexts and places allowed 'proximity and uniqueness of viewpoint for each spectator to become natural features of the performance experience' and, characteristically, it was work in which 'the withdrawal to the proscenium arch and the creation of stage illusion have no primacy'.[24] Thus, in work created initially in and for rural communities, Brith Gof located themselves as practitioners operating outside conventional theatre auditoria, performing at sites such as chapels, barns, and markets, making work that chimed with Welsh performance traditions in a way that was 'particular but not parochial' (p. 5). At the same time, preconceptions regarding familiar patterns of audience and performer relationships were often altered, with performances structured in such a way as to take into account the audience's sensibilities and preconceptions – either working in accord or at odds with them.

Advocating theatre as a nexus of relationships based in performance, Brith Gof was an embodiment of the performative turn in Welsh theatre that saw practitioners and companies such as Eddie Ladd and Marc Rees, originally performers with Brith Gof, follow their own creative practice and others such as Cwmni Cyfri Tri (succeeded by Arad Goch) and Y Gymraes under Sêra Moore Williams, arise out of the same artistic context of experimental and alternative theatre in the late 1980s.[25] Crucially, Brith Gof was also very much part of the broader artistic community of Europe, its work echoing other experimental practices associated with minority cultures and reflecting the influence of folk culture on contemporary theatre since the 1960s, for instance in the work of Odin Teatret, Farfa and Teatr Ósmego Dnia, practitioners with whom Brith Gof collaborated.[26] The company was uncompromising in its adoption of elements of traditional Welsh performance, making an indigenous claim on theatrical performance, albeit transformed through the spectrum of contemporary experimental theatre practice. During the 1980s, the decade of 'intercultural theatre' in Europe, the company also adopted theatre techniques from other countries that were merged with Welsh texts and mythology. This extra-cultural leaning was an opportunity to dwell on theatre-craft in ways not usually experienced in Western theatre traditions. It resulted in work such as *Blodeuwedd* (1982), a performance based on the Mabinogi story of the woman made from flowers, performed on a wooden Nō style stage and integrating the Japanese martial art Kendo and Balinese Legong dance.[27] Though a schoolchild when I saw this production, the impressions that remain are of the highly stylised movements, the precision with which the performance unfolded and the mediation of a well-known story in a way that was immediately understood by its audience. This instantaneous recognition of meaning through visual image, as opposed to an understanding achieved primarily through listening, was a revelation at the time.

Although the emphasis was aesthetic, emplacing performance in spaces other than the theatre auditorium was a political stance. Brith Gof did not conceive of the theatre space as 'a neutral vessel of representation',[28] but rather as the remnant of a dominant discourse that had alienated audiences in Wales. This was a recurrent theme for the company, for whom Wales's purpose-built theatres were 'problematic in one way or another',[29] or seen as 'colonial outposts'.[30] Because the company was starting from a different theatrical premise, one that recognised the power relationships inherent in the theatre architecture itself, the theatre building was obsolete. By emplacing itself outside theatre auditoria the company exposed the depoliticising nature of such buildings in practice and the hidden machinations of power that they conceal. In contrast to provision made for formal theatre spaces, from entertainment on the one hand to the presentation of dramatic works of cultural significance on the other, the work that Brith Gof made and the experience it provided, incited the audience member's capacity to think deeply about certain perceptions of the past through an aesthetic response. This was usually intensely moving and often deeply political in terms of the vectors of relationships employed within the performance itself. The way the work was designed in and for specific places was a primary factor in making this theatre so central to the audience's experience, accessing the resonances of place through performance, or rather, creating new resonances in the interconnections made during the performance itself, between the place as a historical and social entity, the performance space including all the people present and the space as a site, in terms of its architectural and spatial characteristics. In performance work that inhabits spaces outside formal theatre architecture or the notional 'empty space' of the studio theatre, the place of performance is an explicit presence, imparting its own meanings into the performance. Between the site as place and the performance conceived within it, previous histories come to bear on the work in ways that are both consciously signalled and unconsciously wrought, arising perhaps by chance. In this way the performance weaves a text composed of the history of the site as place, participants' memories of place, including the meaning of this place to them, the performance possibilities of the site itself, and the work that is emplaced there. These elements interact to provide a threshold occasion, a spatial poetics, where something moves away from itself to become something other in a process of emergent meaning – through performance the space is revealed in terms of *place*. This process of *poiesis* is not a peculiarity of the site-specific that is particular to Welsh performance, though the history of site-specific practice in Wales has shown a commitment to constructing work formed from this kind of deep interweaving, which engages with the collective memory of the audience. Although definitions of site-specific performance cover a broad range of practices outside formal theatre buildings, as Fiona Wilkie has examined in detail,[31] my use of the term here is based on the premise that these performances necessarily bear traces of the past for the participants, as the previous events of the 'place' are often not only implicated physically/architecturally or by reference to the site's past or present function (as factory, chapel etc.), but also within the performance itself, constituted of the participants and the material of performance. The embodiment of collective memory and its relationship with place has been a condition of the site-specific in Wales. The fact that the connections between social actors in performance are capable of galvanising memory is a basis for many of the ideas formulated around place, memory, art and performance in a Welsh context.

Brith Gof's early work reflected the particular cultural modes of recalling memory in Welsh culture, for instance in the various Mabinogi performances, *Branwen* and *Rhiannon* (1981) and *Manawydan* and *Blodeuwedd* (both 1982), in the work of the eighteenth-century poet and hymn writer in *Ann Griffiths* (1983–5) and of writer D. J. Williams and poet Gwenallt in *Rhydcymerau* (1984–5).[32] These works resonated with notions of a shared cultural history that is emplaced and, via Welsh narratives and poetry, also sought to convey such embodied memories. Common traits or motifs in these memory texts are commemorations and memories in triad form, genealogies, intricate stories of the naming of places, onomastic stories, poetic traits that act as mnemonics, culturally specific ideas of place such as *bro, y filltir sgwâr*, *yr aelwyd* (region, square mile, hearth), and so on – particular ways of knowing and telling the stories of life inculcated by a culture. While literature may access ideas of place deeply, the experience of being situated *in place* during the performance itself ensures a doubling of this effect. Edward Casey speaks of place as a conduit for memory, of the way places 'furnish convenient points of attachment for memories . . . and . . . provide situations in which remembered actions can deploy themselves.'[33] The places concerned in Brith Gof's performances were the places of habitual work, the places of Welsh rural life – even when transposed to other spatial contexts, these performance works signalled the daily existence that Welsh-speaking audiences recognised as part of their collective memory. Casey's definition of place as 'a mise en scène for remembered events' (p. 189), approaches space as a meaningful set of situated relationships that assist in retaining or guarding the memory of certain events that have happened within its perimeters. It is because place acts in this way that performance situated in place is able to access and contain such a dense network of references to the past; it becomes a channelling device, a support for the excavation of the inextricable associations between place, space, history, memory and people that Mike Pearson, Cliff McLucas and Michael Shanks have referred to as 'deep maps', or in more detail,

> attempts to record and represent the grain and patina of place through juxtapositions and interpenetrations of the historical and the contemporary, the political and the poetic, the factual and the fictional, the discursive and the sensual; the conflation of oral testimony, anthology, memoir, biography, natural history and everything you might want to say about a place.[34]

In the work described here the frames of reference and the narrative structures that hold signs and meanings, all the textures out of which the performance is woven in the moment, are in direct contact with, and are embedded, in the place itself, which becomes not just the site of performance or backdrop against which a 'text' is played out, but one of the primary components of that text. Here, place is not imaginary or representational, it is a historical, social and cultural entity in which we are embedded. Our understanding of place informs and participates in the experience of performance. In this way, emplaced performance can be a portal into contemporary experiences of history and the work charged with the relationships we forge with the past through our own identity and sense of community in place.

Brith Gof's span of work can be read in terms of a trajectory of different responses to place in performance. Initially, the performance was about witnessing a particular historical moment intersecting with the present. In the early work, such as *Gernika!* (1983), based on the bombing of the Basque town during the Spanish Civil War, the spatial relationship between performers and spectators and the use of commonplace, familiar actions associated with rural life, though in an unfamiliar context, was profoundly moving for the audience.[35] In the performance at Chapter (in an old school gymnasium, before its conversion into a studio space) the audience sat in traverse and a series of scenes unfolded, in which a group of villagers dwelling outside Gernika following the bombardment remember their lives. Because the audience members were looking across at each other, as well as at the action, we recognised in each other the implications of the performance for all present. This aspect was heightened at the time by the fact that many in the audience wept openly under the stark lighting. Eleri Rogers, writing in *Y Cymro*, spoke of the images remaining in the memory 'i ddeffro'r hen wylo yn y gwaed' (to awaken the old weeping in the blood).[36] In *Rhydcymerau* (1984), performed at the old market in Llanbedr Pont Steffan, Ceredigion, during National Eisteddfod week, the memory of life in the now vanished village of Rhydcymerau was performed in song, daily chores and child's play across the length of the hall.[37] The marketing material told us that the very name Rhydcymerau 'creates a rich pattern in the mind: faces and voices; stories of work and play; the traces of a long tradition of agricultural and religious life; signs too of the effects of changes in one's world (the obvious and the hidden) on landscape and community', and asked, 'As deathly as the external landscape is, is there still hope hidden in the deep in the woven fabric of memories?'[38] The majority of the audience would have been familiar with Gwenallt's poem *Rhydcymerau*, the name of the Welsh village appropriated by the Forestry Commission in the 1950s, where 'the seedlings of the Third War were planted' ('*Plannwyd egin coed y Trydydd Rhyfel*').[39] The performance drew directly on the poem's imagery and on D. J. Williams's autobiographical account of a Welsh country upbringing in the same square mile.[40] The audience sat in traverse, watching the man and woman (mother and son?) perform their daily lives, while on one side of the audience two men used a longsaw to cut a tiny coffin out of an enormous tree trunk held horizontally on a large trestle. This was brought to the man and woman at the end of the performance and child's clothes were placed inside it, making the impression of a small body. At the same time, the church bells chimed on the hour, as per usual, but in the context of what the audience had witnessed in the preceding hour they were tolling for the death of a community. In this moment our remembrances and our present lives, including our hopes for the future, collided. The performance language was not new; the movements and gestures, songs and voices, the images and series of events enacted were not at odds with indigenous Welsh performance traditions. The performers used buckets, clothes and a clothesline, as well as agricultural equipment, such as a seed-sowing machine and, in an ironic gesture, old techniques of woodworking. Despite the familiar artefacts, what we were witnessing revealed a complex connection that was deeply affecting. This connection between an image of what was and the implications of its loss for who we are now is achieved through the use of material artefacts connecting traditional everyday customs (washing clothes, playing leapfrog over buckets) with their place in memory as representations of home and hearth. Everyday objects operated like knives, penetrating the veil of representation that we believe to be there on the surface. The very materialism of the objects, coupled with the fact that they were not implanted behind the frame of a proscenium arch stage, ensured that we questioned the world before us, forcing a double-take that undid the strength of the representational fiction usually bound up with stage materials as signifiers. And in the encounter of a theatrical language with the historical subject matter, the place in which it is performed, and the audience itself, a new cultural consciousness was formed, one which was aware of the possibilities of aesthetics for identity. This is a company statement from 1986:

> When history is experienced as contemporaneous, information from the 19th century might have a current resonance. A traditional society experiences the particulars of change: we can see things happening. This singular viewpoint may be important to help understand what is happening in majority cultures in the west, where the deep sense of loss and displacement is widely felt though more difficult to locate. And whilst we concentrate on the various forms of repression, we always celebrate resistance, following the example of those who struggle in more severe situations.[41]

10. *Rhydcymerau* (Brith Gof), performers Lis Hughes Jones,
Matthew Aran and Nic Ros.
Source: Brith Gof Archive, NLW. Photo: Marian Delyth.

By 1987, the connection between the past and its relationship with the politics of the present is more apparent in Brith Gof's work. *Pandaemonium: The True Cost of Coal, Gwir Gost Glo* (1987), a collaboration with Theatr Taliesin, put the contemporary closure of the mining industry across south Wales into sharp relief through a performance that told of a Welsh mining disaster from 1913.[42] In the largest chapel in Wales, Tabernacl, in Treforys near Swansea, the 'audience' filled the pews, members of three large choirs sat facing us in choral stands behind the pulpit, and we sang the anthemic hymn *Llef* ('O Iesu Mawr!')[43] as one congregation, waiting for word of what happened in the Senghennydd mining disaster in which 426 men were killed. Taking us into that moment of waiting for any news from the place below the earth, the programme tells us: 'It is October 1913. On Wednesday over 400 men walked out of the blazing pit. An equal number are still unaccounted for. It is now Sunday evening.'[44] Enacting the 'Sunday evening' was a device supported by the rhythms of a Nonconformist service with its 'hymn sandwich' structure; the hymns, the prayer, and the sermon, as natural as breathing to the chapel goers present. Yet the performance also presented behaviour that was not entirely at ease within the space; piercing shouts and wailing interspersed with quiet weeping, singing and desperate praying reminded us that this was a performance above and beyond the usual chapel service. In a transgression of the chapel space, men struggled between floor and gallery to rescue those still living and the dead, with ladders, ropes, pulleys and bare hands. This was not a commemorative event but a form of remembrance, not a re-enactment but an evocation of communal loss and it resonated loudly in contemporary consciousness, for at the end the female performers returned to the *sedd fawr* (the raised pews under the pulpit) in their contemporary clothes to unfurl the banner of a women's support group from the 1984 miners' strike. There was a profound sense of loss and yet of communal consensus, and hope. As we sang, looking across towards the miners' choir facing us, it was deeply felt, an extreme empathetic response to a local and national event imprinted in our memory. Maurice Halbwachs states that the main forms of commemorative memory reside in the family, in religious behaviour and in social classes and their traditions. In *Pandaemonium* these were intertwined within a performative structure that is fractured and that brought moments of isolated and heightened action together in a deeply meaningful way for the participants. Rather than understanding and acknowledging a representation of a truth we participated in a ritualised and multilayered evocation of who we are, with implicit corporeal understanding of how the space, place and performance all operate.

Brith Gof's initial performer-centric pieces were superseded over time by design-led works on an epic scale performed across Europe, South America, North America and Asia, a significant shift away from the intimacy of the earlier works to an aesthetics of grand scale. Proxemics remained as important as ever, but the complexity and scale of the event saw the relationship of audience-member and performer take on a different dimension.[45] The journey from chapel (*Anne Griffiths* in 1983; *Pandaemonium* in 1987), cattle-market (*Rhydcymerau*, 1984), and village square (*Pedole Arian*, 1984; *Iddo Fe*, 1985) and towards the railway station (*Pax*, 1990–1), the deserted factory (*Gododdin*, 1988–9), and abandoned foundry (*Haearn*, 1992) was perhaps an echo of the company's move from the rural to the urban, from Aberystwyth to Cardiff, in the late 1980s. The move towards industrial and design-focused architecture in their work also coincided with Cliff McLucas becoming co-artistic director in 1989. Then, the spatial context became highly designed, and scenography a primary consideration. The inter-relationship between performer and technology, or 'man and machine', became a recurrent thematic function within many large-scale works. Both *Gododdin* (1988–9) and *Haearn* (1992) presented this interrela-tionship, as did *Pax* (1990–1), all of them monumental works that were among the first theatre performances to be referred to as site-specific theatre, in an application of the visual art term used to describe the interdependence of artwork and site in the 1960s and early 1970s.

In the process of investigating the emergence of the late twentieth-century return to the site-specific in art, Miwon Kwon defines the tendency as one that distinguished itself from past practices that had 'reached a point of aesthetic and political exhaustion'.[46] Although there has been an attempt to reclaim or redefine the 'art-site' rela-tionship, with artists applying terminology such as 'audience-specific', 'community-specific' and so on, Kwon believes that site-specificity itself has become a site of contestation, in which competing positions regarding the site and art's relationship to it are being problematised (p. 2). She also suggests that the term site-specific has been used uncritically as a category, perhaps as a symptom of the way in which experimental and politically committed practices become assimilated into the dominant culture. Kwon defines the site-specific as having an implicit differential function and quotes Henri Lefebvre in order to emphasise the dependence of site-specificity on articulating difference: 'Inasmuch as abstract space [of modernism and capital] tends towards homogeneity, towards the elimination of existing differences or peculiarities, a new space cannot be born (produced) unless it accentuates differences.'[47] According to Kwon it is not surprising that the 'efforts to retrieve lost differences, or to curtail their waning, become heavily invested in reconnecting to uniqueness of place – or more precisely, in establishing authenticity of meaning, memory, histories, and identities as a *differential function* of places'.[48] This differential function is to be found as a political component within late twentieth-century Welsh site-specific practice in theatre performance, where articulating the changing meaning of place for Welsh identity, due to political, economic and other social factors, became a component of the work itself through its emplacement at specific sites.

Gododdin (1988), the first example of large-scale site-specific work performed in various exterior locations across Europe was, according to Mike Pearson at the time of its performance, 'a political imperative.'[49] 'Y Gododdin' is a poem recorded in the thirteenth century (but thought to have been composed between the seventh and the early eleventh centuries), attributed to the poet Aneirin and found in the manuscript *Llyfr Aneirin* (The Book of Aneirin). The epic poem is a series of elegies to the Brittonic men of the Gododdin tribe who died at the battle of Catraeth (possibly Catterick, north Yorkshire) in the year 600, and tells of the Gododdin's feasting for almost a year at Din Eidyn (Edinburgh) and their suicidal campaign launched against the Angles. Of the three hundred men who went to battle, only a few survived to tell the tale, one being the bard himself.[50] Brith Gof's *Gododdin*, composed in collaboration with industrial music group Test Dept and performed during a particularly cold December in the cavernous hall of the disused Rover car factory in Cardiff, made a compelling link between the demise of the tribe as described in the battle epic and the decline of our own. What or who 'our own' tribe could be is open to conjecture. Whether a disenfranchised industrial community who worked in factories such as this one, as some have suggested,[51] the Welsh people seen as descendants of the Brythoniaid, or another imagined community, the nature of your identification depended on where you stood at the time.

At the beginning of the performance audience members situated themselves on one side of a vast circle demarcated by breeze blocks, perhaps too wary to venture further into a vast panorama of natural elements – sand and trees, interrupted by metal, carcasses of cars, oil barrels, car scraps. As soon as we stood on the sand, smelling the trees in the cold, wondering at the nature of the event (it is all encompassing), the frenetic performers entered on a tall chariot that moved into the space to the banging of drums. This was about posturing and the physical strength of the warrior – oil drums are thrown by men standing on car bonnets in displays of physical prowess, directly reflecting the poem's praise of the warriors before their downfall. Over time, however, very slowly and seemingly inevitably, for this is about the demise of a people, the arena flooded with water and the performers were lost in the sludge of water and sand, their clearly defined patterns of military behaviour, their battle stances and regimentation disappearing in the encroaching waters. Accompanied by a cacophony of drums and wailings and an elegaic libretto, sung by Lis Hughes Jones, each performer's actions seemed to be against no one but herself / himself – or possibly an unseen opponent. Hammering home the realisation that the performers were struggling alone in the impossibility of the situation, in the literally difficult physical conditions of play, Pearson states: 'The audience is watching real responses, which is not to suggest that all around her is reactive. The performer may be vulnerable but has a range of rejoinders: those planned, those extemporized and those informed by previous experience.'[52] In the disused factory, the experience became subsumed by the sense of an all-pervading enemy. With glaring clarity, as the performance proceeded towards its end and the death of the tribe, we make the association between the site and its recent history and the significance of the poetry. It is all, together, an almost insurmountable effort for performer and watcher – a last stand against an overwhelming enemy.

Brith Gof's work did not always reveal a correlation between audience and space, and sometimes the performance was self-consciously conflicting. In *EXX-I* (1990), for instance, the audience were herded around the studio space in Chapter Arts Centre, Cardiff, as several huge corrugated metal sheets forming steep ramps, on which the three performers stood, 'sailed' around the space via pulleys operated by the performers themselves. The ramps were precarious and the performers occasionally fell or slid down them. The audience avoided the careering

metal sails, creating a perpetual swirl of people, and dodged a ram-
paging performer with a supermarket trolley. We heard the recorded
voices of Saunders Lewis and R. S. Thomas against performer Lis
Hughes Jones's desperate praying into a handheld microphone as she
huddled on top of a metal sail. We were told repeatedly in English to
'get out of the way'; we were corralled and almost threatened by the
confusion and the imposition. We were physically rattled throughout;
we could make out Saunders Lewis's statement that it would take nothing less than a revolution to save the Welsh language, and we felt the
extreme tension of habitual experience, of cultural struggle, played out
explicitly in space and in the human body. While the physical presence
of the performers and our entrapment in the space was a threatening experience, what we heard, and its searing importance culturally,
held us in thrall. There was an embodied understanding of the tension
between discomfort in space/place and the resolute decision and desire
to stay put; such a juxtaposition was mediated in the process of seeing
chaos unfold without apparent meaning (performers fell from their
ramps, removed their clothes and washed their bodies, rampaged with
trolleys, threw buckets), and hearing highly sophisticated and poetic
writings with which we make statements about our sense of belonging. And we found a moment of relief when we were offered a burning
match from one of the performers, who charged us in hushed tones,
to accept it. Was this moment of conciliation an act of remembrance
or an incitement to revolt? Or both?

Towards the end of Brith Gof's 'Disasters of War' series, which
included both *Gododdin* and *EXX-I*, there was a growing unease
amongst some of the Welsh audience about the apparent shift in
references away from the Welsh-speaking community and towards
something far more conceptual (variously described as 'international',
'urban' or 'design-led').[53] Roger Owen suggests that there was also an
artistic incompatibility between the artistic directors' respective visions,
which Owen reads in terms of a tension between the body and the
scenography as main loci of performance.[54] Both *Gododdin* and *EXX-I*
had also begun to complicate the relationship between the Welsh cultural context and broader political questions, such as colonialism and
cultural hybridity, which *EXX-I* mediated via its uncompromising dramaturgy, and this was reflected in the audience's experience, including the
unwillingness of some people to accept it. These productions stood as a
bridge between the small-scale work much beloved by Welsh-speaking

community audiences and the later performance work that was explicitly defiant, and challenged the audience to react. This later work usually operated on a vast scale and with the visual and aural experience of a total artwork; it employed numerous fields of theatrical elements all tethered to a central thematic, which was often complex in itself, a conglomeration of different ideas, narratives and histories, though it continued to be a theatre of place and memory, one in which the constituent parts were structured so as to bring different meanings to bear in and on place. During this time, some members of the company left due to the perceived shift away from what they considered to be the company's main remit, making work that was imbued with the cultural references of the Welsh-speaking audience, and for them.[55] There is a suggestion in this moment of breakdown and change that emphasis on theatre as visual event, where the human body is relegated to the role of a figure within the design-led space, negates or interferes with the relationship between performer and audience member, a relationship based in a mutually shared background. I would argue however that the work continued to hold the same cultural resonances, but that our aesthetic response was, in the later work, filtered through highly structured performance modes and spatial forms that represented, conceptually, the political and cultural ideas at the heart of the work. Consequently, the emotional impact was not always as immediate (the moments of cultural recognition were not as instantaneous), and the scale and complexity of the spatial and visual framework, as well as the performance's time-based structure, demanded a different response.

According to art historian Peter Lord, Brith Gof were the first company to show 'the creative potential of new ways of working which might arise from a post-colonial state of mind', a stance shared by other companies across Europe that was indicative of a broader 'post-colonial ethos'.[56] While a consideration of Wales as postcolonial is often contested in historical terms, there are analyses in the study of Welsh culture that reveal it to be a valid conceptual stance.[57] Kirsti Bohata's theoretical readings demonstrate that postcolonial paradigms may be employed to 'reveal the ways in which the Welsh have been subjected to a form of imperialism over a long period of time, while also acknowledging the way the Welsh have been complicit in the colonization of others'.[58] Bohata refers to the fact that in postcolonial studies Wales is often completely absent, with England and Britain used interchangeably as the key terms to refer to the whole of the United Kingdom, reflecting the Anglocentricity of British scholarship, which often disguises English cultural hegemony by its use of 'British' as an inclusive term. Encouraging a consideration of postcolonialism in the Welsh context as moving away from 'the reductive, linear model of conquest, colonization, resistance, independence and post-coloniality' (p. 9), Bohata releases us to concentrate on the discourse of Anglocentric cultural imperialism and its effects on Welsh history up to this day. Here, postcolonialism is a form of remembrance that offers

> a structure within which the past can be interrogated with the aim of (re) constructing the present. It is a strategic methodology, a self-conscious act of cultural and historical imagination and, as such, is rich with possibilities for peoples whose stories and histories have been suppressed, neglected, untaught. (p. 15)

She also draws attention to the importance of ensuring that such stories are subject to contestation, as the nostalgic impetus may threaten social awareness or critique, obliterating the possibilities of critical knowledge sought in the dismantling of imperialism. In considering Brith Gof in a postcolonial context, I am following Bohata's defninition of postcolonialism as both a conceptual stance and a form of remembrance. While Brith Gof's postcolonial stance is present in the early small-scale work, in so far as it embodied a critique of the spatial dynamics of theatre in Wales, postcolonial content can be seen more clearly in performances of a different scale, which utilise Welsh and English alongside each other and access a breadth of material written in the context of eighteenth- and nineteenth-century imperialism, for example Mary Shelley in *Haearn* (Iron; 1992), Swift and Defoe in *Y Pen Bas/Y Pen Dwfn* (The Shallow End/The Deep End; 1994) and Edmund Burke, Thomas Paine and Jac Glan-y-Gors in *Prydain: The Impossibility of Britishness* (1996). *Haearn* is particularly significant as it presented the inter-relationship between the site and the elements brought to it in performance. According to Pearson, McLucas had begun to 'characterize site-specific performance as the coexistence and overlay of two basic sets of architectures, those of the extant building or what he later called the *host*, that which is at site . . . and those of the constructed scenography or the *ghost*, that which is temporarily brought *to* site.'[59] *Haearn* was situated in a disused foundry at the British Coal Works in Tredegar, south-east Wales, built in 1913, the year of the greatest output from the south Wales coalfields. Pearson and McLucas explained that in separating out the elements of the 'ghost' *Haearn* one could detect seven overlaid and interpenetrating 'architectures' or orders of material, some conceptual and some spatial, and that these were conceived in order to maximise the charge in their relationships, that is, in the dynamic spaces between them. Spatial architectures included 'The Valley/The Mirror', composed of the audience on one side, and the choir and brass band from Tredegar on the other, set against the backdrop of a historical film of people at work in the steel works of south Wales. Another architecture is described as 'the two women': the actor playing Mary Shelley, Victor Frankenstein and Frankenstein's creature, who was situated only two metres away from the audience and facing them, and the singer, located a hundred metres away from the audience, relating stories of the Greek demigods Hephaestus and Prometheus and their project to create man and woman. Conceptual architectures included the mythical, historical and personal narratives and the way they wove in and out of each other, and the body as conceived in medical and industrial sciences of the time as a biological, mechanical set of components. There was also the climate, incorporating heat, rain, wind and snow; the grid, on which all movement vectors in *Haearn* were based; and 'the times' (literal, metaphorical, classical, historical).[60] While it might not be possible to detect these architectures as clearly denoted structures within the performance, inasmuch as only some of them come to the fore while others recede, audience members are aware of a complexity and depth of material from which they glean a kind of 'structure of feeling' compacted into the space, time and relationships of the performance. *Haearn* was a dense visual text, restrictive in terms of the movement seen and almost stifling in atmosphere, despite the cold. While the audience could move freely in *Gododdin*, in *Haearn*, we sat on bleachers at one end of the 100-metre-long windowless foundry space, gazing at layers of scenographic structures within the brick building, including an enormous gantry crane that spanned the width of the space and brought the gods in and out of focus quickly above us. And despite the fact that it rained, snowed and blew a gale, we were somehow 'outside' it, gazing in at the creation of a monster: industrial man. Directly in front of us, on three chairs placed on ladder towers and occupied in a sequence by performer Nia Caron, the words of Mary Shelley, of Victor Frankenstein, and lastly, of Frankenstein's monster were performed

– a progression from a personal to an internalised grief and then exter-nalised agony. On the foundry floor a relentless, impersonal and almost brutal display of industry exhibited its human costs in the creation from foundry moulds of 'man' and 'woman', who were then hoisted by ropes and pulleys, compelled to move and, in the final snowstorm, were attached to the walls by long bungee ropes, unable to reach each other through the blizzard for any kind of human consolation. The recurrent human cost was reinforced by the myth of Prometheus and Hephaestus, and underscored by the narrative of Mary Shelley's novel *Frankenstein*. *Haearn* was an amalgamation that deconstructed the formation of the modern industrial and machinist world to reveal, in physical terms and in ways that directly affected the audience's sensibil-ity, how the relationship between worker and machine became so important during the industrial revolution that the values of humanity eroded away. The semi-derelict site in which the performance played out not only reflected the erosion of values understood during the performance, it embodied it – here was a place that contributed directly to the human and cultural costs that the performance dealt with. Emplacing the work here prompted McLucas to state that after *Haearn* 'site as a term was beginning to include meaning and historical part narrative as well as the formal built architecture, and *place* began to feel like a more useful term than the more abstract term site'.[61] Place signifies a strong tie with the memory already associated with the site in question, and the performance situated in place references the mem-ory associated with it explicitly and at the same time enables a new memory or remembrance through the aesthetic statements con-structed during the performance. Pearson refers to this when he says that 'Performance itself can be a rearticulation of site'.[62] Describing a sort of 'rescue archaeology' of cultural identity, he emphasises that any approach to site-specific work must take into account 'the endless narratives, the political aspirations and disappointments, which have accumulated' around the site' (p. 156). In some productions this rela-tionship was foregrounded in formal ways, as it was in *Tri Bywyd* (Three Lives; 1995), performed at Esgair Fraith, Clywedog, an aban-doned farm in a conifer plantation near Llanbedr Pont Steffan in Ceredigion, where the audience sat on scaffolding placed high in the forest, watching the performance from above as three stories of three lives unfolded in three overlapping zones within one space.[63] In the dark and the cold we watched the brightly lit performance through the

11. *Tri Bywyd* (Brith Gof), the scaffolding in the trees and within the ruin.
Source: Cliff McLucas Archive, NLW. Photo: Cliff McLucas.

mist; it was as though a theatre had been erected in the middle of the forest itself – not in a clearing, but *in* the trees. I was constantly drawn to the ruins of the isolated farmhouse, Esgair Fraith, at the lower right-hand side of the landscape before us; here the performance told of rural poverty and suicide, set in 1956. At audience eye level, square cubes of scaffolding 'held' other rooms up in the trees; these enabled us to see 'place' as defined over and through the landscape, through the ruin and into the trees, each cube a kind of room or box for 'domestic' vignettes, incorporating narrative, movement, source material and sound in a multi-layered text. One cube is Lletherneuadd Uchaf, in 1869, a cottage in the village of Llanfiangel-ar-Arth, Carmarthenshire, home of Sarah Jacob, 'the Welsh Fasting Girl'. Another cube bears the story of 7 James Street, Butetown, Cardiff docks, the site in 1988 of the murder of Lynette White, a young prostitute. While each cube tells of a different place and event entirely, the effect of the simultaneous performance of each narrative, interspersed throughout the performance, is a 'bleeding' of the lives presented one in to the other. And through the filter of the place itself, and the ruins of an old farmhouse, something else was channelled, something to do with our understanding of the relationship between rural and urban and their interdependence in Welsh culture, history and memory, as well as the co-presence of both the Welsh and English languages and their implications for our identities over time.

Defining and creating performance work in this way as a 'field of activities', Brith Gof were at the forefront of the process of hybridisation in theatre, where art forms work together and each one engages with the narratives of the site. In this, the site is not a backdrop or an illustration and there is no single viewpoint. Although inherently visual, this is not about the setting of a specific image and there is no clearly defined pictorial mise-en-scène; this is about the coming together of certain artistic vocabularies. Site-specific work enables a fluid set of relationships between place, public and performance, and the result is not stable or unchanging, but open to interpretation. In this process language acquires a different meaning; it is not simply about direct exposition – language may be sound, structure, noise, or conversation. As their productions developed Brith Gof's use of language became more complex. In *Camlann* (1993), an examination using Arthurian mythology of the war in former Yugoslavia, spectators were divided into Welsh and English speakers, each group following

performers in different areas of the warehouse and only gradually coming together. Here, languages formed a perpetual score and were heard
together, conceivably as conflicting sounds, each potentially a double
of itself. In *Arturius Rex* (1994) this device was taken further, with
Welsh and English spoken at the same time and the spectator free to
find and follow the voice of her choice. In *Prydain: The Impossibility of
Britishness* (1996), in which Britishness was projected as a hindrance
to the revolutionary discourse on human rights and freedom, the performance incorporated the notion of revolution as a compositional
element: the audience was separated into two groups, some to become
actively involved and others to witness. In this situation, the audience
member was asked to reflect on what it was they were witnessing.
Welsh and English were present, but half-heard or overheard amongst
the commotion, the spectator having to negotiate between languages
and perhaps taking sides. Here, language becomes a component in the
self-conscious split of identity alignment, an aspect disclosed in the
construction of the performance itself.

Site-specific practice in Wales at the end of the twentieth century
can be seen as a project to retrieve social relations in space. More
than the liberation of the theatre event from a site that masks a power
relationship, this is theatre as performance that claims its own set of
relationships as negotiated between performer, audience and site in a
place that is claimed or reclaimed as meaningful to us. This is a form
of activism, a performance that is explicitly created for a given site – a
place – the aesthetic and political meanings of which emanate from the
interrelationship of text, performer, audience and place. Site-specific
practices in Wales have accessed social and cultural practices that
reveal people's investment in place, their commitment to something
that contributes to the making of the space as *place*. This might be
called 'spirit of place', but this is too self-consciously nostalgic, for in
this work it is not only what has happened in this place before that
counts. What is happening here now in relation to what has happened before is the primary signifier of the piece and the reason why
this work is implicated in processes of cultural identity. Contributors
– performers, audience members – are involved in a process where
the performance evokes memory of place, and taps into the relationship between memory and place in order to forge new meanings and
to articulate what is known in a new way (*poiesis*). The performance
is encountered through spatial practice as a process of interrogating

the memory and of unearthing relationships between the place itself and memory. What these places become for us in performance has a bearing on how we define who we are.

This identity function within the site-specific in Wales has been heightened and, in practice, problematised, by the establishment of two national theatre companies following devolution. How these companies inhabit spaces outside theatre auditoria reveals much about the influence of the site-specific practices pioneered by Brith Gof, but also the differences in what the site-specific entails in post-devolutionary Wales. In the national theatre work, the interrelationships between performance constituents is at times less developed and the site often used as a backdrop, a representation of place as well as the place itself. Perhaps the claim on place is no longer in jeopardy since devolution; perhaps the claim on place is less meaningful for the community, or perhaps the audience's claim on theatre is less urgent, considering the emergence of what Roger Owen has called 'a *faux*-populist institutionalisation of Welsh theatre'.[64]

National theatres and their places

The project of self-determination that is implicit in devolution for those who desire it (rather than those who bestow it) has led to the establishment of several important institutions, including a Welsh-language national theatre, Theatr Genedlaethol Cymru (ThGC) in 2003, followed by an English-language company, National Theatre Wales (NTW) in 2009. In what appeared to be a calculated attempt at inclusion, the establishment of two distinct companies performs the validity of representing both bilingual and Anglophone experiences of Welshness.[65] The establishment of a national theatre company was debated by academics prior to its/their formation, though the critique tended to dwell on the redundant nature of the debate, 'because politicians see it as part of the nation building project'.[66] The 1999 Arts Council of Wales 'Drama Strategy for Wales' had already paved the way for a reduction in revenue funding and consequently in the number of funded theatre companies across Wales, with an emphasis on professional quality theatre increasing its reach across 'under-provided' for areas. Theatr Genedlaethol Cymru was the first large company to step out of this context. Its establishment is mentioned explicitly in the Welsh Government's document '*Iaith Pawb*: A National Action Plan for a Bilingual Wales' (2003), which declares its intention of creating a 'high profile vehicle' for live theatre, similar to the visual represen- tation of the Welsh in films such as *Hedd Wyn* (1992), *Gadael Lenin* (1994) and *Solomon a Gaenor* (1999), which placed Welsh (specifi- cally Welsh-language) film on the cinematic map, if rather briefly.[67] In 2002–3 the Arts Council of Wales allocated an initial £250,000 to fund two Welsh-language productions, and subsequently to 'set up the company that will take the development forward and bring live drama to Welsh-speaking audiences throughout Wales'.[68] A further £1.5 million was made available over the following two years to enable the Arts Council of Wales to establish and run the new company, the aim of which was to ensure 'coverage across Wales' and to 'enhance the status and profile of Welsh language theatre' (p. 50). The advent of ThGC is directly related to the Welsh-language policy of govern- ment and the vision of sustaining Welsh-language culture in the widest sense and promoting the Welsh language is therefore a core part of ThGC's mission.

The establishment of the English-medium National Theatre Wales in 2009 came as part of the Labour/Plaid Cymru coalition govern- ment agreement of 2007 on a 'progressive agenda' towards an inclusive 'one Wales'.[69] NTW produces work in English and is not part of any specific drive towards language acquisition, though their online state- ment specifies that the company's work reflects 'the many cultures and languages of contemporary Wales'.[70] There is obviously a question regarding how exactly it is able to do this when its specific remit is to work through the medium of English. The word 'reflect' is surely the answer, inferring a representation that takes place beyond spoken language; theatre is able to access and channel cultural connotations through means other than the spoken (or written) word, or at least in addition to it. In this way, the cultural content may acknowledge the Welsh language and context though the medium is English. In an early article to accompany the establishment of the company, the first artistic director John E. McGrath writes of Welsh writing in English as 'a negotiation' and of the company's aim 'to perform the question of language'.[71] The company's first few years of production work have revealed that this is Welsh material, reflecting the common adage that people are speaking Welsh 'through the medium of English', a refer- ence to the residual Welsh words, syntax and general cultural context of the English spoken. The Welsh language inevitably haunts NTW's performances; it is referenced in the connotations of colonial history in a performance on the Epynt mountain range of *Persians* (Pearson/ Brookes, 2010), so redolent of loss is the place itself, or in the language and vocabulary used in Dafydd James and Ben Lewis's *The Village Social* (2011), and in the inventive bilingual turn in Gruff Rhys's *The Insatiable, Inflatable Candylion* (2015).[72]

It could be argued that a separation of theatrical outputs based on language is artificial and self-defeating, dividing artistic outputs according to linguistic differences. This is based on the perception of theatre as a performance of dramatic works, which prioritises the language on the page as primary signifier. That this is at odds with the history of theatre practice in Wales over the past forty years adds weight to the argument that government-led projects are overwhelmingly geared towards specific representations of nationness and can be poor at exploring 'hybrid' identities. In relation to exploring the daily experience of bilingual Wales explicitly, both companies are hindered by their linguistic separateness. ThGC, operating in Welsh, has made repeated attempts at reaching out to a wider audience through synopses and surtitles, and more recently the specially developed translation app Sibrwd (whisper), while NTW, operating in English, is unable to play to Welsh-language audiences without closing off a fundamental aspect of their experience of life. For me, as a bilingual audience member, the existence of two companies ratifies the experience of a linguistic split and does nothing to assist the coming together of differing awarenesses of Welshness within one's self. This has implications for what collective memory can mean in the places in which performances occur, for whom, and for the way it is accessed through theatre. The establishment of two national theatre companies in Wales has hindered the possibility of a potentially exciting theatrical hybridity, which has not yet been fully explored in Welsh theatre, apart from early explorations in the work of Ed Thomas, e.g. *Adar Heb Adennydd* (1989) / *The Myth of Michael Roderick* (1990), and Ian Rowlands, e.g. *A Marriage of Convenience* (1996). More recent exceptions include Gary Owen's *Amgen / Broken* (2009), and Alun Saunders's *A Good Clean Heart* (2015), both plays that use the metaphor of the brother/twin as a device for discussing bilingual identity. More generally, in terms of linguistic registers, we have seen the naturalness of Wenglish in Dafydd James's *Llwyth*.[73] This critique of the division in linguistic provision should not be read as an abnegation of theatre that operates through one language alone. It is rather a desire to see an amelioration of the schizophrenic split in Welsh theatre, which tends to normalise one cultural practice over the other and in which there is the potential danger of Welsh becoming totally peripheral and English entirely normative. It also represents a longing to witness and participate in theatre that is able to reflect and discuss the experience of contemporary cultural identity, rather than reify cultural aspirations alone. Increasingly, for many people, particularly the young, who have a working if not completely fluent knowledge of Welsh, the daily experience of bilingualism is very real, and the awareness of each language impinges on cultural expression in both. M. Wynn Thomas refers to this experience when he writes of the condition of translating as 'cynnyrch cyffindir iaith', that is, as a product of being on the frontier between languages. Discussing the notion that Welsh speakers in Wales 'live our interior lives, as well as our public lives, on the borderline between two languages and two cultures',[74] Thomas describes a dual or two-fold identity based on bilingualism:

> Inside every one of us there are two languages and two societies keeping fellowship (*cadw seiat*) perpetually – and sometimes keeping riot. Every soliloquy (*ymson*) we have is a contention/competition (*ymryson*) – and no word will come from our mouths without its mute partner – the 'foreign' word that is its beloved and opposing bedfellow.[75]

Thomas proceeds to discuss the fallacy perpetuated by Welsh speakers: the idea that we are 'able' to speak English, rather than accepting the fact that we have been living in and through two languages for a considerable time, historically. He describes the speech act for those with such a dual identity as one of competition, because on the linguistic stage the bilingual speaker cannot ever be alone with one language; thoughts from each cultural and linguistic context collide and jostle, and speech is constantly permeated with the presence of two languages. The problem of competition entails having to exclude one language when speaking the other; the partner language is present, however, lurking beneath the spoken words and constantly informing them. This condition is so fundamental to the bilingual Welsh/English speaker that the lack of a theatre that communicates to and for this experience is surprising. While the cultural and political impetus of sustaining a Welsh-language dramatic canon and safeguarding it through its performance on the main stage circuit in Wales has understandably been of paramount importance, it is peculiar that contemporary performance, from the point of view of representing contemporary cultural experience, has not yet explored the experience of bilingual culture more fully. The language of theatre as an artistic medium is more extensive than the language of the dramatic text, but herein lies one of the central problems; while one national company is able to operate beyond the confines of the primacy of the dramatic text, it is very difficult for the other, such has been the investment in developing a Welsh-language canon and its representation on the national stage. This concerns much more than language preservation, however; it involves cultural ideals regarding the nature and purpose of theatre as an art form, as well as questions of representation. Taking the point of view that everything and all is translatable through theatre as an experience, perhaps it would be useful to accept the use of both (and all) languages on the national stage, without threatening any specific audience's linguistic experience. Perhaps such ventures take time.

Inevitably, national institutions reverberate with questions of identity. But what form should a national theatre take? Can it offer a framework within which national identity may come into being continually in a perpetual process of imagination, reflecting definitions of nationness over and over? Can it be a sphere in which to articulate and contest such questions? Or does a national theatre exist to affirm specific cultural ideals? The diverse and divergent quality of nationness in a Welsh context, lends itself to a potentially rich variety of representations and responses. However, the means by which we might do this are divided. The two national theatre companies of Wales represent different attitudes towards place that make their approaches markedly different. National Theatre Wales (NTW) began its first year programme in 2009 by undertaking a 'theatrical mapping' of Wales, and declaring that 'The nation of Wales is our stage: from forests and beaches, from aircraft hangars to post-industrial towns, from village halls to nightclubs . . .You'll find us round the corner, across the mountain and in your digital backyard.'[76] John McGrath spoke of nation as place above all else: 'you can look at a nation through history, through identity, but really we thought what a nation is is a place – so let's explore what place means,'[77] suggesting also that this could be a way through the language 'minefield.'[78] In this context, the attempt to emplace twelve productions in twelve different locations during the first year was not only ambitious but a central part of the attempt to define what a national theatre might be to the entire nation. Taking its cue from National Theatre Scotland, which was established with no home building, a small core staff base and a company dedicated to collaboration and partnership, NTW took 'place' as the starting point for theatrical collaboration. The meaning and the implications of 'place' as a central concept is not analysed in detail, however, and there is a sense in which NTW's 'theatrical mapping' of the country, alongside declarations regarding 'exploring' the land through theatre, might suggest a power relationship between institution and audience, one which unintentionally bears imperialistic undertones. Such a suggestion is undercut, however, by the company's serious drive to operate in an open and democratic way through its online community, though this community interface inevitably operates through the medium of English (such is its remit), and unwittingly conforms to a set of linguistic power relations.

Despite its formation six years earlier in 2003, Theatr Genedlaethol Cymru launched itself as a national theatre for the main stage in order to represent the Welsh classics to the widest audience possible, though it too began experimenting with its own version of the site-specific, albeit with a difference of agenda and audience. Much has been made of NTW's lack of a theatre venue as home for the company, but virtually nothing has been mentioned about ThGC's similar status in terms of a base. Situated in Carmarthen, the company operates from a building on a university campus, which it shares with the headquarters of Coleg Cymraeg Cenedlaethol (national Welsh college), which works to develop and support Welsh-medium provision across the universities in Wales. Here ThGC have their offices and a rehearsal space, though they perform in and through most of the receiving houses in Wales. While there are similarities in terms of contexts of operation, the responses of the two companies to a sense of place in performance are notably different, although both seek to emplace work in various locations beyond traditional theatre buildings and to attract new audiences. An overwhelming distinction in relation to place is revealed in NTW's extreme sense of the local, and ThGC's sense of performing to the nation *in toto*; the first an attempt to be minoritarian and localised, the latter an attempt at majority performance. In 2015, the companies came together to produce, a bilingual (or trilingual, including the Spanish material) production, {150}, directed by Marc Rees, to mark the one hundred and fiftieth anniversary of the Welsh settlement in Argentina. *{150}* drew from the Welsh emigration of 150 people to Patagonia in 1865 and the subsequent stories and histories mythologised by the Welsh back home and the emigrant/immigrant Welsh (subsequently Argentinian) population of Patagonia. Self-consciously referencing Brith Gof's performance work *Patagonia* (1992), the production was a layered and episodic exploration of the history of *Y Wladfa* (the Settlement), with the audience split in two to follow the action around the enormous Royal Opera House scenery and costume stores in Abercwmboi. Using languages interchangeably, the performance forged a linguistic soundscape against which different actions and historical scenarios unfolded. These were mostly solo pieces by performers representing historical figures, though there were also more abstract formal pieces of dance and movement and excerpts of a television production called *Galesa*, shown on expansive screens, about a Patagonian actor, Elizabeth Fernandez's return home after having played a Patagonian character in the Welsh soap opera *Pobol y Cwm*, which was broadcast in full following the production run. The use of the cavernous storehouse, its shelves packed high with stage props of all sorts, reinforced the notion that this is about a community in the process of leaving. Some shelves held artefacts relating to the performance itself, signified by the brightly coloured translucent Perspex boxes in which they were housed. Some were containers labelled with the emigrants' names and home addresses, reminding us of the fact that the performance was happening a stone's throw from their former homes. The vast building contributed to the general aesthetic of the piece but the performance was not invested in creating new meaning for the place itself. It is, after all, the props store for the Royal Opera House, which is located over 200 miles away in London. The venue operated as an empty container – a storage space – and within it excerpts of history came together in a living exhibition format, a kind of museum of formative historical moments, presented by narrators giving the background and punctuated by dance, singing and recitation. This was site as holding vessel, here representing the non-place or threshold between departure and arrival for the emigrant. There was no certainty that this place, as property of the Royal Opera House, could ever hope to represent the local, and it is within this disjunction that there was a potential reflection on identity and displacement. The use of the storehouse was almost circumstantial, however, and

12. *{150}* (ThGC and NTW), actor Gareth Aled in performance, seen through the storage space at Royal Opera House Stores, Abercwmboi.
Source: National Theatre Wales. Photo: Simon Clode.

the production's site-specificity was missing the internal connections and contentions that enable a complex interaction between the site as space and as place.

NTW's pledge of performing across Wales in spaces other than (though occasionally inclusive of) theatre auditoria has to some extent reawakened an interest in the site-specific. This version of the site-specific is not emphatically political in the way it relates to discourses of space and place, though there is within it a clear focus on community and audience. 'Immersive theatre' is the recurrent phrase in reviews and accounts of NTW's first year, though 'site-based' and 'site-responsive' have also been used.[79] Josephine Machon defines immersive theatre as 'physical, sensual and participatory', part of 'an immersive practice that arises from the fusion of installation arts and physical and visual theatres of the 1980s', which owes 'its sensual aesthetic primarily to a mix of ingredients involving landscape, architecture, scenography, sound and direct, human contact'.[80] While there is much in common here with site-specific performance, a key constituent of the immersive experience is the social context surrounding the performance itself, that is, how it has been set up and promoted outside and beyond the performance, and often as an event that merges with everyday life. For instance, it may be set up via online groups, on Facebook or Twitter, and the participant will purchase tickets online, submitting to a set of instructions on how to get to the performance location, which is most likely to be a venue or locale within which there is total immersion in a different world, or a game with its own specific rules (pp. 54–5). This development of an online community has been central to the community practice inherent in NTW's philosophy of participation in theatre as a democratic project and a crucial step in the evolution of the audience participant's relationship with the performance event and the company as a whole. In this process NTW have committed to the concept of their community as co-creators in the work, appearing to democratise the production process. This has been clearly discernible in the experience of attending NTW productions. For instance, community was at the heart of the experience of NTW's *Tonypandemonium* (2013) by Rachel Trezise, performed in Treorci's Park and Dare theatre in the south Wales valleys during the venue's centenary year. The performance told the story of a daughter's relationship with her alcoholic mother, but this was not a sociopetal presentation of interpersonal relationships presented through the mise-en-scène of a proscenium arch theatre. Its emphasis on community as one body saw the spatial mechanics of the large Edwardian proscenium arch theatre of the Park and Dare Hall, its existence originally funded by and for the mine workers,[81] completely subverted. Mathilde Lopez's production over-set the stalls with decking so that the playing area incorporated the entire ground floor space in the theatre, including the 'stage space' proper, which resulted in the absence of a divide between stage and auditorium. The effect was that of bringing the community and the performance space itself far closer together in a conscious theatrical representation of the performance as product of community. On this vast open platform, audience members sat in the round, in rows of chairs, sofas and armchairs, merging the representation of living room with the audience space. Tables, lamps and other furniture were dotted amongst the audience, an immersive device that developed in other ways during the performance. The main character in this semi-autobiographical play was performed by several young women from the area, of various ages, representing the character's process to maturity. All of them stepped out of and back into the audience, a device that supported the sense of performers and audience as one community. In a similar way NTW and Wildworks's *Passion* (2011) in Port Talbot, directed by Michael Sheen and Ben Mitchell, saw an entire community stage Christ's Passion throughout the town itself. Here, in a strange melding of virtual and actual, everyday life and mythology, Hollywood star Michael Sheen played 'Teacher', an amnesiac homeless man, in a retelling of the Passion play, with a group of actors and the people of Port Talbot as cast and crew – over a thousand community volunteers in all. WildWorks, founded by Ben Mitchell in 2005, is renowned as a company which focuses on site-specific work, described as 'landscape theatre, large scale spectacular performances and arts works that flow out of their locations'. The material is wrought by 'probing the feelings, thoughts, stories and memories of people . . . and by attending carefully to the place, the genius loci, and working in a spirit of mutual hospitality with the people who inhabit the physical space'.[82] *Passion* was a performance about memory, a theme woven into the narrative itself, 'hewn with tenderness from the memories of locals', according to critic Lyn Gardner,[83] and heightened by the fact that Port Talbot's long-lost son, Sheen himself, had returned. Playing Teacher, the amnesiac, Sheen provided hope by listening to the accounts of the lives of the people of Port Talbot:

13. *Passion* (NTW and WildWorks), scene in the shopping
centre with Michael Sheen and Julie Hobday, Port Talbot.
Source: National Theatre Wales. Photo: Ian Kingsnorth.

In an underpass, two fierce boys, crouching on piles of rubble, tried to
remember themselves. In Llewellyn Street, where a terrace of houses
has been destroyed to build a bypass, a resident summoned up his
exiled neighbours: as he described their lives, figures appeared under
the arches of the flyover, loitering in a nether region, an anti-cathedral
of concrete pillars and a vaulted roof.[84]

When Teacher is crucified he exclaims 'I remember. I remember!', letting forth a torrent of final utterances formed from local reminiscences,
the name of a shop, the smell of a slaughterhouse, etc. Addressing Port
Talbot from the cross, was Michael Sheen giving the townspeople
their memories repeated back to them as an affirmation, a moment of
solidarity through a collective communal remembrance? According to
Lyn Gardner, it was like watching a town discovering its voice through
a shared act of creation. The emphasis on the social context, the fact
the performance inhabited the entire town, the local people performing and attending, meant that *Passion* operated through a relational
aesthetics in which the lines between mimetic representation and daily
life were blurred, if present at all. In effect, this was a large-scale social

event, set up by the artist/the company, where the townspeople's own involvement constituted the artwork. *Passion* demonstrated the fact that site-specific performance can reside and emerge from the confluence of people, place and event, and here, its site-specificity was Port Talbot itself and its people.

Once hijacked as form alone, however, 'site-specificity' loses its power to redefine community and to establish a sense of place. Without this imperative, site-specific performance, defined as nothing more than performance outside theatre auditoria, does not contribute at all to the process of emplacement involving collective memory and operates as a pseudo-stage, unable to expose or add to the cultural significance of place. Such a performance becomes nothing more than an experience of a different kind of stage, where meaning is contingent on images made against the site as a theatrical backdrop rather than formed from the specifics of *place*, which was the case with ThGC's *Blodeuwedd* (2013), and NTW's *Mametz* (2014), for instance, both performed outdoors. Saunders Lewis's classic play *Blodeuwedd* (1948), directed by Arwel Gruffydd and performed at Tomen y Mur, near Trawsfynydd, Gwynedd, was described as an 'outdoor performance' and was situated at the probable seat of Lleu Llaw Gyffes, the play's protagonist. The site's archaeology was referred to in detail in the programme, and on headphones as the audience journeyed to the site, which was historically engaging, but had no immediate bearing on the performance we watched on top of the mountain. The audience occupied at first a raked seating area in the open air, followed by an arena of hay bales overlooking a brook, and a further broad seating arrangement in the final act. Being situated so gave the audience the sense of viewing a domestic scene against the landscape's depth of field – cars came into the frame from afar and so on within a wide cinematic backdrop. Originally written for the narrow formality of a 'straitened stage',[85] however, the play's tightly woven unity of place and action, the formality of its presentation – though against a picturesque setting on the mountaintop – suggested that the overall effect could have been replicated in a theatre auditorium, more or less, though less spectacularly. In the same year, the production was indeed staged in auditoria in a tour of Welsh main stages, with the same staging replicated in the front-on theatre space.

In *Mametz* by NTW, directed by Matthew Dunster and performed at Great Llancayo Upper Wood, near Usk in Monmouthshire, the

performance site – a farmhouse, outbuildings and the nearby wood –
while dramatically appropriate, held no specifically apparent resonance
in relation to the First World War or to the Somme. But we accepted
this landscape as representative of the agricultural land of France and
the woodland as illustration of Mametz wood. The performance served
as a gentle memorialisation, one born from an elegiac poem based
on a visit to Mametz Wood by the poet and dramatist Owen Sheers.
This was a play in which time bends (an elderly man walks back from
the shop with his plastic bags and into the trenches as he remembers
them), and a performance in which the initially passive audience eventually climbed across and through the stage, which opened to reveal
a stairway into the hellish woods beyond. When we walked into the
forest during the final part of the performance, a backdrop was set up
between the trees – a large canvas with an enlarged sepia photograph
of a soldier, while tree trunks placed horizontally in rows formed a
theatre in the woods. Despite the earlier attempt at deconstructing
the stage frame the final theatrical configuration together with the
representational unity of the play worked to provide a convention-
ally unified stage for the unfolding representation. This is not to say,
however, that classical drama cannot work in a site-specific context,
as Mike Pearson's production of *Persians* (2010) for NTW revealed.

Persians was staged at the British Army's military training ranges
at Sennybridge, Powys, a site with no public access. This performance represented an aesthetic project, where theatre emerges from
a disjunction between compositional elements, reflective of the philosophically discordant partnership of the 'site-specific' with 'national
theatre', a dissonance that reached its pinnacle in *ILIAD* (2015), staged
at Y Ffwrnes theatre in Llanelli. The *Persians* text, based on the earliest extant play in Western drama, tells of the battle between the
Greeks and the Persians at Salamis, an event in living memory for
the dramatist Aeschylus, having taken place eight years prior to the
first ever staging of the play in 472 BC. While Aeschylus celebrated
Athenian victory, the play is a tragedy that unravels to reveal a deep
empathetic response to those who have been vanquished. The parallel
with the history of the land on which NTW's *Persians* was performed
was not lost on those who knew the history of the communities of the
Epynt mountain range, displaced by forced eviction by the Ministry
of Defence in 1939 to allow for a military training zone of several
thousand acres. This loss was not directly referenced in the production

– there would have been no need to do so. In the context of the history of the Welsh language, such acts are recognised as assaults against an already fragile cultural and linguistic community. Iorwerth Peate, who was asked to survey the last traces of Welsh life in the area before the military moved in, described it as 'a community that had been murdered'. During his final visit in 1940 he reports seeing the few remaining people in the process of moving, including a woman over eighty years old who had 'dragged an old chair to the furthest corner of the yard and was sitting there like a statue, gazing towards the mountain with tears streaming down her cheeks'. Peate felt as though he had 'interrupted a sacrament'; the old woman tells him to return to Cardiff with haste, as 'it is the end of the world here'.[86] 'Cilieni', the shell of a village, is now a collection of desolate buildings, mostly without facades, and used for 'fighting in built-up areas' training. Against this history, what does it mean to have the audience standing in the middle of the village with the chorus before them 'rejoicing in war and announcing "no one can withstand this tsunami of the Persians in full rage"'?[87] Later on, as the audience are emplaced in a viewing area overlooking the facade-less house in which Atossa, mother of the defeated Xerxes, resides, the audience view the gradual disintegration as the mother queen, as well as the chorus and even the ghost of Darius, her husband returned from the grave, accept with horror that grief is all that remains. It is an unrelenting threnody on the futility of war that chimes with the biblical quotation from Isaiah 2:4, inscribed in Welsh on a plaque in the ruins of Capel y Babell in the village: 'They shall beat their swords into mattocks and their spears into pruning-knives; nation shall not lift sword against nation nor ever again be trained for war.' The operation of communal memory here was entirely a matter of context. For those who knew the history of Epynt, *Persians* was charged with pathos.

In an entirely different context, NTW's *ILIAD* (2015), directed by Pearson and Brookes, represented the apotheosis of the discord between site-specificity and theatrical event in that its central problematic was how to make a site-specific performance based in a theatre auditorium. The fractal poetry of Christopher Logue's *War Music* (based on Homer's *Iliad*), together with the repeated dismantling and reconstitution of the staging, assisted in deconstructing the theatrical event from the inside. During the eight-hour long performance of four parts,[88] the physical compositional elements of plastic chairs, tyres and flat wooden platforms are reorganised constantly by the performers, with the audience altering position in response, creating a fluid continuum of spatial movement. This is punctuated by moments of stillness when the fractal and explosive poetry is spoken into suspended microphones. The real dynamic throughout, however, is to be found in the tension between the experience of audience as witness/spectator and audience as participant, with audience members negotiating where to place themselves and whom to watch throughout. At times the audience members are themselves positioned to represent the dead. That the poetry is spoken as a narrative of war and encapsulates in its theatrical time frame the associated siege at the end of the Trojan war (we are all in this theatre overnight after all), makes the process of waiting and watching even more affecting. But how precisely is this production in a purpose-built theatre space, 'site-specific'? A large performance space with the seating rake pulled back, the studio theatre becomes a site in which the implications for defining and delimiting theatrical activity are exposed. In recognising the elements within the space and utilising them as theatrical constituents – screen, chairs, stages, microphones, monitors, performers, audience members etc. – the performance is an exercise in form, or a lesson in constructing meaning from within with all the formal elements available at the site, in which we as audience become formal constituents. Unmasking the theatrical and stripping the elements of the theatre event down to the bare bones exposes the necessary relationships between participants. *ILIAD* is a self-conscious retelling of what performance entails – between performer and performer, performer and witness, and witnesses together. This works with the relentlessly unforgiving interpretation of the *Iliad* in the poetry itself, an apposite construction of Logue's *War Music* in motion, a telling of the formal experience of the poetry through theatre. Here, site does not become place – it is consciously and at all times relegated to site as site, the antithesis of auditorium as representational space. But is it site-specific? The performance's ontology is literally bound with the spatial context in which the performance is taking place and there is no gap between site and the event itself. *ILIAD* was a compelling exercise in form that took the deconstruction of the event to an extreme. It did not attempt to access memory of place; this was happening after all in a new theatre venue that had opened only two years previously. Audience communality here was based in the theatrical experience itself.

14. *ILIAD* (NTW), view of performers Llion Williams, Guy
Lewis and Richard Lynch, with audience sitting.
Source: National Theatre Wales. Photo: Farrows Creative.

Theatr Genedlaethol Cymru: Wales as Place / The Place of Wales

Theatr Genedlaethol Cymru have staged two productions to which
the term site-specific has been applied, *Y Bont* (2013) and *Tir Sir Gâr*
(2015). *Y Bont* (the bridge), directed by Arwel Gruffydd, 'staged' the
1963 sit-in by the students of Aberystwyth and Bangor university col-
leges on Pontrefechan Bridge in Aberystwyth, a historically important
protest and the first event organised by Welsh-language pressure group
Cymdeithas yr Iaith Gymraeg as part of the campaign to gain equal
status for the Welsh language. Following Saunders Lewis's instrumental radio broadcast, *Tynged yr Iaith* (the fate of the language), in
1962, which predicts the demise of the Welsh language unless 'revolutionary' steps are taken to defend its use, the group sought ways of
obtaining police summonses, specifically so that they could request
them in Welsh.[89] The students' attempts at being arrested for plaster-
ing the town's post office with Welsh-language leaflets had failed and
blocking the traffic into town by sitting in the road across the bridge
became a last ditch attempt during a day of civil disobedience. ThGC's

203

performance was an episodic voyage by bus into a town populated by 'students' that re-enacted some of the key events, culminating with audience and performers on the bridge itself. The performance bordered on re-enactment, an aspect that was suppressed by the inclusion of a contemporary love story between a Welsh-speaking woman and a man who is learning Welsh, which also anchored the performance in a contemporary context. Beginning from Aberystwyth Arts Centre on the hill overlooking the town, the audience are led to a series of vintage buses and listen to interviews from the 1960s, including Saunders Lewis's radio lecture, through headphones. We pass groups of students in period clothes walking down the hill and when the bus drives past the old police station on the seafront, we witness some sort of protest / intervention, with leaflets being stuck on the door. On the promenade, we see pairs of men and women on bicycles, each man seated on the bicycle seat and each woman sitting on the handlebars in a recurrent image of the initial moment of rule-breaking designed to incur a summons. We proceed back into town and disembark to walk down Great Darkgate Street past the post office, where there is a re-enactment of the daubing of the building's facade with leaflets demanding Welsh-language services. Following this we disband anti-climactically to one of several cafés, designated randomly by coloured lanyards worn by each audience member. The original café from where the bridge protest was plotted, Home Café on Pier Street, is attended by the lucky ones. The desire for authenticity in re-enactment is such that the theatrical representation can't hope to match the longing for what once happened. Sitting in the Penguin Café, I drink tea, eat a Welsh cake and watch interviews with members of the Welsh Language Society who took part in the original protest, shown on monitors. On cue, the disbanded audience reforms, flowing together into a mass of people, now directed to walk down Bridge Street towards the bridge itself. Walking over the crest of the road we see in the distance the students on the bridge and there is a remarkable moment when there is an awareness of the audience's mobility as commemoration. Hundreds are moving towards the people on the bridge. That the 'students' on the bridge are mostly actual students (many are my own students), heightens a sense of remembering 'forward', of retracing the past in re-enactment as a remembrance and a continuation, reflecting Rebecca Schneider's question of whether 'remains' might be understood as that which resides in embodiment, in 'bodies striking poses, making gestures, voicing calls,

15. *Y Bont* (ThGC), re-enacting the protest at Aberystwyth Post Office.
Photo: Lisa Lewis.

reading words, singing songs, or standing witness'[90] On the bridge I am struck by a powerless feeling that this is a commemorative re-enactment, as though the remembrance removes the ability to retread the protest as protest. This perceived lack is underlined by the dramatic intervention of the love story between Welsh-speaker and Welsh learner, who now emerge from within the crowd on the bridge. Their dialogue is not entirely audible or visible; people attempt to listen, but the silent stillness of commemoration is deafening and the lovers' story is insignificant compared to the physical feeling of re-treading such a symbolic past event. The profound sense of remembrance ensures that the protest is suspended in amber. Consequently, the performance, as theatre, is unable to elicit the same kind of jolt as Saunders Lewis's interventional radio broadcast and remains in the realm of memory. At the end, our headphones repeatedly instruct us to 'cross the bridge' so that we can return to the buses. In crossing, I'm aware for the first time of a liminoid moment, as though the act of crossing the bridge is more meaningful than the protest itself. This locates the bridge as a significant threshold; it made me realise that the protest cannot be repeated and we are left to reflect back on it as a moment in history. What then is the relationship of the bridge protest with our lives today? Perhaps, tellingly, this relationship resides in the embodied moment of performance. The actual students on the bridge, performing students on the bridge, told of the moving moment of connection when they saw the sheer volume of the people appear on the crest of the hill at Bridge Street, and the fact that they kept coming in what seemed like an unstoppable flow. On the bridge itself, we the audience also saw this recognition in the performers' eyes; they were moved and at the same time were charging us to be moved, searching for our own responses.

Tir Sir Gâr (2013), directed by Marc Rees in collaboration with writer Roger Williams, dealt explicitly with significant changes in ways of life and the potential impact of these changes on rural Welsh-speaking communities. Beginning in Carmarthen town, the audience were ferried by bus out and into the land of Carmarthenshire itself (the title of the piece) and the Carmarthen County Museum at Abergwili. The house in which the museum is situated was once the palace of the bishop of St David's, where the New Testament was first translated into Welsh. The performance presents a dramatic play, situated episodically around the museum. The play is a family scenario following the father's death, when the children articulate their inability or unwillingness to take on the farm, and tells of the erosion of agricultural ways of life, specifically the decline of traditional dairy farming. The dramatic scenes are interspersed with installations – short video episodes showing rural traditions, visible as the audience moves between rooms. That the museum is based in a house complicates the representation. It is possible to see clearly the rooms' original function – the kitchen, the hall and so on – which gives the performance an unexpected sense of theatricality. The fact that we are also in a museum, however, and that artefacts of local importance are exhibited, places the audience in a position of gazing on, and is slightly at odds with the dramatic representation. The exhibitionary context establishes a distanciation – we are witnesses to a dramatisation of historical fact, but we are never too close to the drama. At one point only do the empty house, the museum and the dramatic content coalesce in a haunting scene in the kitchen, where the mother sees her dead husband as a young man and washes his body. The final funeral scene in the palace chapel is the closest moment of integration between audience and event, where we sit in pews and sing, participating in a familiar scene. This momentary recognition is shattered by the appearance of the father's ghost, come to warn us that the old ways must be kept alive. That his message is a pipe dream is irrelevant; the paradox at work is the unnerving contrast between the plight of the farm and the fact that we are distanced by the installation – we are looking on, witnessing as unseen and passive observers, unable to change the events as they unfold in the cold glare of the museum's exhibits. Memory here is employed in order to consider carefully and rationally the consequences of turning away from a former way of life and all it represents. There is no deep process of remembrance, but there is a hard look at the consequences of changes in ways of life due to demographic shifts and changing social contexts. This is brought home prophetically in the words on the funeral leaflet we are given during the final scene, 'Daw Pawb a Phopeth ym Mhobman i Ben / Everything, Everyone, Everywhere Ends.' This is performance as commemorative act for a way of life, but it does not, for me, engage with memory, and nothing is internalised. The mimetic playing out of dramatic scenes may be responsible for this and the production, despite itself, takes us into a representation of a crisis, rather than an awareness that it is happening now. Mimesis is not forthcoming in supplying material for collective memory because as a form it is associated with the discursive internal world of the closed drama. While this form has historically offered the opportunity for a reflection on life, it is becoming increasingly difficult for it to do so after the problematisation of representation that manifested itself in Welsh contemporary performance at the end of the twentieth century. The stark reality at the end of *Tir Sir Gâr*, where we depart having accepted that everything must end, leads on to the question of the role of memory as constituted in performance and in a world of unravelling social circumstances. What is the role of collective memory here, if it does not support the continuation of ourselves as people? Perhaps the internalisation of memory and place will happen under a different set of performative circumstances altogether.

Crossings in performance and technology: memory and *kinesis* in the work of Eddie Ladd

Some of the most important performance work in relation to questions of people, memory and place has, to an extent, taken place in the national theatres' shadow, and in the performance work of Eddie Ladd.

Although Ladd has collaborated with Theatr Genedlaethol Cymru on a production, *Dawns Ysbrydion* (2015), and was a performer in *{150}*, the National Theatre Wales and ThGC joint production, it is her own solo work that resonates most implicitly with questions of identity and memory in relation to home, nationness and embodiment.[91] These elements present themselves increasingly through the use of specific technologies often used in order to locate a junction between image and the process of creating an image and, by implication, between identity and the process through which it is constituted. Ladd's work accesses ideas regarding the subjugation of people and unfolds them through an intermedial process, where the actor's performance in time is emplaced to interact with technology in such a way as to invoke memory, through the body – in tandem with other textual elements – the choreography, the music, the spatial makeup of the site, the words and the energy. In one of her best-known performance pieces, *Scarface** (2000),[92] Ladd reworks the persona of Al Pacino's Tony Montana from Brian de Palma's film *Scarface* (1983), to camera, in front of a CSO (colour separation overlay) blue screen, the results of which are mixed live with sound and superimposed on to a film, shown on a different screen, of her parents' farm – her childhood home – in Cardiganshire. The audience watch the 'end product' at the same time as they watch Ladd's live movements before the camera in a triangular demarcated area. The film begins with a panning shot of an elderly couple washing a car on a yard in front of a farmhouse. They are Ladd's parents, but the imagery seems so mundane that this information is not immediately of importance to the audience member. The audience are at this time also given the bold title 'SCARFACE*' across the screen, as the camera moves through the door into the porch and further into the house, and a heavily pulsing drone by Welsh hip hop group Tystion is heard turning the empty domestic setting into an ominous and almost dramatic space. This is the point of realisation that the compositional aspects have begun to merge. The initial opening statement by the performer, spoken live, 'This is my gift to Al Pacino. / This is where I am from. We're going to do it here', is a confessional moment announcing the thoroughly embodied nature of the performance. It is also the first signpost that the performance will merge site, place and questions of identity in colliding moments of compressed and juxtaposing signs.[93] Ladd's live movements in front of the camera on stage are captured and transposed on to her home 'background' film as we watch, in a haunting and violent meditation on colonial oppression, in which the power struggles associated with nationness (in relation to Wales/ UK and Cuba/USA) are reflected against each other. Ladd 'becomes' actor Al Pacino playing Cuban drug lord Tony Montana, meticulously reworking his physicality and intonation, so that the entire sequence including stunts, is performed to camera. Such is the investment in the live performance, with much energy tightly contained within a very specific frame and range of movement, that this could also be understood as a study in acting for camera. The 'seen in the moment' mechanics of the entire performance emphasise character as construction, but the fully assimilated piece, shown on the composite screen, is a cinematic imagining of the self as fantastical character juxtaposed against a rural landscape. *Scarface** acknowledges ideas of memory and nationness and what it means to reject, need or hold on to a sense of home. It reveals deep desires regarding emplacement that reverberate in the performer's body, against the very place (on screen) in which she was raised. While the contrast between Ladd's rural home in Cardiganshire and the Hollywood tale of a gangster's brutal life and inevitable fall seems paradoxical, these disparate elements are far more congruent and compatible than they at first appear. Much of the aesthetic interest of the piece derives from this juxtaposition. Ladd has made several references to the postcolonial interpretation of the piece, and the correlation between a 'peasant' from Cuba (as referred to in Brian de Palma's film) and one from Wales.[94] Jodie Allinson refers to this as 'the experience of the colonized subject who aspires to the ideals as displayed by the colonizing culture', and describes the way the production explores this aspect in terms of its intermediality.[95] This is complex Welsh- and English-language performance, which deals directly with the Welsh speaker's predicament, yet also recognises the pull or extension of an 'American Wales', the culture most associated with industrialised and urbanised south Wales.[96] Ladd's home near Aberporth, located in a predominantly Welsh-speaking area, is removed from this experience yet the effects of Anglo-American culture on the self we desire to be is inescapable. Ladd's work shatters the conventional clichés regarding language and place in Wales and shows the Welsh speaker as utterly complicit in the desire to be different, or other than (myself) – not only in relation to the language of the oppressor, but also in terms of the globalising forces of mass media and their influence on individual identity. *Scarface** divulges the fact that to make sense of identity we must reveal and acknowledge the way in which we seek to project such images of ourselves.

This aspect is developed further in *Club Luz* (2002), a performance set during club night in which the audience sits in an auditorium watching a single performer (Ladd) on a raised platform covered with a reflective black floor. Twelve electro songs are played throughout. Samuel Fuller's B-movie *Shock Corridor* (1963) is the background film, in which the character of Trent, a black man institutionalised in a mental hospital, believes himself to be white and a Grand Wizard of the Ku Klux Klan. What transpires before us is a carefully constructed performance in which the condition portrayed in the film is transposed to a current Welsh context through embodiment. Ladd dances and sings into a microphone on a stand, which at first seems innocuously straightforward, but the self-possessed movements and the songs start to leak a certain desperation, and the lone performer 'walks the theme through songs on the colonised split brain, alienation, aspiration, grief, extreme solutions and the redemptive power of pop' (explained in Welsh as 'gwaredigaeth canu pop a'r SRG' – the deliverance of pop music and the Welsh Rock Scene).[97] In the interweaving of music, film and choreography Ladd faces the aspirational anguish involved in attempting to assume the Other that we desire to be; she struts at the microphone with confidence, but the self-assured nature of the performance is questioned within itself, breaks down and becomes a repetitive action that pains the body. The unrelenting nature of the movement becomes literally breath-taking, such is its pace, adding to the sense of hopeless desire. There is a return to a quietude of certainty though, felt through the desire mediated by the music, which holds *Club Luz* in check. This is perhaps what Ladd is referring to when she talks of redemption through pop music. A meditation on a condition deeply embedded in Welsh identity, the performance prises apart the anxiety and self-loathing of an induced colonial state. The uniqueness of this work is that it feels like a resistance to a process of interpella-tion in Welsh culture, where the self becomes fixated on the Other (in whose gaze I gain identity). Here the Other could be described as the colonial Other of Anglo-American popular culture, seemingly superficial enough to be negligible, but masking a greater and more insidious imperial force with which it is associated, that of the British state and its negation of Welsh identity. This is a hegemony in which the oppressed not only tolerate their oppression but are complicit in it. Ladd's work, which deals head on with these processes, ultimately rejects this position for the self, and through a process of complex mirroring, turns the situation on its head, reformulating the relationship of power, or disarming it as it is pulled apart in the work itself. There is no removal of the oppressed, but a raging against it which places her performances in the realm of the redemptive, the work a study in complicity, rage and transformation. Any sense of an inferiority complex revealed in the work, in which the self is evaluated according to the values of the coloniser, is blown apart by the inventiveness of the artwork. What this does for the spectator is to pry open and discomfort notions of complicity in forms of subjugation, and the experience is ultimately affirming. In this process, memory is reconstituted, is no longer simply an object of the past that encapsulates past traditions or identities, but a reassembling – memory refracted through a contemporary rendering of what it means to be Welsh. This is solo work that has the quality of parable or even an individual confessional, and in experiencing it we become absolved.

Ladd's work also deals explicitly with the concept of place and space. In a series of works bearing the name 'Stafell' (Room), the result of a NESTA award and collaboration with media and technology artist Michael Day in exploring web-based performance, Ladd created three pieces on the idea of a room, mediated through different technologies.[98] These works emplace deeply felt conundrums around Welsh identity alongside history regarding the colonial power relations between Wales and the British government into different spatial forms. Across the three *Stafell* productions this network of relationships, played out in space, is witnessed live (by an audience, an individual cameraman, a choreographer, as well as the performer herself). It is mediated by film and emplaced further into a perpetual loop in time on the Internet and placed into a responsive digital environment during live performance, all of which entangles and confounds notions of space in relation to the series of performances and complicates the idea of place. In the first piece, *Stafell A* (2003), Ladd created a 24-minute piece of choreography to a soundtrack and within a three-room set based on Roman Polanski's psychological horror film *Repulsion* (1965), which follows a young woman, played by Catherine Deneuve, during her spell staying in her sister's apartment as she starts to relive traumas of her past. *Stafell B* (2004), a live show, incorporated dance to the accompaniment of music and text material heard on headsets. The text

16. *Stafell C*. Eddie Ladd performs on the set built for the three pieces of the *Stafell* project with a view of *Stafell C*, the completed work, in foreground.
Photo: © Keith Morris/*www.artswebwales.com*

is multilayered and diverse, including material on Owain Williams's bombing of the Tryweryn reservoir site in 1963, elements of Catherine Deneuve's performance in the film *Repulsion* and material relating to the presence of MI5 in a Welsh-language hall of residence at the University College of Wales Aberystwyth. Images from this performance are set into a permanent website, which randomly mixes the images and sound in an endless continuation of the piece as an online artwork; no two viewings of the work online can ever be the same. In *Stafell C* (2006), Ladd worked within a responsive digital environment designed by Michael Day. The dance movement and music are improvised in the moment of performance. The live constituent is set alongside video material by Lee Hassall, who operates the roaming camera during the performance. Working with Hassall, or next to him, is choreographer Margaret Ames, who responds to Ladd's work in the moment of live performance, moving between active engagement as witness-commentator and onlooker. Ladd describes Ames's role as moving 'between supporting that performance and watching almost in the same way as the audience which negotiates between the live work and the setting as it likes'.[99] The audience also negotiate between the view of the wide set, the performer's movements within it and the work captured on screen. All three *Stafell* works deal explicitly with memory and confound its relationship with space in performance. *Stafell B* in particular unsettles this relationship by removing human agency almost completely. The web-based iteration repeats in different patterns the constituent elements of the work that have been captured electronically, and the random and arbitrary combination of signs takes the work out of the context of the personal and the located and into the realms of cyberspace. It is a new art work. This is a re-emplacing of the work as formal artwork, devoid of place, memory, and identity. Or is it? For the people who understand its context the significance cannot be removed, and the random cyclical composition, much like a prayer wheel, reinforces and repeats the original performance's meaning as it has been explained to us (either in performance or by association through explanation by Ladd while the Internet piece is viewed).[100] As the performance deals with issues of paranoia and trauma in the context of Welsh identity, its random and endless reformation accelerates and intensifies the assertion of these issues. It is as though its arbitrary and unplanned quality gives it its own life, free from the need of continual personal articulation, which unwittingly strengthens what we believe it articulates and gives it energy of its own. In this endless performance, which combines notions of place associated with Welsh culture, with formal space (the rooms) and the cyberspace of the Internet, something shifts and we understand the value of performance as *kinesis*, the breaking and reworking of the performance and its emplacement into a different space. This is performance as cultural intervention, where the implicit meaning of the work diminishes through time even as we cleave to what we understand to be its essential meaning. It leaves us in an entirely different place from conceptions of performance that root us to specific place; it upsets the concept of memory completely, is not governed by the performer and yet is a variation of Ladd's own artistic construct. According to Alice Rayner, cyberspace 'offers more than a new landscape for performance; it challenges the very meaning of "space"', for what performance in cyberspace is able to achieve is a resistance to space, or a resituating of it 'in the fugitive dimension of time'. [101] By locating her apparently endlessly forming performance in cyberspace, Ladd makes a claim for the role of time in relation to the artwork, and even though the piece will diminish in the end, its recurrent reformulation on the

Internet is, for the time being, a statement of the fragility of the art-work. Ultimately, even in its computerised and seemingly impersonal rerouted permutations, the piece reminds us of the deep and binding connections between people, memory and place, connections that we insist are emplaced within this artwork, even when they are all but banished from the medium. The central quality of this work, that of time, ensures that we are able to bind ourselves to a semblance of memory of the work, whatever our vantage point, through experience of the piece in the moment, now. This piece sits in a peculiar relation to performance on the Internet, or 'cyberformance', which Christina Papagiannouli defines as 'the intermedial negotiation between theatre and Internet', with 'liveness and interactivity' its main characteristics, based on the live nature of theatre and the interactive medium of the Internet. Papagiannouli asserts that in cyberformance, 'liveness is no longer an aesthetic choice, but rather a basic trait that is directly con-nected to the interactive and participatory character of the Internet, as without real-time engagement the notion of co-presence is weak, and thus, liveness is meaningless.'[102] Ladd's *Stafell* takes us further into a deep consideration on the nature of liveness and interactivity in rela-tion to the work. Unlike usual cyberformance, in which there is a live exchange between participants, the performance in *Stafell*, if it is a performance and irrespective of whether or not it is watched, exists in its own space and time, set apart from the spectator in an endless random loop, which becomes meaningful as and when the spectator endows it with meaning, probably during the act of watching it. Or does the very fact that we know it to be repeating itself ad infinitum mean that this artwork becomes itself as artwork through its very repetition? In its ambiguous status as artwork – (where does it exists and for whom?) the piece serves as a meditation on the act of recep-tion. The computer-run 'performance' seems to release us from the necessity of interpretation, but does nothing to relieve the process of attempting to define the artwork in relation to ourselves, which happens in our mind even when we are not present before it. Such is the power of that which has been internalised by us in the moment of remembering.

AFTERWORD

The chapters within this book, though pursuing different manifestations of the performance of Welsh culture – through museum exhibit, heritage performance, festival and theatre – have attempted to locate performance as a general and unifying function of Welsh culture, a function that both reveals and sustains distinct relationships between people, memory and place. While it could be said that all culture is performative, a position taken up within performance studies and anthropology, my stance here is that, for the most part, the performance of culture in the Welsh context reveals an urgent desire to redefine tradition, to perform heritage anew, to review and re-articulate the meaning of identity through the fluidity of festival or the experimental space of theatre performance, in which identity can be freely explored. This is not necessarily due to a desire to represent a Wales that is perpetually emergent, always on the precipice of existence and willed into being. Rather, this drive to culturally reinvent is an inherent shape-shifting characteristic within Welsh culture. Its capacity to reconstruct and redefine in specific social contexts is responsible for the creative scope of Welsh culture as it mediates questions of identity – who we are, how we talk about ourselves, how we remember and recall our relationship with others and with our history. Emyr Humphreys follows this creative drive in his book *The Taliesin Tradition*, which concentrates on a particular thread, that of the poetic tradition. This tradition has an implicit connection with the performative aspects of culture; the *cyfarwydd* or storyteller-poet was an accomplished performer who carried the oral tradition into the literary form in the sixth century, when it first became written tradition. While evidence of the 'Taliesinic' is present through the centuries, its most remarkable quality, according to Humphreys, is the 'less conspicuous . . . manner in which at all times it has contrived to be a major factor in the maintenance, stability, and continuity of the Welsh identity and the fragile concept of Welsh nationhood'.[1] The poetic tradition is defined by Humphreys in terms of a powerful tendency that exceeds 'a conservative expression of poetic art' (p. 3). Indeed, he defines its more profound function as being 'a crucible of myth', with the construction of myth a necessary 'major creative activity among a people with unnaturally high expectations reduced by historic necessity, or at least history, forced into what is often described as a marginal condition' (p. 3). Here the force of the poetic tradition echoes the function of *poiesis*, that of unfolding a thing out of itself, of unveiling what is already there, of a transformation or threshold occasion when something moves away from its standing as one thing to become another. More than its literal meaning (to make), *poiesis* refers to the creative emergence of that which is in the process of being made, as in a moment of flowering, or of birth.

Humphreys also elaborates on the way in which the poetic tradition sustains a sense of authority and power 'sufficient to breathe forms of life into the national being when independent military and political power have long withered away' (p. 2). While culture becomes a supreme carrier for identity when the political will towards self-determination is weak or not forthcoming, the chief role of the performance of culture for the Welsh people has been to allow a place for voicing identity in such a way that what is performed becomes internalised, a part of the way in which we come to understand who we are. This internalisation is related to how implicated we have become in the very processes of culture. This is not culture as set apart from the people, as remote or situated on higher ground; this is culture as belonging to the people, not as content, substance or form, but as a living breathing reflective relationship inhabited by people in the moment of performance. The performance of culture is not a substitute for the political reality of Wales, even though there seems to be an assumed correlation between the vitality of Welsh culture and a lack of political self-determination, as though the overflow of culture ensures a strength of identity missing in the political realm. While Wales is not yet a completely self-confident political entity, its multitudinous culture has ensured the perpetuation of the idea of Wales through performance, in and between the people who participate in it. This is not to say that Wales exists because it is performed into being; it is rather a recognition of the fact that the powerful and incontrovertible force of culture is manifestation of the people them-selves as *cenedl*.

Events taking place in the sphere of heritage at the time of writing point towards the need for a greater understanding of the implications of heritage for the definition of who we are. The announcement of an 'iron ring' sculpture at Flint Castle, to celebrate the 'year of legends', as Visit Wales, the tourist arm of the Welsh Government has called 2017, has resulted in strong condemnation from a substantial num-ber of commentators and the public. The result of a million-pound competition announced in 2016 by CADW, the body responsible for safeguarding scheduled listed monuments in Wales, in collaboration with the Welsh Government, the contentious design made direct ref-erence to the encircling of Wales by strategically positioned castles built by Edward I, the English king who was to bring about the polit-ical assimilation of Wales into England. Designed by Gloucestershire and London based architects, it referred to the iron ring, literally and figuratively. It bluntly acknowledged the annexation and con-quest of Wales by England and without a trace of awareness of the implications and significance of this history to contemporary Welsh identity. Instead, the statement released following the furore around its announcement coolly referenced the idea that artworks may be con-tentious and, with a postmodern ambivalence, refused to acknowledge any implicit meaning for local people. An initial statement alluding to Shakespearean heritage, with reference to the play *Richard II* and the surrendering of Richard's crown to Henry IV at Flint Castle, located the Welsh site and the proposed sculpture within the English tourism circuit. Those responsible for the artwork were either unaware of the contemporary cultural connotations or felt certain that the historical distance (between the thirteenth century and today) precluded any deeply-felt meaning in the present. Indeed, some who championed such an artistic intervention in Flint at any cost seemed to be entirely ambivalent to the sculpture as artwork, preferring to support the plan as an example of government investment in the area, one that was bound to bring tourist footfall and jobs. Such an attitude seemed to be oblivious to the way in which Welsh communal memory has been sustained through the idea of place and revealed in performances that connect people and their memory of place. The breakdown of commu-nication between people, government agencies, and an architectural company exemplified the collapse in understanding that is possible when heritage is reframed according to values that are entirely alien to the meaning internalised by people through collective memory. People define their identities in the relationship of memory and place, and seek to participate in performances that reference this relationship. That the ethical, let alone the cultural implications of emplacing an iron ring sculpture at the site of a castle in Wales were not understood reveals the work that remains to be done in translating experiences of being Welsh.

Performance is a vital, necessary activity in the process of defining ourselves to each other. Its ephemerality makes it appear as though it is lost after the event, and because its presence is so fleeting, the significance of performance is frequently overlooked. In actuality, performances that bind people, memory and place are expressions of cultural ideas, beliefs and tendencies and reveal the ways in which a community of people define themselves and attend to change. Disclosing much more than social values and relationships, such performances reveal how cultural identity is constituted over and over through a constant process of participation. It is the performance of culture and the very processes involved in its playing out between multiple participants that support the ability to deal with change and to enable a transformative experience for members of the group.

NOTES

Introduction

1. Dwight Conquergood, *Cultural Struggles: Performance, Ethnography, Praxis* (Ann Arbor: University of Michigan Press, 2013), pp. 15–25 (p. 18).
2. Conquergood, *Cultural Struggles*, p. 43.
3. Elin Diamond, *Performance and Cultural Politics* (London: Routledge, 1996), p. 1.
4. See Richard Schechner, *Performance Studies: An Introduction* (London: Routledge, 2002) p. 1.
5. Victor Turner, *From Ritual to Theatre: The Human Seriousness of Play* (New York: PAJ Publications, 1982).
6. Clifford Geertz, *The Interpretation of Cultures: Selected Essays* (New York: Basic Books, 1973).
7. 'Cultural specialists': used by the anthropologist Milton Singer to describe those trained or paid to take part in cultural performances. Milton uses the term to refer to the performers themselves but it could equally be used to refer to all participants in cultural performance, especially if the performance is defined as a collaboration between its participants. Milton Singer, *When a Great Tradition Modernizes: An Anthropological Approach to Indian Civilization* (Chicago: University of Chicago Press, 1972).
8. Victor Turner, *The Ritual Process: Structure and Anti-Structure* (Ithaca: Cornell University Press, 1977), p. 337.
9. Conquergood, *Cultural Struggles*, p. 17.
10. D. Conquergood, 'Poetics, Play, Process and Power: The Performative Turn in Anthropology', *Text and Performance Quarterly*, 1 (1989), 82–95 (83).
11. Conquergood, *Cultural Struggles*, p. 56. *Poiesis*, from the ancient Greek, to make, is the process of reconciling thought with matter and time (and hence the root of 'poetry'). In relation to the work of art it is to bring something from concealment into the created work, a process of unveiling in order that something can be known and led into presence. For Martin Heidegger, it is a type of threshold occasion where something moves away from itself to become something other, a kind of bringing forth that is

capable of producing community understanding. Martin Heidegger, 'The Origin of the Work of Art' (1950), *Basic Writings* (London: Routledge, 1993), pp. 139–212.

12. Turner, *From Ritual to Theatre*. Turner had formulated crucial ideas on the nature of 'social drama' and on cultural performance, providing an analysis of humankind as *homo performans*, an influential theory of life as performance.

13. Homi K. Bhabha, *The Location of Culture* (London: Routledge, 1994), pp. 146–9; referred to in Conquergood, *Cultural Struggles*, p. 57.

14. Conquergood, *Cultural Struggles*, p. 57.

15. Edward Said, *Orientalism* (Harmondsworth: Penguin Books, 1979), p. 93, quoted in Conquergood, *Cultural Struggles*, p. 47.

16. Conquergood, *Cultural Struggles*, p. 48.

17. Jane Aaron, *The Welsh Survival Gene: The 'Despite Culture' in the Two Language Communities of Wales*, National Eisteddfod Lecture (Cardiff, Institute of Welsh Affairs, 2003), p. 1.

18. See further and in relation to literature specifically, M. Wynn Thomas, *Internal Difference: Literature in Twentieth-Century Wales* (Cardiff: University of Wales Press, 1992) and M. Wynn Thomas, *Corresponding Cultures: The Two Literatures of Wales* (Cardiff: University of Wales Press, 1999).

19. According to the 2011 Census, 19% of the population of Wales speaks Welsh. In Gwynedd, a predominantly Welsh-speaking county, 65.4% (77,000) of the population speaks Welsh, while in Cardiff it is only 11.1% (36,735) and in Swansea 11.4% (26,332). We see this pattern across Wales, where traditionally Welsh-speaking heartlands have a relatively high percentage of Welsh speakers (Ceredigion 47.3% or 34,964 people; Carmarthen 43.9% or 78,048 people), meaning that here one can habitually exist through the medium of Welsh, whereas the percentages in counties in the south-east are low. However, there is a significant number of Welsh speakers in the south-east (Rhondda Cynon Taf 12.3% or 27,779 people; Caerphilly 11.2% or 19,251 people; Neath Port Talbot 15.3% or 20,698 people); while the combined number in the counties further east (Blaenau Gwent, Torfaen, Monmouthshire, Newport) is 35,707. The gradual increase in the south-east can be attributed to the success of Welsh-medium education.

20. *The Cambridge History of British Theatre*, edited by Baz Kershaw (2004), is one of the few comprehensive texts to consider Welsh and Scottish drama alongside the English, and within which Welsh contributions deal explicitly with Welsh- and English-language theatre.

21. Raymond Williams, *Problems in Materialism and Culture* (London: Verso, 1980), p. 43.

22. The AHRC-funded research project on Welsh performance, 'What's Welsh for Performance?', led by Heike Roms, took its provocative name

from this well-debated issue. See *www.performance-wales.org* (accessed 9 October 2015).
23. See Simon Shepherd, *The Cambridge Introduction to Performance Theory* (Cambridge University Press, 2016), p. vii.
24. Turner, *From Ritual to Theatre*, p. 91.
25. 'Theatr', *Geiriadur Prifysgol Cymru: A Dictionary of the Welsh Language*, Rhan LXI (Cardiff: University of Wales Press, 2002), p. 3690.
26. 'Perfformiad', *Geiriadur Prifysgol Cymru*, Cyfrol III (1987–1998), pp. 2273–4.

Chapter 1: People, memory and place: ideas for a consideration of Welsh performance
1. P. Morgan, 'Keeping the Legends Alive', in T. Curtis (ed.), *Wales: The Imagined Nation, Essays in Cultural and National Identity* (Bridgend: Poetry Wales Press, 1986), pp. 19–41 (p. 22).
2. Morgan, 'Keeping the Legends Alive' p. 19.
3. The census of 1911 shows for the first time a decline in Welsh speakers, relative to the population.
4. T. Brennan, 'The national longing for form', in Homi K. Bhabha (ed.), *Nation and Narration* (London: Routledge, 1990), pp. 44–70 (p. 45).
5. Raymond Williams, *The Year 2000* (New York: Pantheon, 1983), quoted in Brennan, 'The national longing for form', p. 45.
6. Benedict Anderson, *Imagined Communities, Reflections on the Origin and Spread of Nationalism* (London: Verso, 1983). Anderson's idea of 'imagined communities' posits connections between building the nation and historical memory and at the same time constitutes a significant attack on essentialist models of culture. For Anderson, nation states give expression to nations that seem to 'always loom out of an immemorial past, and still more important, glide into a limitless future' (p. 19). In this, nations are 'imagined' not because they don't actually exist or are false, but specifically because they are a form of community, and it follows that not even the community of 'the smallest nation' will know, meet or hear about 'most of their fellow-members . . . yet in the minds of each lives the image of their communion' (p. 15). Anderson also notes that nations are imagined as limited, being defined by borders or boundaries, and sovereign, that is, having legislative authority. It seems that for Anderson, the imagined tradition exists to serve the perpetuation of the nation, which is already defined and delimited in terms of its territory and legislation.
7. Brennan, 'The national longing for form', p. 47.
8. R. Williams, 'Wales and England', in D. G. Williams (ed.), *Who Speaks for Wales?* (Cardiff: University of Wales Press, 2003), pp. 16–26 (p. 23).
9. J. R. Jones, *Prydeindod* (Llandybïe: Llyfrau'r Dryw, 1966), p. 9.
10. Jones, *Prydeindod*, p. 14. Translation my own.

11. Jones also stated that it would not be enough to add the bind of self-government to the interpenetration of language and land in order to fulfil the conditions of formal nationhood, because such conditions could be given to us by an external power (i.e. the British state). In whichever way independence should arise, Wales would not be ready until the will to full nationhood is awakened in the people. J. R. Jones, *A Raid i'r Iaith ein Gwahanu?* (Talybont: Y Lolfa, 1978), pp. 10–11.

12. The immediate impact of devolved government on culture included the forging of cultural flagships in the form of national bodies and companies such as Theatr Genedlaethol Cymru and National Theatre Wales and at the same time involved policy changes and new laws, such as the Welsh Language Measure of 2011. Despite these developments, however, the consequences of devolution for culture more generally are still emerging and this is partly because cultural institutions formed by Arts Council policy take time to establish their orbits of influence and grow into their creative stances in tandem with the movements of culture at large. See Anwen Jones's work on the emergence and development of new national theatres, Anwen Jones, *National Theatres in Context: France, Germany, England and Wales* (Cardiff: University of Wales Press, 2007) and A. Jones, 'Cymru, cenedligrwydd a theatr genedlaethol: dilyn y gwys neu dorri cwys newydd?', in A. Jones and L. Lewis (eds), *Ysgrifau ar Theatr a Pherfformio* (Cardiff: University of Wales Press, 2013), pp. 103–18.

13. Homi K. Bhabha, 'DissemiNation: time, narrative, and the margins of the modern nation' in Homi K. Bhabha (ed.), *Nation and Narration*, pp. 291–322, p. 292.

14. Homi K. Bhabha, *The Location of Culture* (London: Routledge, 1994), p. 140.

15. Waldo Williams, 'Cofio', *Dail Pren* (Aberystwyth: Gwasg Aberystwyth, 1957), p. 78. Translated by A. Llwyd as 'One fleeting moment as the sun is setting, one gentle moment as the night falls fast, / To bring to mind the things that are forgotten, Now scattered in the dust of ages past.' Cymdeithas Waldo Williams (the Waldo Williams Society); see *www.waldowilliams.com* [accessed 30 October 2015].

16. Paul Connerton, *How Societies Remember* (Cambridge: Cambridge University Press, 1989), pp. 39–40.

17. See Maurice Halbwachs, *On Collective Memory* (London: University of Chicago Press, 1992); first published as *Les cadres sociaux de la mémoire* (Paris: Presses Universitaires de France, 1952).

18. Aleida Assmann, 'Re-framing memory. Between individual and collective forms of constructing the past', in K. Tilmans et al. (eds), *Performing the Past. Memory, History and Identity in modern Europe* (Amsterdam University Press, 2010), pp. 35–50 (p. 36).

19. Samuel Beckett, *Endgame* (London: Faber and Faber, 2009 [1958]), pp. 12, 22.

20. Joseph Roach, *Cities of the Dead, Circum-Atlantic Performance* (New York: Columbia University Press, 1996), pp. 3–4.

21. Herbert Blau, *The Audience* (Baltimore: Johns Hopkins University Press, 1990), p. 382, quoted in Roach, *Cities of the Dead*, pp. 3–4.

22. Marvin Carlson, *The Haunted Stage: The Theatre as Memory Machine* (Ann Arbor: University of Michigan Press, 2003), p. 2.

23. E. Diamond (ed.), *Performance and Cultural Politics* (London: Routledge, 1996), p. 1.

24. Erika Fischer-Lichte, *The Transformative Power of Performance: A New Aesthetics* (London: Routledge, 2008).

25. Aleida Assmann, *Cultural Memory and Western Civilization: Functions, Media, Archives* (Cambridge: Cambridge University Press, 2011), p. 19.

26. Diana Taylor, *The Archive and The Repertoire, Performing Cultural Memory in the Americas* (Durham and London: Duke University Press, 2003), p. 143.

27. Hebrews, 12:1, *New English Bible*, p. 289.

28. Waldo Williams, 'Pa Beth yw Dyn?', *Dail Pren*, p. 67, translated by E. Humphreys in M. Elfyn and J. Rowlands (eds), *The Bloodaxe Book of Modern Welsh Poetry* (Northumberland: Bloodaxe Books, 2003), p. 129.

29. J. R. Jones, *Ac Onide, Ymdriniaeth mewn ysgrif a phregeth ar argyfwng y Gymru gyfoes* (Llandybïe: Llyfrau'r Dryw, 1970), p. 137. Translation my own.

30. *Trioedd Ynys Prydain* (The Triads of the Island of Britain) is a collection of related texts from the medieval period, found in various manuscripts, which form a summary of Welsh bardic knowledge on the mythology, folklore and early traditions and histories of Wales and the Island of Britain. As with other triads, the rhetorical form is classified into units of three listing names of traditional heroes and events, and each triad is given a heading indicating the thematic link of the three entities on the list. The triads operated as an aide memoire for the bard in remembering myths and legends and the traditions related to them. The early bard was a *cyfarwydd* (storyteller) as much as a poet and bardic lore was transferred via oral tradition. Thus, the triads were an essential part of the bard's training and knowledge. See Rachel Bromwich (ed.), *Trioedd Ynys Prydein. The Welsh Triads* (Cardiff: University of Wales Press, 1978).

31. The bardic tradition, in essence a performative practice, is the basis for one of the earliest forms of European literature and operated *as* memory as well as being dependent on it. The ancient meaning of the word *cerdd* (poetry or music in contemporary Welsh use) was 'art' or 'craft', though according to John Morris-Jones the word did not retain this meaning except in the phrases *cerdd dafod* (poetry, literally 'the art of the tongue'), and *cerdd dant* (a musical form, literally 'string arts'). John Morris-Jones, *Cerdd Dafod* (Oxford: Clarendon Press, 1925; Cardiff: University of Wales Press, 1980), p. v.

32. J. R. Jones, *Ac Onide*, pp. 138–9. Translation my own.

33. R. Williams, 'Welsh Culture', in D. G. Williams (ed.), *Who Speaks for Wales?*, pp. 5–11 (p. 5).
34. R. S. Thomas, 'Reservoirs', from *Selected Poems 1946–1968* (London: Granada, 1983), p. 117.
35. S. M. Low, 'Embodied Space(s), Anthropological Theories of Body, Space and Culture, *Space and Culture*, 6/9 (2003), 9–18 (10).
36. Low, 'Embodied Space(s), Anthropological Theories of Body, Space and Culture', 15, in reference to the work and ideas of S. Rockefeller, *Where are you going? Work, power and movement in the Bolivian Andes* (unpublished PhD dissertation, University of Chicago, 2001).
37. See Edward Casey, *Remembering, A Phenomenological Study* (Bloomington: Indiana University Press, 2000), p. 184.
38. Describing the moment of his fight with 'Giant Death', the poet tells of the croak of the raven from Pendist Mawr Crag on Snowdon's slopes and the cries that will come too from Nant-y-Betws and Drws-y-Coed and from Cae'r Gors bridge when the result of 'the contest' is announced. He tells of a scar appearing on the face of Llyn Cwellyn and on Llyn y Gadair, a wrinkle that wasn't there before; of a crack that appears in the gable-end of Tŷ'r Ysgol when the news is told in the telephone's ear; of a crick that will come to Snowdonia's muscles, and the cramp of his death flowing through the Gwyrfai River. And lest we read this as the proud conceits of a mad-man, he explains – there are pieces of himself scattered across '*y fro*'. T. H. Parry-Williams, *Detholiad o Gerddi* (Llandysul: Gwasg Gomer, 1972), p. 110. See also R. Gerallt Jones, *Writers of Wales: T. H. Parry-Williams* (Cardiff: University of Wales Press, 1978), pp. 95–6.
39. Waldo Williams, *Dail Pren*, p. 93; see also, *The Peacemakers: Selected Poems*, translated by Tony Conran (Llandysul: Gomer Press, 1997), pp. 120–1.
40. J. R. Jones was influenced by theologian Paul Tillich's 'crisis of meaning-lessness'; see Paul Tillich, *The Courage to Be* (London: Yale University Press, 1952).
41. In this Jones was influenced by Simone Weil's *L'Enracinement, Prélude a une déclaration des devoir envers l'être humain* (Paris: Gallimard, 1949), translated to English as *The Need for Roots, Prelude towards a declaration of duties towards mankind* (London: Routledge and Kegan Paul, 1952).
42. J. R. Jones, *Ac Onide*, p. 155. Translation my own.
43. Henri Lefebvre, *The Production of Space* (Oxford: Blackwell, 1991), pp. 93–4.
44. H. Lefebvre, 'Reflections on the politics of space' in R. Peet (ed.), *Radical Geography* (London: Methuen, 1978), p. 224, pp. 339–52 (p. 341).
45. Edward Soja, *Postmodern Geographies, The Reassertion of Space in Critical Social Theory* (London: Verso, 1989).
46. Lucy R. Lippard, *The Lure of the Local, Senses of Place in a Multicentered Society* (New York: New Press, 1997), p. 7.

47. P. Nora and L. D. Kritzman (eds), *Realms of Memory: The Construction of the French Past, Volume 1, Conflicts and Divisions* (New York: Columbia University Press, 1996), p. 14.

48. L. D. Kritzman, Foreword, 'In Remembrance of Things French', in Nora and Kritzman (eds), *Realms of Memory*, p. ix.

49. Nora and Kritzman (eds), *Realms of Memory*, p. 1.

50. John Davies, *A History of Wales* (Harmondsworth: Penguin, 1994); Kenneth O. Morgan, *Rebirth of a Nation: Wales 1880–1980* (Oxford University Press, 1981); Gwyn A. Williams, *When Was Wales? A History of the Welsh* (Harmondsworth: Penguin, 1985).

51. Assmann, *Cultural Memory and Western Civilization*, p. 292.

52. Interview with Baron Elystan-Morgan, *Tryweryn: 50 Years On*, broadcast 19 October 2015, BBC One Wales, 10.35 p.m.

53. In 1956 Liverpool City Council sponsored a private member's bill in order to obtain authority for the flooding of the village of Capel Celyn by Act of Parliament, thereby avoiding the need for planning consent from local Welsh authorities. The bill was passed in 1957, despite the opposition of Welsh MPs. The community of Capel Celyn then spent the following eight years attempting to prevent the decision, to no avail.

54. Assmann, *Cultural Memory and Western Civilization*, p. 292.

Chapter 2: *Amgueddfa*: museum

1. I. Peate, 'Gwerth Amgueddfa', *Lleufer: Cylchgrawn Cymdeithas Addysg y Gweithwyr*, 2/1 (1946), 14–16 (14).

2. The word *amgueddfa* includes the adjective '*cu*' denoting dear or beloved, also used to refer to that which is precious.

3. Edward Williams, *Cyneirlyfr* (1826), quoted in I. Peate, 'Gwerth Amgueddfa', 14. Translation my own.

4. 'Cywreinfa' appeared in *Seren Gomer* and *Y Brython*, cited by I. Peate in 'Gwerth Amgueddfa', 14.

5. Peate, 'Gwerth Amgueddfa', 14. Translation my own.

6. Barbara Kirshenblatt-Gimblett, *Destination Culture: Tourism, Museums and Heritage* (Berkeley and Los Angeles: Routledge, 1998), p. 3.

7. Richard Handler, *Nationalism and the Politics of Culture in Quebec* (Madison: University of Wisconsin Press, 1988), p. 14.

8. S. J. Macdonald, 'Museums, national, postnational and transcultural identities', *Museum and Society*, 1/1 (2003), 3.

9. D. Preziosi and C. Farago (eds), *Grasping the World, the Idea of the Museum* (Aldershot: Ashgate, 2004), p. 13.

10. D. Preziosi, 'Narrativity and the Museological Myths of Nationality', in B. M. Carbonell (ed.), *Museum Studies: An Anthology of Contexts* (Oxford: Wiley-Blackwell, 2012), pp. 82–91 (82).

11. Tony Bennett, *The Birth of the Museum: History, Theory, Politics* (London: Routledge, 1995); see also, E. Cooper-Greenhill, 'The Museum: the socio-historical articulations of knowledge and things' (unpublished PhD thesis, University of London, 1988).

12. Bennett, *The Birth of the Museum*, p. 3.

13. Bennett locates the emergence of the fixed-site amusement park as somewhere between the opposing values attributed to the museum and the travelling fair; see Bennett, *The Birth of the Museum*, pp. 1–13.

14. Bennett refers to James Silk Buckingham's three bills, written in response to the 1834 report by the Select Committee on Drunkenness, proposing that local committees could levy rates in order to establish walks, paths, playgrounds, halls, theatre, libraries, museums and art galleries, so as to 'draw off by innocent pleasurable recreation and instruction, all who can be weaned from habits of drinking.' Bennett, *The Birth of the Museum*, p. 20.

15. Philip Fisher, *Making and Effacing Art: Modern American Art in a Culture of Museums* (Cambridge: Harvard University Press, 1991), p. 7, cited in Michelle Henning, *Museums, Media and Cultural Theory* (Maidenhead: Open University Press, 2006), p. 12.

16. H. R. Leahy, 'Watching me, watching you: performance and performativity in the museum' in A. Jackson and J. Kidd (eds), *Performing Heritage: Research, Practice and Innovation in Museum Theatre and Live Interpretation* (Manchester: University of Manchester Press, 2011), pp. 26–7.

17. Eilean Cooper-Greenhill, *Museums and the Shaping of Knowledge* (London: Routledge, 1992); I. Karp and S. D. Lavine (eds), *Exhibiting Cultures: The Poetics and Politics of Museum Display* (London: Smithsonian Institution Press, 1991); P. Vergo (ed.), *The New Museology* (London: Reaktion Books, 1989).

18. See further J. D. Harrison, 'Ideas of museums in the 1990s', in G. Corsane (ed.), *Heritage, Museums and Galleries* (London: Routledge, 2005), pp. 38–53 (pp. 43–4).

19. Leahy, 'Watching me, watching you: performance and performativity in the museum', p. 27.

20. Nina Simon, *The Participatory Museum* (Santa Cruz, California: Museum 2.0, 2010), p. ii.

21. M. Giebelhausen, 'The architecture *is* the museum', in J. Marstine (ed.), *New Museum Theory and Practice* (Oxford: Blackwell, 2006), p. 42.

22. Bernhard Schneider, *Daniel Libeskind, Jewish Museum Berlin* (London: Prestel, 2007), p. 6.

23. The NMAI is bound to the earth through a variety of references, is aligned with the cardinal directions, references the Native universe and the architecture directs attention towards specific celestial beliefs – the main entrance is east-facing and the central dome opens to the sky.

24. A term used by the Anishinaabe cultural theorist Gerald Vizenor in *Manifest Manners: Narratives on Postindian Survivance* (Nebraska: Bison Books, University of Nebraska Press, 1999). 'Survivance' has become a term of importance in American Indian Studies and is used within the NMAI exhibit.
25. See C. K. Dewhurst, 'Folk Museums', in J. H. Brunvand, *The Study of American Folklore: An Encyclopedia* (London: Taylor & Francis, 1996), pp. 575–7. Also, J. G. Jenkins, 'The Use of Artifacts and Folk Art in the Folk Museum', in R. M. Dorson (ed.), *Folklore and Folklife: An Introduction* (Chicago: University of Chicago Press, 1972), and C. K. Dewhurst, P. Hall and C. Seemann (eds), *Folklife and Museums: Twenty-First Century Perspectives* (London: Rowman & Littlefield Publishers, 2016).
26. Amgueddfa Cymru museums include National Museum Cardiff, St Fagan's National Museum of History, National Waterfront Museum (Swansea), Big Pit National Coal Museum (Blaenafon, Torfaen), National Slate Museum (Llanberis, Gwynedd), National Roman Legion Museum (Caerllion, Newport), and National Wool Museum (Dre-fach Felindre, near Llandysul).
27. Iorwerth Peate, *Canu Chwarter Canrif* (Dinbych: Gwasg Gee, 1963), p. 62. An excerpt from a translation reads: 'Will you come again, old people, to your kitchen / from fold and cowshed, from tending to the crops? / (Hurry up, my girl, and fetch the bellows / to kindle flames within the glowing peat.) / My only answer is the ticking of the clock, / Are they all away from home? . . . tick tock, tick tock.' I. Peate, 'Museum Piece (The old-time kitchen in the National Museum)', translation by J. P. Clancy in M. Elfyn and J. Rowlands (eds), *The Bloodaxe Book of Modern Welsh Poetry, 20th-century Welsh-language poetry in translation* (Northumberland: Bloodaxe Books, 2003), p. 103.
28. Iorwerth Peate, *Amgueddfeydd Gwerin, Folk Museums* (Cardiff: University of Wales Press, 1948), p. 5.
29. Richard Bauman, *Folklore, Cultural Performances, and Popular Entertainments* (Oxford: Oxford University Press, 1992), p. 29.
30. Richard Bauman, *Verbal Art as Performance* (Long Grove, Illinois: Waveland Press Inc., 1977), p. 47.
31. R. Williams, 'Base and Superstructure in Marxist Cultural Theory', *New Left Review*, 82, 3–16 (10–11), quoted by Bauman in *Verbal Art as Performance*, p. 47.
32. P. Burke, 'Popular Culture in Norway and Sweden', *History Workshop*, 3 (1997), 145, cited in Bennett, *The Birth of the Museum*, p. 115.
33. T. Bennett, 'Museums and "the people"', in M. Wallace (ed.) *The Museum Time-Machine* (London: Routledge, 1988), p. 70.
34. M. Sandberg, 'Effigy and narrative: looking into the nineteenth-century folk museum', in L. Charney and V. R. Schwartz (eds), *Cinema and the Invention of Modern Life* (Princeton, N. J.: Princeton University Press, 1995), p. 321.

35. Iorwerth Peate, 'Astudio Bywyd Gwerin: a'i ran mewn amddiffyn gwareiddiad', *Syniadau* (Llandysul: Gwasg Gomer, 1969), pp. 9–23, (23). Translation my own.

36. Peate, 'Astudio Bywyd Gwerin', pp. 9–23; see also I. Peate, 'The Study of Folk Life: and Its Part in the Defense of Civilization', *The Advancement of Science*, 15 (1958), 86–94, reprinted in *Gwerin*, 2/3 (1959), 97–109. Further related writing: I. Peate, 'A Folk Museum for Wales', *Museums Journal*, 34 (1934), 229–31; I. Peate, 'Re-erected Buildings at the Welsh Folk Museum', *Museums Journal*, 52 (1953), 74–6.

37. See John Davies, *The History of Wales* (London: Penguin Books, 1993), pp. 398–508; and Gwyn A. Williams, *When was Wales? A History of the Welsh* (London: Penguin Books, 1985), pp. 173–81.

38. Daniel G. Williams, *Black Skin, Blue Books: African Americans and Wales 1845–1945* (Cardiff: University of Wales Press, 2012), p. 48.

39. Iorwerth Peate, *Diwylliant Gwerin Cymru* (Dinbych: Gwasg Gee, 1975 [1942]), p. 132. Translation my own.

40. Peate, *Diwylliant Gwerin Cymru*, p. 132. Translation my own.

41. Iorwerth Peate, *The Welsh House: A Study in Folk Culture* (Liverpool: Hugh Evans / Brython Press, 1944), p. 4. Italicized in the original.

42. Catrin Stevens, *Iorwerth C. Peate* (Cardiff: University of Wales Press, 1986), p. 29.

43. See I. Peate, 'Welsh Folk Culture', *Welsh Outlook* (1933), 294–7; 'Diwylliant Gwerin', *Transactions of the Honourable Society of Cymmrodorion* (1937), 241–50. See further D. A. Bassett, 'The Making of a National Museum (Part III)', *Transactions of the Honourable Society of Cymmrodorion* (1984), 217–316 (263, note 184).

44. See I. Peate, 'The place of folk culture in the Museum', *Museums Journal* 41 (1941), 45–50; 'Folk Studies in Wales', *Welsh Review*, 3 (1944), 49–55; 'The study of folk life: and its part in the defence of civilisation', *Advancement of Science*, 15 (1958), 86–94.

45. Peate, 'Astudio Bywyd Gwerin', *Syniadau*, p. 11. Translation my own.

46. Peate is referring here to a definition of folk society put forward by Robert Redfield, as elaborated upon in G. M. Foster's article 'What is Folk Culture?', *American Anthropologist*, 55 (1953), 159–73.

47. Peate, *Amgueddfeydd Gwerin*, p. 35.

48. Davies, *The History of Wales*, p. 602.

49. Peate, *Amgueddfeydd Gwerin*, p. 13. Peate lamented the snail's pace at which the British museum community was to adopt this stance. The attempt in 1912 by F. A. Bather of the British Museum, Henry Balfour and others to arouse interest in a project using the Crystal Palace in London as a centre for a British Folk Museum had failed. In Wales, there were similar attempts at encapsulating folk culture, but it was more piecemeal and grew from small collections into an overall project. Local historian T. C. Evans (or Cadrawd, to give him his bardic name) and artist

T. H. Thomas (Arlunydd Pen-y-garn) collected old implements and utensils and sketched interesting objects and buildings and it was this collection that became the basis for a small 'Welsh Bygones' collection at the Cardiff Municipal Museum, displayed in 1913 at a temporary exhibition in City Hall.

50. In 1926, the 'Welsh Bygones' collection was exhibited for the first time in a small gallery opposite the main entrance of the National Museum in Cathays called the Welsh Bygones Gallery, a name Peate disliked (see Iorwerth C. Peate, *Rhwng Dau Fyd, Darn o Hunangofiant*, Gwasg Gee, 1976, p. 131). It was this collection of objects that eventually grew into the National Folk Collection. In 1930 the museum council sent two of its members to Sweden, who returned and placed before the council a report pressing for the creation of a Folk Museum in Wales. The principle was accepted and two years later the collection was enlarged and named the National Folk Collection. It included a series of reconstructions – four farmhouse rooms, a smithy and a wood-turner's shop – all set up in the museum building. A sub-department of Folk Culture was instituted in 1932 and in 1936 became the full Department of Folk Life. In 1943 the council declared the creation of the Welsh Folk Museum to be one of the chief needs of post-war reconstruction and in 1946 the earl of Plymouth offered St Fagan's Castle and its eighteen acres of gardens and grounds to the National Museum of Wales as a centre for the Welsh Folk Museum. This consisted of an Elizabethan mansion and, in the end, one hundred acres of land. See Douglas A. Bassett, 'The Making of a National Museum (Part III)', *Transactions of the Honourable Society of Cymmrodorion* (1984), 217–316.

51. The reconstruction of the Welsh farmhouse kitchen was the inspiration for Peate's sonnet *Y Gegin Gynt yn yr Amgueddfa Genedlaethol* (translated by Joseph P. Clancy as 'Museum Piece'), quoted at the beginning of the section on Sain Ffagan Amgueddfa Werin Cymru.

52. Iorwerth C. Peate, *Sylfeini* (Wrecsam: Hughes a'i Fab, 1938), p. 105. Translation as in Catrin Stevens, *Iorwerth C. Peate*, p. 56.

53. Peter Lord, *The Aesthetics of Relevance* (Llandysul: Gomer, 1992).

54. D. Smith, 'Labour History and Heritage', *Social History Curators Group Journal*, 18, (1990/1), 5.

55. H. Francis, 'A nation of museum attendants', *Arcade*, 16 January (1981), 8–9.

56. Bennett, *The Birth of the Museum*, p. 110.

57. J. G. Jenkins, 'Interpreting the Heritage of Wales', *Folk Life: a Journal of Ethnological Studies* 25 (1986/7), 5–17. Jenkins believed that a romantic and highly selective view of Wales was at play at the museum and his criticism of the collecting practices at work instigated a significant change in policy. See also, J. Geraint Jenkins, *Getting Yesterday Right: Interpreting the Heritage of Wales* (Cardiff: University of Wales Press, 1992).

58. Heavy industry is represented at former sites of industry turned into museums, the National Slate Museum at Llanberis and the Big Pit National Coal Museum, both operated by Amgueddfa Cymru.

59. I am indebted to Matthew Davies (former education officer and site manager at Sain Ffagan), for this discussion on Rhydycar Terrace.

60. Peate, *Amgueddfeydd Gwerin*, p. 61

61. Gaston Bachelard, *The Poetics of Space* (Boston: Beacon Press, 1994 [1964]), p. 7.

62. Peate is quoting A. G. Ling, 'Peasant Architecture in the Northern Provinces of Spain', *Journal of the Royal Institute of British Architects* (1936), 845.

63. Peate juxtaposes 'the non-professional architecture' of 'a nation bereft of its sovereignty', and the rise in eighteenth- and nineteenth-century Europe of the professional architect, whose influence in Wales is 'felt only on the houses of the rich and on the public buildings of the prosperous towns and cities' (p. 3). That the 'rich' were 'almost universally anglicized' and the town's industrial areas 'were then breaking away from traditional peasant culture to become anglicised but *deraciné* areas' meant that there was hardly an incentive for professional architects in relation to the rural Welsh community (pp. 3–4). Because of this, Peate can state clearly that there is no Welsh architecture, for the buildings are by Welsh or English architects working 'in a supra-national tradition which has not found a particular Welsh expression' (p. 4). In terms of establishing a discourse on Welsh architecture in relation to the Welsh house much was accomplished since Peate's time by Peter Smith; see Peter Smith, *Houses of the Welsh Countryside: A Study in Historical Geography* (Royal Commission on the Ancient and Historical Monuments in Wales, 1975), and by Gerallt Nash in relation to buildings re-erected at Sain Ffagan; see Gerallt Nash, *Timber-framed Buildings in Wales* (Cardiff: National Museums and Galleries of Wales, 1995).

64. G. Bagnall, 'Performance and performativity at heritage sites' *Museum and Society*, 1/2, (2003), 87–103 (87).

65. Aleida Assmann, *Cultural Memory and Western Civilization: Functions, Media, Archives* (Cambridge: Cambridge University Press, 2011), p. 122.

66. P. Nora (ed.), *Realms of Memory: The Construction of the French Past, Volume 1, Conflicts and Divisions* (New York: Columbia University Press, 1996), p. 15.

67. For an in-depth treatment of the implications of this name change see Rh. Mason, 'Nation Building at the Museum of Welsh Life', *Museum and Society*, 3/1 (2005), 18–35.

68. For Amgueddfa Cymru's operational plan see *http://www.museumwales.ac.uk/our_plans/operational_plan_2014-15/* [accessed 25 March 2016].

69. In 2012 Sain Ffagan Amgueddfa Werin Cymruy was awarded £11.5 million by the Heritage Lottery Fund towards 'Making History', a £25.5 million project to transform the museum, extending the timeline of history told at Sain Ffagan to over 230,000 years.

70. D. Smith, 'Labour History and Heritage', 3–6; see also, H. Francis, 'A nation of museum attendants', 8–9.

71. The Battle of St Fagan's (1648) has been commemorated at the museum by a large-scale battle re-enactment on several occasions. The section of land that was part of the village and that has since been excavated remained within the village boundary up to 1855, when the castle grounds were extended.

72. Kirshenblatt-Gimblett, *Destination Culture*, pp. 20–1.

73. Christopher Baugh, *Theatre, Performance and Technology, the development of scenography in the twentieth century* (London: Palgrave, 2005), pp. 11–12.

74. Peter Szondi, *Theory of the Modern Drama* (Cambridge: Polity Press, 1987), p. 8.

75. He also discusses his visit to the open-air Maihaugen Museum at Lillehammer (est. 1904), and the National Folk Museum of Norway (est. 1894). Iorwerth Peate, *Amgueddfeydd Gwerin*, pp. 29, 31.

76. Hazelius had collected material to illustrate the life of people in all parts of Sweden and worked towards establishing a Museum of Swedish Folk Life, which opened in Stockholm in 1873. Skansen, which opened in 1891, was the second part of his scheme and was designed as a representation of the landscape, peoples and culture of Sweden in an open-air site to which old houses and buildings from different provinces were moved and re-erected, and their natural environment and setting re-created.

77. Peate, *Amgueddfeydd Gwerin*, p. 19.

78. Kirshenblatt-Gimblett, *Destination Culture*, p. 40.

79. P. Widén, 'National Museums in Sweden: A Story of Denied Empire and a Neutral State', in P. Aronsson and G. Elegnius (eds), *Building National Museums in Europe 1750–2010. Conference Proceedings from EuNaMus, European National Museums: Identity Politics, the Uses of the Past and the European Citizen*, Bologna, 28–30 April, 2011, EuNaMus Report No 1 (Linköping University Electronic Press), *http://www.ep.liu.se/eep_home/index.en.aspx?issue=064*, pp. 881–902 [accessed 4 January 2017].

80. Bennett, *The Birth of the Museum*, p. 130.

81. R. Williams Parry, 'Gwae Awdur Dyddiaduron', *Cerddi'r Gaeaf* (Dinbych: Gwasg Gee, 1952). 'Closer than the historian to the perfect Truth is the dramatist, who is all lies.' Translation my own.

82. See *https://museum.wales/stfagans/makinghistory/galleries/* [accessed 19 January 2017].

83. The Festival programme included folk dancing, a craft exhibition and demonstrations and a performance of Saunders Lewis's play

Blodeuwedd, as well as public lectures. See D. A. Bassett, 'The Making of a National Museum (Part III)', *Transactions of the Honourable Society of Cymmrodorion* (1984), 217–316 (265).

84. J. Geraint Jenkins, *Morwr Tir Sych: Hunangofiant* (Aberystwyth: Cymdeithas Lyfrau Ceredigion, 2007), p. 85.

85. Jenkins, *Morwr Tir Sych*, p. 107.

86. A major funded research project on heritage and performance in the UK, called 'Performance, Learning and Heritage', was conducted by the Centre for Applied Drama, Manchester University in collaboration with the Centre for Museology, University of Manchester, and funded by the Arts and Humanities Research Council, July 2005–November 2008. The project investigated the use of performance for educational purposes at several 'regional' sites, including Llancaiach Fawr Manor in Caerffili, south Wales. See A. Jackson and J. Kidd (eds), *Performing Heritage* (Manchester: Manchester University Press, 2011). The full project report can be found at: *http://www.plh.manchester.ac.uk/*

87. Perhaps influenced by Ralph Waldo Emerson's 1838 address, in which he stated that 'Truly speaking, it is not instruction but provocation, that I can receive from another soul'. Freeman Tilden, *Interpreting Our Heritage* (Chapel Hill: The University of North Carolina Press, fourth edition, 2007), p. 18.

88. C. E. Parry, 'Theatre-in-Museum at the National Museums and Galleries of Wales, 1990–2002' (unpublished MPhil thesis, University of Wales Aberystwyth, 2003), pp. 100–14.

89. These are customs associated with *calennig* or New Year traditions. See Trefor M. Owen, *Welsh Folk Customs* (Cardiff: National Museum of Wales, Welsh Folk Museum, 1978), pp. 48–55 and Iorwerth C. Peate, *Diwylliant Gwerin Cymru*, pp. 96–100.

90. Aberystwyth University and the University of Glamorgan have conducted modules on live interpretation and museum performance on site, and both Cardiff University and Trinity College Carmarthen have performed on site. Between 1995 and 2003 some of this work was directed by Matthew Davies, (then education officer and subsequently site manager at Sain Ffagan), and Lisa Lewis (then lecturer at Aberystwyth University).

91. During my time as lecturer in the Department of Theatre, Film and Television Studies, Aberystwyth University (1991–2002), I taught a module on live interpretation and museum performance, written collaboratively with National Museum Wales staff, including Matthew Davies.

92. Richard Schechner, *Performance Theory* (London: Routledge, 1988), pp. 158–9.

93. Parry, 'Theatre-in-Museum at the National Museum and Galleries of Wales, 1990–2002', pp. 83–84.

94. The Experience of Worship project website *www.experienceofworship.org.uk* [accessed 7 January 2017] has further information, including videos of the enactments.

95. Colin Ford was director of the National Museum of Photography, Film and Television in Bradford from 1983–92.

96. Parry, 'Theatre-in-Museum at the National Museums and Galleries of Wales, 1990–2002', pp. 77–81.

97. Mike Pearson, *Site-Specific Performance* (London: Palgrave Macmillan, 2010), p. 66.

98. Mike Pearson, *Brith Gof: A Welsh Theatre Company, 1. 1981–5,* (Aberystwyth, 1985), p. 25.

99. Pearson, *Site-Specific Performance*, p. 66.

100. E. Edwards, 'Dramateiddio Tirlithriad', *Barn* 405 (1996), see *www.theatre-wales.co.uk* Translation my own.

101. Marc Rees, *shed * light, http://.r-i-p-e.co.uk* [accessed 19 November 2015].

102. Rees, *shed * light, http://r-i-p-e.co.uk* [accessed 19 November 2015).

103. Bedwyr Williams, a Welsh artist who uses performance, text and multimedia in often humorous and satirical works. His work has been shown widely internationally and represented Wales at the 55th Venice Biennale. See further *www.bedwyrwilliams.com*

104. The *cywydd* is a traditional Welsh poetic metre written in *cynghanedd* believed to have originated in the fourteenth century, from which time most recorded examples date. Dafydd ap Gwilym (*c.*1315/1320–*c.*1350/1370) was perhaps the foremost poet of Wales and of Europe in the Middle Ages. *Trafferth mewn Tafarn* (trouble in a tavern) is a humorous *cywydd* telling of his slapstick exploits in a country tavern.

105. At the time of writing the Vulcan Public House from Adam Street, Cardiff, one of the few remaining buildings from New Town, once Cardiff's Irish area and now mostly demolished, is being rebuilt at the museum.

106. Mason, 'Nation Building at the Museum of Welsh Life', 22.

Chapter 3: *Treftadaeth*: heritage

1. *Geiriadur Prifysgol Cymru*, LVII (Cardiff: University of Wales Press, 2001), 3577. Early examples of the usage of the word occur in a religious or theological context.

2. See further B. Dicks, 'Encoding and Decoding the People, Circuits of Communication at a Local Heritage Museum', *European Journal of Communication* (2000), 15/1, 61–78.

3. S. Macdonald, 'A People's Story? Heritage, identity and authenticity', in C. Rojek and J. Urry (eds), *Touring Cultures, Transformations of Travel and Theory* (London: Routledge, 1997, pp. 155–75 (p. 175).

4. Nina Simon, *The Participatory Museum* (Santa Cruz, California: Museum 2.0, 2010). On 'the people's museum' movement, see also S. Macdonald

and R. Silverstone, 'Rewriting the Museum's Fictions: Taxonomies, stories and readers', in D. Boswell and J. Evans (eds), *Representing the Nation: A Reader – Histories, heritages and museums* (London: Routledge, 1999), pp. 421–34.

5. Laurajane Smith, *Uses of Heritage* (London: Routledge, 2006), p. 71.
6. L. Smith, 'The 'doing' of heritage: heritage as performance', in A. Jackson and J. Kidd (eds), *Performing Heritage: Research, Practice and Innovation in Museum Theatre and Live Interpretation* (Manchester: Manchester University Press, 2011), pp. 69–81 (69).
7. Smith, *Uses of Heritage*, p. 83.
8. M. Crang, 'Magic Kingdom or a Magical Quest for Authenticity?', *Annals of Tourism Research*, 23/2 (1996), 415–31; R. Handler and W. Saxton, 'Dyssimulation: Reflexivity, narrative, and the quest for authenticity in "living history"', *Cultural Anthropology*, 3/3 (1988), 242–60; Robert Hewison, *The Heritage Industry: Britain in a Climate of Decline* (London: Methuen, 1987); David Lowenthal, *The Past is a Foreign Country* (Cambridge University Press, 2009 [1985]); Paul Reas, Stuart Cosgrove and Val Williams, *Flogging a Dead Horse: Heritage, Culture and its Role in Post-Industrial Britain* (Manchester: Cornerhouse, 1993); D. Uzzell and R. Ballyntyne, 'Heritage that hurts: Interpretation in a postmodern world', in D. Uzzell and R. Ballyntyne (eds), *Contemporary Issues in Heritage and Environmental Interpretation* (London: Stationery Office, 1998).
9. Patrick Wright, *On Living in an Old Country* (London: Verso, 1985), p. 70.
10. Hewison, *The Heritage Industry*, p. 83.
11. Raphael Samuel, 'Living History', in Raphael Samuel, *Theatres of Memory: Present and Past in Contemporary Culture* (London: Verso, 2012 [1994]), pp. 169–202.
12. Samuel, 'Heritage-Baiting' in *Theatres of Memory*, pp. 259–73
13. The idea of resurrectionism was developed by French historian Jules Michelet in the 1840s as a 'history which aimed to give a voice to the voiceless and speak to the fallen dead' (R. Samuel, *Theatres of Memory*, p. xxi), and also echoes, according to Samuel, E. P. Thompson's idea 'of history as a gigantic reparation, rescuing the defeated from the "enormous condescension" of posterity'. (Samuel, *Theatres of Memory*, p. xxi).
14. Samuel, *Theatres of Memory*, p. 191.
15. B. Kirshenblatt-Gimblett, 'Afterlives', *Performance Research* (1997), 2/2, 1–9 (4).
16. Bella Dicks, *Heritage, Place and Community* (Cardiff: University of Wales Press, 2000).
17. J. Geraint Jenkins, *Morwr Tir Sych, Hunangofiant* (Aberystwyth: Cymdeithas Lyfrau Ceredigion, 2007), p. 98.
18. Samuel, *Theatres of Memory*, p. xxii.

19. A. Escobar, 'Culture Sits in Places: Reflections on globalism and subaltern strategies of localisation' in *Political Geography*, 20 (2001): 139–74 (140), reference in Smith, *Uses of Heritage*, p. 75.
20. Smith, *Uses of Heritage*, p. 75.
21. *Celtica* (Norwich: Jarrold Publishing, 1997), p. 5.
22. See Susan Pitchford, *Identity Tourism: Imaging and Imagining the Nation* (Bingley: Emerald Group, 2007).
23. H. White, 'The Fictions of Factual Representation', in D. Preziosi and C. Farago (eds), *Grasping the World: The Idea of the Museum* (Aldershot: Ashgate, 2004), pp. 22–35 (22).
24. Engraved on a stone on the pathway from the welcome centre at Castell Henllys, site of an Iron Age fort and its reconstruction in Pembrokeshire. The site uses costumed interpreters.
25. A. Robertshaw, 'Live Interpretation', in A. Hems and M. Blockley (eds), *Heritage Interpretation* (London: Routledge, 2006), pp. 42–3.
26. Scholarly writing on the practice of living history at museums and historic sites includes Richard Handler and Eric Gable, *The New History in an Old Museum: Creating the Past at Colonial Williamsburg* (London: Duke University Press, 1997); Scott Magelssen, *Living History Museums: Undoing History through Performance* (Maryland: Scarecrow Press, 2007); Stephen Eddy Snow, *Performing the Pilgrims: A Study of Ethnohistorical Role-Playing at Plimoth Plantation* (Jackson: University Press of Mississippi, 1993); and Kevin Walsh, *The Representation of the Past: Museums and Heritage in a Post-modern World* (London: Routledge, 1992).
27. See the report on the Arts and Humanities Research Council funded 'The Performance, Learning and Heritage Project', (2005–8), Centre for Applied Theatre Research, University of Manchester. *http://www.plh.manchester.ac.uk* [7/1/2017].
28. Catrin Stevens, *Iorwerth C. Peate* (Cardiff: University of Wales Press, 1986), p. 1.
29. Jay Anderson, *Time Machines: The World of Living History* (Nashville: American Association for State and Local History, 1984), p. 45.
30. Barbara Kirshenblatt-Gimblett, *Destination Culture: Tourism, Museums, and Heritage* (London: Routledge, 1998) p. 190.
31. Williamsburg was chosen because of the dilapidated but 'original' state of its buildings in the 1920s.
32. Handler and Gable, *The New History in an Old Museum*, pp. 3–27.
33. The theatrical production department at Colonial Williamsburg re-create historically 'accurate' productions of eighteenth-century plays, based on period prompt books, the physiological model of the humours, stage blocking in the eighteenth century and what is known from archaeological and historical data.
34. Magelssen, *Living History Museums*, p. xiii.

35. P. Smith, 'A la Ronde: eccentricity, interpretation and the end of the world', in Jackson and Kidd (eds), *Performing Heritage*, pp. 158–71 (p. 165).
36. Magelssen, *Living History Museums*, p. 53; see also Gilles Deleuze and Félix Guattari, *What is Philosophy?*, Columbia University Press, 1994), 153, 155–6.
37. Magelssen, *Living History Museums*, p. 53.
38. S. Magelssen, 'Introduction', S. Magelssen and R. Justice-Molloy (eds), *Enacting History* (Tuscaloosa: University of Alabama Press, 2011), pp. 6–7.
39. Its solitary existence does not reflect a general lack of theatre and performance that engages with Welsh heritage, for this aspect has been pursued historically by theatre for young audience companies across the country. The prevalence and importance of theatre in education (T-i-E) in Wales, the only country in the British Isles, until 2010, with a fully funded T-i-E company, with a broad reach into most sectors, including the museum, in each county, has meant that heritage performance has been served in Wales by a range of theatre and education providers, funded by the Arts Council of Wales and the local education authorities. This relationship between county council and educational theatre can be traced back to 1976 and the decision by the Arts Council of Wales to support the establishment of a theatre-in-education group in every county. That Llancaiach Fawr Manor is owned and run by Caerffili County Council is related to this historical endorsement of educational theatre through local authorities.
40. *Llancaiach Fawr Manor* guidebook (Norwich: Jarrold Publishing, 2002), no page numbers.
41. See, for instance, Robert Minhinnick, *A Postcard Home: Tourism in the Mid-'Nineties* (Llandysul: Gwasg Gomer, 1993), p. 25.
42. Lauren Berlant, *The Queen of America Goes to Washington: Essays on Sex and Citizenship* (Durham: Duke University Press, 1997), p. 1. Berlant is referred to in a discussion on re-enactment in I. McCalman and P. A. Pickering (eds), *Historical Re-enactment: From Realism to the Affective Turn* (Basingstoke: Palgrave Macmillan, 2010), p. 6.
43. The number and variety of battle re-enactors rose sharply towards the end of the twentieth century and by 2004 there were over six hundred battle re-enactment groups listed in the British journal *Call to Arms*, an increase of 150 groups since the year 2000. See Robertshaw, 'Live Interpretation', in A. Hems and M. Blockley (eds), *Heritage Interpretation* (London: Routledge, 2006), p. 43.
44. Crang, 'Magic Kingdom or magical quest for authenticity?', 415–31.
45. P. Burke, 'A Short History of Distance' in M. S. Phillips et al., *Rethinking Historical Distance* (Basingstoke: Palgrave Macmillan, 2013), pp. 21–34 (p. 21).
46. L. Clemons, 'Present Enacting Past: The Functions of Battle Reenacting in Historical Representation', in S. Magelssen and R. Justice-Malloy (eds), *Enacting History*, pp. 10–21 (p. 10).

47. Hewison, *The Heritage Industry*, p. 43.
48. Clemons, 'Present Enacting Past: The Functions of Battle Reenacting in Historical Representation', p. 10.
49. Rebecca Schneider, *Performing Remains: Art and War in Times of Theatrical Reenactment* (London: Routledge, 2011), p. 32.
50. J. R. Jones, *Ac Onide* (Llandybïe: Llyfrau'r Dryw, 1970), p. 138. Translation my own.
51. Fortress Wales, 3–4 May 2009, Margam Country Park, Neath Port Talbot. The castle lawns presented a series of arena events by various re-enactment groups including the Wyoming Wild Bunch, the Companions of the Longbow, Regia Anglorum, the Freemen of Gwent, Sons of the Dragon, the Confederation and Union Re-enactment Society, Vikings of Middle England, the Welsh Horse Yeomanry, the South Wales Borderers, WW2 Re-enactment, 2nd Devon's, Stahl Krieger 'Steel Warriors', 5th Duke of Cornwall's, 4th Wiltshire Living History, Birmingham PALS, Glamorgan Home Guard, SS Toten hopt, An airfield somewhere in . . . , the Welsh Sons of the Dragon, La Columna, Modern Army, the Marcher Stuarts, the Courtweve Household, Sir Henry Vaughan's Company of the Sealed Knot, Companions of the Forest, Nostalgia, and Monmouthshire Muzzleloaders.
52. Silures (a group that operated in South Wales during the 1990s and 2000s); Brigantia, Iron-Age Celtic re-enactment, see *http://ironage-history.com/brigantia/*; Ancient Celtic Clans, see *www.celticclans.org*; Meibion y Ddraig/ Sons of the Dragon, medieval Welsh archers, see *www.sonsofthedragon.co.uk*; Cardiff Castle Garrison, medieval re-enactment, see *https://cardiffcastlegarrison.wordpress.com*; the Freemen of Gwent, medieval re-enactment group, see *freemenofgwent.com*; Blaeddau Du (Vikings), see *www.blaeddaudu.co.uk*; The Montgomery Levy, see *https://sites.google.com/site/historymattersorg/Home/the-montgomery-levy*. Other Welsh re-enactment groups include South Wales Borderers WW2 Re-enactment Group, *http://www.webster.uk.net/Hobbies-and-Interests/Re-enactment-WW2-SWB/Home.aspx*; Brotherhood of Aman Re-enactment Society (BOARS), 12th–13th century, *http://boarsreenactors.wixsite.com/boars*; the Marcher Stuarts Living History and Military Group (seventeenth-century Tudors and Stuarts and fifteenth-century Tretower Court, Crickhowell, Powys), *www.marcherstuarts.com*; Age of the Princes, Middle Ages, *www.ageoftheprinces.co.uk*. [all accessed 8 January 2017]. This list is far from exhaustive, and there are many other groups operating in Wales.
53. *thewelshtommies.weebly.com* [accessed 7 January 2017].
54. Firing Line: Cardiff Castle Museum of the Welsh Soldier. The museum is dedicated to commemorating over three hundred years of history, from the Battle of Waterloo in 1815 to recent wars in Iraq and Afghanistan. See *www.cardiffcastlemuseum.org.uk* [accessed 30 November 2015].

55. M. Kirby, 'On Acting and Not-acting', in P. Zarrilli (ed.), *Acting (Re) Considered, A Theoretical and Practical Guide* (London: Routledge, 2002), pp. 40–52.
56. The bicentenary re-enactment 'The Fight for Canada! 1812–1815' at Firing Line: Cardiff Castle Museum of the Welsh Soldier, 25–6 August 2012. The voiceover dramatisation was performed by University of Glamorgan students and staff and directed by Richard Hand.
57. Paul Connerton, *How Societies Remember* (Cambridge University Press, 1989), p. 102.
58. Connerton, *How Societies Remember*, pp. 5 and 72.
59. Schneider, *Performing Remains*, p. 37.
60. Freddie Rokem, *Performing History: Theatrical Representations of the Past in Contemporary Theatre* (Iowa City: University of Iowa Press, 2000), pp. 2–3.

Chapter 4: *Gŵyl*: festival

1. Alan Llwyd, 'Yr Eisteddfod', in Moses Glyn Jones (ed.), *Cerddi Prifeirdd*, 2 (Swansea: Gwasg Christopher Davies, 1979), p. 52.
2. Jürgen Straub (ed.), *Narration, Identity and Historical Consciousness* (New York: Berghahn, 2005).
3. The National Eisteddfod is attended by between 150,000 and 200,000 people, depending on where it is held; approximately 6,000 people take part in the competitions, all of which are in Welsh.
4. B. Stoeltje, 'Festival', in R. Bauman (ed.), *Folklore, Cultural Performance, and Popular Entertainments* (Oxford University Press, 1992), pp. 261–71 (p. 261).
5. Stoeltje, 'Festival', p. 261.
6. W. J. Gruffydd, 'Nodiadau'r Golygydd', *Y Llenor*, 16/2 (1937), 66.
7. Alan Llwyd, *Y Gaer Fechan Olaf, Hanes Eisteddfod Genedlaethol Cymru 1937–1950* (Llandybïe: Gwasg Dinefwr, 2006), p. 75.
8. Jan Morris, *Wales: Epic Views of a Small Country* (London: Penguin Books, 1998), p. 166.
9. Stoeltje, 'Festival', p. 262.
10. The damage caused by the publication of this report was captured in a play by R. J. Derfel, *Brad y Llyfrau Gleision* (The Treason of the Blue Books, 1854) and subsequently the report and its implications were immortalised as the Blue Books, in reference to the play and to the colour of the covers of the actual report.
11. *Reports of the Commissioners of Inquiry into the State of Education in Wales* (London: HMSO, 1848), p. 3
12. Hywel Teifi Edwards, *The Eisteddfod* (Cardiff: University of Wales Press, 1990), pp. 20–1.
13. See further Hywel Teifi Edwards, *Eisteddfod Ffair y Byd* (Llandysul: Gomer Press, 1990).

14. Arnold van Gennep, *Rites de Passage. Étude systématiques des rites* (Paris: Edition A & J Picard, 2011 [1906]).
15. Victor Turner, *The Forest of Symbols: Aspects of Ndembu Rituals* (Ithaca: Cornell University Press, 1970 [1967]).
16. The liminal state is found in the activities of 'churches, sects, and movements, in initiation rites of clubs, fraternities, masonic orders, and other secret societies, etc', while liminoid phenomena are more likely to be found in 'the leisure genres of art, sport, pastimes, games, etc.' Victor Turner, *From Ritual to Theatre: The Human Seriousness of Play* (New York: PAJ Publications, 1982), p. 55.
17. The year 1789 marks the beginning of the modern eisteddfod, a consequence of the Gwyneddigion Society's response to the promptings of Thomas Jones of Corwen regarding the importance of the eisteddfod to the regeneration of Welsh language and culture in the face of the anglicisation of the Welsh gentry. The project was halted due to the Napoleonic wars but was revived in 1818 following the formation of several societies for the advancement of Welsh culture. See Edwards, *The Eisteddfod*, p. 15. It was not until the second half of the nineteenth century that the eisteddfod took off in local and national contexts. The first National Eisteddfod was held at Aberdare in 1861.
18. Iolo Morganwg's influence was substantial – he was a sincere scholar and most knowledgeable on the literature and history of Wales. He was also a brilliant imitator, particularly of poetry, and proceeded to devise traditions, poets and poetry that never existed. See G. A. Williams, 'Iolo Morganwg: Bardd Rhamantaidd ar gyfer cenedl nad oedd yn cyfrif', in G. H. Jenkins (ed.), *Cof Cenedl V, Ysgrifau ar Hanes Cymru* (Llandysul: Gwasg Gomer, 1990), pp. 57–84; see also G. H. Jenkins (ed.), *A Rattleskull Genius: The Many Faces of Iolo Morganwg* (Cardiff: University of Wales Press, 2009).
19. E. Hobsbawm, in E. Hobsbawm and T. Ranger (eds), *The Invention of Tradition* (Cambridge University Press, 1983), p. 1.
20. See R. P. Evans, 'Mythology and Tradition', in T. Herbert and G. E. Jones (eds), *The Remaking of Wales in the Eighteenth Century* (Cardiff: University of Wales Press, 1988), p. 151.
21. Ceri W. Lewis, *Iolo Morganwg* (Caernarfon: Gwasg Pantycelyn, 1995), p. 187.
22. Lewis, *Iolo Morganwg*, p. 189.
23. Lewis, *Iolo Morganwg*, p. 233.
24. *Uchelwyr*: the landed gentry of Wales and the descendants of the princes of Wales.
25. The formation of the French republic, and indeed of the United States of America, was profoundly influential during this period. Iolo Morganwg admired the efforts to secure freedom and independence in America, 'where first since the world began, appears . . . a government founded on

the true principles of Liberty, Justice and the Rights of Humanity'. Lewis, *Iolo Morganwg*, p. 135.

26. Williams, 'Iolo Morganwg: Bardd Rhamantaidd', p. 59. Translation my own.

27. Anwen Jones, *National Theatres in Context: France, Germany, England and Wales* (Cardiff: University of Wales Press, 2007). See in particular chapter four, 'The National Eisteddfod, the national pageant and the Welsh national theatre: friends or foes?', pp. 129–55.

28. Initially, according to Iolo Morganwg's ideas, it was only possible to hold a Gorsedd at four particular times, the vernal equinox, the autumnal equinox, the summer solstice and the winter solstice. See Lewis, *Iolo Morganwg*, p. 189.

29. To facilitate having the Gorsedd Circle on the Maes during the week of the Eisteddfod, it was decided in 2004 to use fake (but realistic-looking) stones.

30. Morris, *Wales*, p. 167.

31. Jones, *National Theatres in Context*, p. 135.

32. Stoeltje, 'Festival', p. 264.

33. Stoeltje, 'Festival', p. 267 and p. 268.

34. Ifor Rees (ed.), *Dŵr o Ffynnon Felin Bach: Cyfrol Dathlu Canlwyddiant Geni Cynan* (Dinbych: Gwasg Gee, 1995), p. 94.

35. For further information see Dafydd Owen, *Cynan* (Cardiff: University of Wales Press, 1979), p. 79.

36. Stoeltje, 'Festival', p. 268.

37. *Y Babell Lên* (the literature tent) is a programme of daily highlights from the venue; *Talwrn y Beirdd* (the bards' cockpit) is a programme of daily highlights from the live poetry competitions held at the literature tent. It is also the name of a BBC Radio Cymru programme that has well-known poets placed in competitive regional teams and performing poetry composed over a short period of time.

38. In 1944 the BBC broadcast several hours of the Llandybïe National Eisteddfod to homes in Wales and to the armed forces. This move was seen as contentious by many at the time, mainly because of the perceived need for a dedicated Welsh Broadcasting Company.

39. Stoeltje, 'Festival', p. 263.

40. 'Eisteddfod Genedlaethol Ryfeddaf Erioed', *Y Cymro*, June 29, 1940, p. 1.

41. The project to explore the history of performance art in Wales, "What's Welsh for Performance?', led by Heike Roms and funded by the AHRC, 2009–11, has revealed the extent of performance art actions and interventions on the Eisteddfod field. See H. Roms, 'What's Welsh for Performance? Constructing an Archive of Performance Art in Wales', *Cyfrwng Media Wales Journal*, 5 (2008), 54–72; see also H. Roms, *What's Welsh for Performance? An Oral History of Performance Art in Wales 1968–2008*, Vol. 1 (Samizdat Press, 2008).

42. The National Eisteddfod in Cardiff in August 2018, will make use of the area and buildings around Roald Dahl Plass in Cardiff Bay as the site.
43. Edwards, *The Eisteddfod*, p. 74.
44. M. Foucault, 'On Other Spaces', *Architecture-Mouvement-Continuité* (1984), 3.
45. I refer here to the large national festival, although there are different forms of the eisteddfod in Wales and the activity itself, although of Welsh origin, is appropriated the world over as a competitive event.
46. Foucault, 'On Other Spaces', 7.
47. Llwyd, *Y Gaer Fechan Olaf*, p. 9.
48. *Cerdd dant* (literally, string music) refers to a vocal (usually composed and rehearsed) improvisation of a counter melody, usually sung in solo or duet form to the accompaniment of the harp, which provides the core melody. *Cyd-adrodd* (literally, co-recital) is a kind of spoken choral recitation in which different voices are used to particular effect in the recitation of poetry.
49. Edwards, *The Eisteddfod*, p. 2.
50. Stoeltje, 'Festival', p. 271.
51. Dwight Conquergood, *Cultural Struggles: Performance, Ethnography, Praxis* (Ann Arbor: University of Michigan Press, 2013), p. 57.
52. Daniel E. Sheehy, 'Tradition and Change', in *The 2009 The Smithsonian Folklife Festival: Giving Voice, Las Americas, Wales* (Smithsonian Institution, 2009), p. 8.
53. Smithsonian Folklife Festival website, *www.festival.si.edu/2009/wales/smithsonian* [accessed: 10 May 2010].
54. Sheehy, 'Tradition and Change', p. 9.
55. See Peter R. Penczer, *The Washington National Mall* (Arlington, Virginia: Oneonta Press, 2007), p. 7.
56. Foucault, 'On Other Spaces', 7.
57. Richard Kurin, *Reflections of a Culture Broker: A View from the Smithsonian* (Washington and London: Smithsonian Institution, 1997), p. 120.
58. S. D. Ripley, quoted in K. Ringle, 'Of Lawyers and Other Folk: Even Barristers Join the Blend at the Smithsonian's Festival of Diversity', *Washington Post*, 25 June 1986, reference in Kurin, *Reflections of a Culture Broker*, p. 110.
59. William S. Walker, *A Living Exhibition: The Smithsonian and the Transformation of the Universal Museum* (Amherst and Boston: University of Massachusetts Press, 2013), p. 116.
60. Walker, *A Living Exhibition*, pp. 121–2.
61. Kurin, *Reflections of a Culture* Broker, p. 110.
62. Coco Fusco, *English is Broken Here: Notes on Cultural Fusion in the Americas* (New York: The New Press, 1995), pp. 41–3. Fusco's list begins

in 1493 with the display of an Arawak person in the Spanish Court, brought from the Caribbean by Columbus.

63. Walker, *A Living Exhibition*, p. 113.

64. Richard Kurin, *Smithsonian Folklife Festival, Culture Of, By, and For the People* (Washington DC: Smithsonian Institution, 1998), p. 41.

65. Ralph Rinzler, quoted in Walker, *A Living Exhibition*, p. 113.

66. Simthsonian Folklife Festival website, *www.festival.si.edu* [accessed 10 May 2010).

67. Barbara Kirshenblatt-Gimblett, *Destination Culture: Tourism, Museums and Heritage* (Berkeley and Los Angeles: University of California Press, 1998), pp. 76.

68. Robert Cantwell, *Ethnomimesis: Folklife and the Representation of Culture* (Chapel Hill and London: University of North Carolina Press, 1993), p. 214.

69. Kurin, *Smithsonian Folklife Festival*, p. 54.

70. In 2008, the year preceding the Wales event, I attended the Festival as an invited scholar of the Department of Folklife and Cultural Heritage, and as representative of the Centre for the Study of Media and Culture in Small Nations at the University of Glamorgan (now the University of South Wales), following Smithsonian curator Dr Betty Belanus's term at the Centre in 2007–8. This provided a view of the mechanics of the Festival and an opportunity to discuss the potential of the Wales exhibit in 2009. The Folklife Festival in 2008 included the programmes 'Bhutan: The Land of the Thunder Dragon'; 'NASA: Fifty Years and Beyond'; and 'Texas: A Celebration of Music, Food and Wine'.

71. *Tŷ Unnos*, literally 'one night house', was a tradition or belief, prevalent between the seventeenth and beginning of the nineteenth centuries, that if a person built a house on common land in one night the land subsequently belonged to them as freehold. The practice arose because of the pressures on land availability due to land enclosures and taxation laws established by landowners.

72. Foucault, 'On Other Spaces', 4.

73. Kurin, *Reflections of a Culture Broker*, p. 130

74. Cantwell, *Ethnomimesis*, p. 228.

Chapter 5: Theatre Places

1. David Wiles, *A Short History of Western Performance Space* (Cambridge: Cambridge University Press, 2003), p. 3.

2. Hans-Thies Lehmann, *Postdramatic Theatre* (London: Routledge, 2006), p. 152.

3. *Anterliwt* (interlude or enterlude), a satirical and moralistic interlude played with two or three performers in makeshift settings. Its golden age was the late eighteenth and early nineteenth centuries. The most famous

writer of interludes was Twm o'r Nant or Thomas Edwards (1739–1810) from Denbighshire. There were numerous other interlude writers of repute and thousands of interludes written.

4. I. Williams, 'Towards national identities: Welsh theatre', in B. Kershaw (ed.), *The Cambridge History of British Theatre, Volume 3: Since 1895* (Cambridge: Cambridge University Press, 2004), pp. 242–72. The 'imported model' to which Williams refers is comprised of 'good quality mainstream theatre in the literary tradition from Shakespeare through Ibsen and Shaw to our contemporary writers' (p. 242).

5. Henri Lefebvre, *The Production of Space* (Oxford: Blackwell, 1984), p. 26.

6. Richard Schechner, *Performance Theory* (London: Routledge, 1988), p. 161.

7. R. Owen, 'Theatr Dewi': Ymddiriedolaeth Theatr Dewi Sant a Phwyllgor Cymreig Cyngor Celfyddydau Prydain Fawr, 1959–67', in H. W. Davies (ed.), *Y Theatr Genedlaethol yng Nghymru* (Cardiff: University of Wales Press, 2007), pp. 129–68 (p. 132–3). Also discussed by Claire Cochrane, 'The Contaminated Audience: Researching Amateur Theatre in Wales before 1939', *New Theatre Quarterly*, 19/2 (2003), 169–76 (170).

8. For a comprehensive history of theatre in Wales, see Ioan Williams, *Y Mudiad Drama yng Nghymru 1880–1940* (Cardiff: University of Wales Press, 2006); Roger Owen, *Ar Wasgar, Theatr a Chenedligrwydd yn y Gymru Gymraeg 1979–1997* (Cardiff: University of Wales Press, 2003); H. W. Davies (ed.), *Y Theatr Genedlaethol yng Nghymru*; Anwen Jones, *National Theatres in Context*; B. Kerhsaw (ed.), *The Cambridge History of British Theatre, Volume III* ; A. Taylor (ed.), *Staging Wales: Welsh Theatre 1979–1997* (Cardiff: University of Wales Press, 1997); N. Ros and G. Harper (eds), *Studies in Theatre and Production*, 24/3 (2004).

9. Extant late fifteenth-century texts include *Y Tri Brenin o Gwlen* (The Three Kings of Cologne) and *Y Dioddefaint a'r Atgyfodiad* (The Passion and the Resurrection), both written as miracle plays and probably influenced by the Chester cycle, and *Yr Enaid a'r Corff* (The Soul and the Body), a morality play. The only Welsh-language Renaissance play to have survived is *Troelus a Chresyd* (*c.*1600).

10. *Mari Lwyd* is a processional performance during which a horse's skull (called *y Fari Lwyd*) is carried by a band of men from door to door, engaging in an improvisational battle of wits. It is associated with *calennig* (New Year customs). For further information see Trefor M. Owen, *Welsh Folk Customs* (Cardiff: National Museum of Wales, Welsh Folk Museum, 1978), pp. 48–55.

11. Williams, *Y Mudiad Drama yng Nghymru 1880–1940* (2006). See also M. Wynn Thomas, 'All change: the new Welsh drama before the Great War', in M. Wynn Thomas (ed.), *Internal Difference: Twentieth-Century Writing in Welsh* (Cardiff: University of Wales Press, 1992), pp. 1–14.

12. See H. W. Davies, *Y Theatr Genedlaethol yng Nghymru* (2007); A. Jones, 'Cymru, cenedligrwydd a theatr genedlaethol: dilyn y gwys neu dorri cwys newydd?', in A. Jones and L. Lewis (eds), *Ysgrifau ar Theatr a Pherfformio* (Cardiff: University of Wales Press, 2013), pp. 103–18.

13. Cwmni Theatr Cymru ('The theatre company of Wales') was the culmination of a constantly evolving project to form a successful national theatre company in Wales, an endeavour which began at the turn of the century and which was sealed by the formation of the company in 1965. There was widespread debate regarding the inclusion of the word 'national' in the company's title and it was never used. See further L. T. Jones, 'Datblygiad Theatr Genedlaethol i Gymru, 1964–82' in H. W. Davies (ed.), *Y Theatr Genedlaethol yng Nghymru* (2007), pp. 169–207. Cwmni Theatr Cymru came to an end in 1984, its demise a combination of financial mismanagement and a chronic lack of funding. See L. Lewis, 'Cwmni Theatr Cymru ac Emily Davies, 1982–4' in H. W. Davies (ed.), *Y Theatr Genedlaethol yng Nghymru* (2007), pp. 208–51.

14. Gwyn A. Williams, *When Was Wales? A History of the Welsh* (London: Penguin Books, 1985), pp. 296–7.

15. The development of a Welsh-language television channel was considered to be so crucial for the future of the Welsh language that its existence was associated from the start with issues of identity and selfhood. This is represented forcefully by the actions of former Plaid Cymru MP Gwynfor Evans (1912–2005), who threatened to fast unto death until the channel was established. Prior to the establishment of the channel, Welsh-language productions were broadcast as part of the regional provision of BBC Cymru Wales and HTV. For a comprehensive history of the founding of S4C, see Elain Dafydd, *Nid Sianel Deledu Gyffredin Mohoni! Hanes Sefydlu S4C* (Cardiff: University of Wales Press, 2016).

16. Dalier Sylw was formed in 1987 by a group of prominent theatre and television artists intent on supporting theatre in Cardiff and utilised the strong network of south Wales based theatre practitioners who had come to reside in Cardiff over the years due to the presence of the BBC. Theatrig, under artistic director Ceri Sherlock, was a direct descendent of the later work of Cwmni Theatr Cymru during artistic director Emily Davies's tenure, and specifically the work that Sherlock had undertaken for the company during this time. Brith Gof was established by Mike Pearson and Lis Hughes Jones in a split from Cardiff Laboratory Theatre in 1981.

17. R. Owen, *Ar Wasgar*, pp. 1–24.

18. M. Pearson, 'My balls/your chin', *Performance Research* 3/2 (1998), 35–41 (39), quoted in Wiles, *A Short History of Western Performance Space*, p. 2

19. Pearson, 'My balls/your chin', 40, quoted in Wiles, *A Short History of Western Performance Space*, p. 2

20. Wiles, *A Short History of Western Performance Space*, pp. 4–5.
21. Cardiff Laboratory Theatre was formed in 1974 by Mike Pearson and Richard Gough. Following Pearson and Jones's split from the company in 1981, Cardiff Lab became the Centre for Performance Research under Gough's leadership.
22. Brith Gof had given over forty performances in thirteen countries by 1990; see C. Savill, 'Dismantling the Wall', *Planet* 79 (1990), 20–8 (22).
23. This project has been sustained by former members of Brith Gof including Mike Pearson and other Brith Gof associates, as well as individual scholars based at Aberystwyth University. See Brith Gof Archives, National Library of Wales; Cliff McLucas Archives, National Library of Wales; and Brith Gof Archive project (which began in 2007), 'Between Memory and Archive'. A range of published works by Mike Pearson refers to Brith Gof's work, including Mike Pearson and Michael Shanks, *Theatre/Archaeology* (London: Routledge, 2001), and Mike Pearson, *Site-Specific Performance* (London: Palgrave Macmillan, 2010). Unpublished PhD theses include G. Ll. Evans, 'Astudiaeth o'r cysyniad o theatr ôl-ddramataidd yng nghyddestun gwaith Cwmni Brith Gof a'i ddilynwyr ac Aled Jones Williams', (A study of the concept of post-dramatic theatre in the context of the work of Brith Gof Theatre Company and its followers and Aled Jones Williams) (2012); R. O'Neill, 'Croesi'r bar: archwilio hunaniaeth y mewnfudwr Prydeinig trwy gyfrwng archif yr artist Cliff McLucas' (Crossing the bar: exploring the identity of the British incomer through the medium of the Cliff McLucas Archive), (2013); H. Roms, 'Identifying (with) performance: representation and constructions of cultural identity in contemporary theatre practice – three case studies' (2001).
24. Mike Pearson, in *Brith Gof, A Welsh Theatre Company* (Brith Gof: 1985), pp. 3–4
25. Eddie Ladd, performer/dancer/theatre maker, one of the most radical performers working in Wales and a former member of Brith Gof; Marc Rees, an artist whose work responds to place and community and also a member of Brith Gof for several years; Cwmni Cyfri Tri, an experimental physical performance group formed by graduates of the University College of Wales Aberystwyth in 1980; Arad Goch, formed in 1989 from the merger of TiE company Theatr Crwban and Cwmni Cyfri Tri; Y Gymraes, a theatre company established by Sêra Moore Williams in 1992. Williams had worked with regularly with Brith Gof as performer and director (from *Manawydan* in 1982 and through the large-scale works, *Gododdin, Pax* and *Haearn*). Williams's own work follows a different path, utilising scripted drama in the context of an experimental devising process with actors, a unique way of working that stood in between the mainstream dramatic provision (all scripted, and almost all written by men) and the experimental ways of working employed by the alternative theatre.

26. Between 1981 and 1985 Brith Gof had collaborated in performance with Paupers Carnival, Cwmni Cyfri Tri, Farfa and Ósmego Dnia, and members of Odin Teatret.

27. Mike Pearson visited Tokyo in 1980 and studied Nō theatre and Kabuki; Lis Hughes Jones had studied Legong dance. See H. W. Davies, 'Case study: refashioning a myth, performances of the tale of Blodeuwedd', in B. Kershaw (ed.), *The Cambridge History of British Theatre, Volume 3*, pp. 273–87 (p. 282).

28. M. Pearson, 'Special Worlds, Secret Maps: A Poetics of Performance' in A. Taylor (ed.), *Staging Wales: Welsh Theatre 1979–1997*, pp. 85–99 (pp. 94–5).

29. M. Pearson in 'Cliff McLucas and Mike Pearson (Brith Gof)', in Nick Kaye, *Art Into Theatre: Performance Interviews and Documents* (London: Routledge, 1996), p. 209.

30. C. McLucas in 'Clifford McLucas and Mike Pearson', in G. Giannachi and M. Luckhurst (eds), *On Directing: Interviews with Directors* (London: Palgrave Macmillan, 1999), p. 83.

31. Fiona Wilkie describes a continuum line on which the different forms of theatrical space lie – from 'in theatre building', to 'outside theatre', to 'site-sympathetic', to 'site-generic' and finally to 'site-specific'. F. Wilkie, 'Mapping the Terrain: A Survey of Site-Specific Performance in Britain', *New Theatre Quarterly*, Vol 18/2, (2002), 140–60.

32. *Branwen* and *Rhiannon*, both productions with drama students of University College of Wales Aberystwyth. *Branwen* (April 1981) was performed at Harlech Castle and *Rhiannon* (August 1981), at the National Eisteddfod Maldwyn; *Manawydan* (April 1982) was a joint production with Cwmni Cyfri Tri that toured Wales and Denmark. *Blodeuwedd* (1982–3) toured Wales; *Ann Griffiths* (1983–5) toured Welsh chapels; *Rhydcymerau* (1984) was performed at the National Eisteddfod Llanbedr Pont Steffan, before touring Wales nationally in 1984–5.

33. Edward S. Casey, *Remembering: A Phenomenological Study* (Bloomington and Indianapolis: Indiana University Press, 2000), p. 189

34. Pearson and Shanks, *Theatre/Archaeology*, pp. 64–5.

35. *Gernika!*, originally produced under the auspices of Cwmni Theatr Cymru as part of their provision for the National Eisteddfod in 1983.

36. Eleri Rogers, review of *Gernika!*, *Y Cymro* (16 August 1983), 13; quoted by Pearson in *Brith Gof*, p. 6.

37. *Rhydcymerau* was performed at the old market, Llanbedr Pont Steffan, August 6–10, 1984.

38. *Rhydcymerau* publicity flyer, author's own copy. Translation my own.

39. Gwenallt, 'Rhydcymerau', in D. Gwenallt Jones, *Eples* (Llandysul: Gwasg Gomer, 1951), pp. 20–1.

40. D. J. Williams, *Hen Dŷ Ffarm* (Llandysul: Gwasg Gomer, 1953).

41. Pearson in *Brith Gof*, p. 3.

42. *Pandaemonium: The True Cost of Coal, Gwir Gost Glo*, Tabernacl Chapel, Treforys, March 24–8, 1987.
43. *Llef,* hymn tune by G. H. Jones (Gutyn Arfon), words by David Charles; see *Caneuon Ffydd* (Llandysul: Gwasg Gomer, 2001), p. 839.
44. *Pandaemonium: The True Cost of Coal, Gwir Gost Glo* programme, author's own copy.
45. 'Proxemics' and 'proxemic relations' are terms used by the American anthropologist Edward T. Hall, and applied in relation to performance by Mike Pearson.
46. Miwon Kwon, *One Place After Another: Site-Specific Art and Locational Identity* (Cambridge, Massachusetts: MIT Press, 2004), p. 1.
47. Lefebvre, *The Production of Space*, p. 52.
48. Kwon, *One Place After Another*, p. 157.
49. Pearson and Shanks, *Theatre/Archaeology*, p. 109. *Gododdin* was performed in a quarry in Polverigi, Italy; Kampnagel, a former mechanical engineering factory in Hamburg, Germany; an ice skating rink in Leeuwarden, Netherlands; Tramway in Glasgow, Scotland; Rover Way factory in Cardiff, Wales. The production was designed as a 'kit of parts', adapted from one setting to the next. See Mike Pearson in Pearson and Shanks, *Theatre/Archaeology*, pp. 106–7.
50. The number of survivors varies according to two different versions that have been merged in the extant manuscript.
51. See Jen Harvie, *Staging the UK* (Manchester: Manchester University Press, 2005), p. 44.
52. Pearson, *Site-Specific Performance*, p. 173.
53. Ioan Williams suggests that the critical response to this production was possibly a contributory factor to the eventual withdrawal of funding to the company by the Arts Council, several years down the line. I. Williams, 'Towards national identities: Welsh theatre', p. 265; see also, N. Ros, '"Llwfrdra" yn Achub Brith Gof', *Golwg*, 27 March 1997, 4; N. Ros, 'Big Changes in Funding are Inevitable', *New Welsh Review*, Spring (1997), 67; 'Ffarwel Brith Gof?', *Barn*, March (2007), 26.
54. R. Owen, *Ar Wasgar*, p. 158.
55. Owen, *Ar Wasgar*, p. 152; also, Lis Hughes Jones, 'Sand and Milk', Theatre-Women-Lives, *Open Page*, 2, 1997, pp. 29–31, *http://www.themagdalena project.org/sites/default/files/OP2_Jones.pdf* [accessed 7 January 2017].
56. Peter Lord, *The Meaning of Pictures, Images of Personal, Social and Political Identity* (Cardiff: University of Wales Press, 2009), p. 202.
57. See J. Aaron and C. Williams (eds), *Postcolonial Wales* (Cardiff: University of Wales Press, 2005); see also Daniel Williams, *Wales Unchained: Literature, Politics and Identity in the American Century* (Cardiff: University of Wales Press, 2015).
58. Kirsti Bohata, *Postcolonialism Revisited* (Cardiff: University of Wales Press, 2004), p. 5.

59. Pearson, *Site-Specific Performance*, p. 35–6.
60. Cliff McLucas and Mike Pearson, paper given at symposium on Welsh research in theatre and performance studies organised by Aberystwyth University, Gregynog Hall, Powys, 1993 (author's own copy).
61. Cliff McLucas, 'The Host, the Ghost and the Witness. Some approaches to site in the theatre works of Brith Gof 1989–1999. The Roehampton Remix' (1998), (Brith Gof Archive, National Library of Wales), pp. 12–13, quoted in Pearson, *Site-Specific Performance*, p. 143. My emphasis.
62. Pearson and Shanks, *Theatre/Archaeology*, p. 159.
63. *Tri Bywyd* was performed at Esgair Fraith, Clywedog, above Llanbedr Pont Steffan, 12–15 October 1995.
64. R. Owen, 'Theatre in Wales in the 1990s and beyond', in B. Kershaw (ed.), *The Cambridge History of British Theatre, Volume 3*, pp. 485–97 (p. 486).
65. The history of national theatre in Wales has been fraught with concerns regarding linguistic exclusion from all sides. Worries concerning the eventual privileging of one language over the other in any joint endeavour have haunted every iteration of a national company, from fears regarding an eventual Anglicization (see Williams, 'Towards national identities: Welsh theatre' in B. Kershaw (ed.), *The Cambridge History of British Theatre, Volume 3*, pp. 242–72), to the falling away of one linguistic provision (usually English, historically) see H. W. Davies (ed.), *Y Theatr Genedlaethol yng Nghymru* (2008).
66. N. Ros, 'Editorial: Performance in postreferendum Wales', *Studies in Theatre and Performance*, 24/3 (2004), 147–8 (147). See also S. Blandford, 'Theatre and Performance in a Devolved Wales', in S. Blandford (ed.), *Theatre and Performance in Small Nations* (Bristol: Intellect, 2013), pp. 53–70.
67. *Hedd Wyn* (1992), directed by Paul Turner, written by Alan Llwyd and distributed by S4C, recipient of the Royal Television Society's award for best single drama and of several BAFTA Cymru awards, and the first film from Wales nominated for an Academy Award. The elegiac film tells of the poet Ellis Humphrey Evans (bardic name, Hedd Wyn) posthumously winning the National Eisteddfod Chair in 1917 after his death at Passchendaele. *Gadael Lenin* (1994), directed by Endaf Emlyn, written by Siôn Eirian and produced by Pauline Williams, won numerous BAFTA Cymru awards. The film tells the story of seven teenagers and three schoolteachers from a Welsh school on a visit to Russia and is a coming-of-age film charting the children's self-discovery; it was the first film from the West filmed in the new Russia. *Solomon a Gaenor* (1999), directed and written by Paul Morrison and produced by Sheryl Crown, is a BAFTA-awarded and Academy-nominated film, recorded back to back in Welsh and English versions. The film tells the love story of a young Orthodox Jew and a young Welsh woman in the south Wales valleys in 1911.

68. *Iaith Pawb, A National Action Plan for a Bilingual Wales* (Llywodraeth Cynulliad Cymru / Welsh Assembly Government, Crown Copyright: 2003), p. 50.
69. *One Wales: A progressive agenda for the government of Wales*, An agreement between the Labour and Plaid Cymru groups in the National Assembly, 27 June 2007.
70. National Theatre of Wales website, *https://nationaltheatrewales.org/about#ourstory* [accessed 14 April 2016].
71. J. E. McGrath, 'Rapid Response', *New Welsh Review*, 85 (2009), 9–14 (14, 9).
72. *The Village Social* toured village halls in Wales in October–November 2011; *The Insatiable, Inflatable Candylion*, based on Gruff Rhys's album *Candylion* (2007), was performed in the SSE SWALEC stadium hall over Christmas and New Year 2015/16.
73. Gary Owen, *Amgen/Broken* (Cardiff: Sgript Cymru, 2009), produced by Sherman Cymru in Cardiff in 2009; Alun Saunders, *A Good Clean Heart* (London: Oberon Books, 2015), produced by Neontopia, at The Other Room, Cardiff in 2015, by Neontopia and Wales Millennium Centre at the Edinburgh Fringe in 2015, and on tour in Wales in 2016; Dafydd James, *Llwyth* (Cardiff: Sherman Cymru, 2010), produced by Sherman Cymru in 2010 and by Theatr Genedlaethol Cymru and Sherman Cymru in 2011 at London, Edinburgh and Taipei, Taiwan. The production toured Wales three times in two years, a rarity.
74. 'Yn byw ein bywydau mewnol, yn ogystal â'n bywydau cyhoeddus, ar y ffin rhwng dwy iaith a dau ddiwylliant.' M. Wynn Thomas, 'Cyfieithu: Cynnyrch Cyffindir Iaith', *Taliesin, Cylchgrawn Llenyddol yr Academi Gymreig*, 118, Spring (2003), 109–13 (109). Translation my own.
75. 'Oddi mewn i bob un ohonom y mae dwy iaith a dwy gymdeithas yn cynnal seiat yn barhaus – ac yn cadw reiat ar brydiau. Ymryson yw pob ymson o'r eiddom, ar un wedd, ac ni ddaw'r un gair o'n genau heb gymar mud – y gair 'estron' sy'n gyfwely cariadus a gwrthwynebus iddo.' M. Wynn Thomas, 'Cyfieithu: Cynnyrch Cyffindir Iaith', 109. Translation my own.
76. National Theatre Wales 'newspaper' pamphlet, 2012, p. 2.
77. Stephen Moss, 'National Theatre Wales: Roving Revolution', *Guardian*, 1 March 2010 *http://www.theguardian.com/stage/2010/mar/01/national-theatre-wales* [accessed 21 April 2016].
78. McGrath, 'Rapid Response', 9.
79. See Emma Geliot and Cathy Gomez, *https://theatreanddance.british-council.org/blog/2016/09/what-gives-theatre-in-wales-its-radical-edge* [accessed 10 January 2017].
80. Josephine Machon, *Immersive Theatres: Intimacy and Immediacy in Contemporary Performance* (Basingstoke: Palgrave Macmillan, 2013), p. xv.

81. The Park and Dare theatre, completed in 1913, was an extension of the Park and Dare Workingmen's Hall, established in 1892 by the miners of the local Park and Dare collieries, who funded it by donating a portion of their monthly pay. The theatre entrance is built to resemble a non-conformist chapel and the theatre space inside is especially ornate. It is the largest remaining workingmen's institute in the south Wales coalfield.
82. *https://www.nationaltheatrewales.org/passion/wildworks* [accessed 9 January 2017].
83. Lyn Gardner, *Guardian*, 24 April 2011.
84. Susannah Clapp, *Guardian*, 1 May 2011. See *https://www.theguardian. com/culture/2011/may/01/michael-sheen-passion-port-talbot-review* [accessed 20 December 2016].
85. Ioan Williams, *A Straitened Stage, A Study of the Theatre of J. Saunders Lewis* (Bridgend: Seren Books, 1995).
86. I. Peate, 'Mynydd Epynt', *Y Llenor*, 20/4 (1941), 183–8 (184). Translation my own.
87. M. Billington, 'The Persians', *Guardian*, 13 August 2010. See *http://www. theguardian.com/stage/2010/aug/13/the-persians-review-brecon-beacons* [accessed 21 April 2016].
88. *ILIAD* was performed at Y Ffwrnes theatre in Llanelli in a collaboration between NTW and Y Ffwrnes, 21 September–3 October 2015.
89. John Saunders Lewis (1893–1985), one of the most prominent figures in twentieth-century Welsh history and culture, a dramatist, poet and literary critic, political activist and founder of Plaid Genedlaethol Cymru, which became Plaid Cymru. He was nominated for the Nobel Prize for Literature in 1970. *Tynged yr Iaith* (The Fate of the Language) was a radio broadcast given by Lewis in 1962 as a response to the census of 1961, which showed a decrease in the number of Welsh speakers in Wales. It warns of the extinction of Welsh as a living language unless steps are taken to sustain it. The broadcast was instrumental in the establishment of Cymdeithas yr Iaith Gymraeg (The Welsh Language Society) in 1962.
90. Rebecca Schneider, *Performing Remains, Art and War in Times of Theatrical Reenactment* (London: Routledge, 2011), p. 33.
91. *Dawns Ysbrydion* (2015–16), by Theatr Genedlaethol Cymru in parternship with Y Galeri, Caernarfon, was inspired by the Ghost Dances performed by some of the American Indian nations at the end of the nineteenth century, and was a response to the incidents around the drowning of Capel Celyn village and valley, to make a reservoir that would supply water to Liverpool. Three performers, including Ladd, moved on a stage covered with white polystyrene sheets, which were broken up as the performance proceeded.
92. *Scarface** has been performed widely in Wales and internationally in New York, London, Montreal, Madrid, Stockholm, Belgrade, Lublin, Zagreb, Brussels, Dublin, Dusseldorf, Glasgow, Göteborg, Oslo, Pristina, Quimper,

Skopje, Vancouver, and Varazdin. A shorter version, *Sawn-off Scarface (Scarface bach)*, has toured more widely still. See H. Roms, 'The lure of the local, the seduction of the global: locating intermediality in Eddie Ladd's *Scarface*', in P. Koski and M. Silva (eds), *The Local Meets the Global in Performance* (Newcastle-Upon-Tyne: Cambridge Scholars Publishing, 2010), pp. 65–80 (pp. 65–6).

93. See in particular the analysis of this moment in Roms, 'The lure of the local, the seduction of the global', p. 65.

94. See Sarah Broughton, 'Eddie Ladd in conversation with Sarah Broughton', *Platfform – Contemporary Performance Practice in Wales*, 1 (Autumn 2003), 8–15. *http://www.sarahbroughton.com/writing/eddie_ladd.htm* [accessed 10 January 2017].

95. Jodie Allinson, 'Training the Interdisciplinary Practitioner: a case study of Eddie Ladd', *Cyfrwng Media Wales Journal* 8 (2011), pp. 23–35 (pp. 25–6); see also J. Allinson, 'Approaches to multimedia theatre: theory, practice, pedagogy' (unpublished PhD thesis, 2011).

96. Developed by political scientist Alfred Zimmern in *My Impressions of Wales* (London: Mills and Boon, 1921), in which the industrial valleys of south Wales are compared with industrial America. Zimmern's analogy is political and historical as much as it is cultural.

97. See Eddie Ladd's website, *www.eddieladd.com* [accessed 10 January 2017].

98. National Endowment for Science, Technology and the Arts (NESTA).

99. See section on *Stafell C* at *www.eddieladd.com* [accessed 10 January 2017].

100. Eddie Ladd interviewed by Lisa Lewis, Cynhadledd Gydweithredol Theatr a Drama y Coleg Cymraeg Cenedlaethol, Atrium, University of South Wales, January 2014.

101. A. Rayner, 'E-scapes: performance in the time of cyberspace', in E. Fuchs and U. Chaudhuri (eds), *Land/Scape/Theater* (Ann Arbor: University of Michigan Press, 2002), pp. 350–70 (p. 350).

102. Christina Papagiannouli, *Political Cyberformance: The Etheatre Project* (London: Palgrave Macmillan, 2015).

Afterword

1. Emyr Humphreys, *The Taliesin Tradition, A Quest for Welsh Identity* (London: Black Raven Press, 1983), p. 2.

BIBLIOGRAPHY

Aaron, Jane, *The Welsh Survival Gene: The 'Despite Culture' in the Two Language Communities of Wales*, National Eisteddfod Lecture (Cardiff: Institute of Welsh Affairs, 2003).

Aaron J. and C. Williams (eds), *Postcolonial Wales* (Cardiff: University of Wales Press, 2005).

Allinson, J., 'Training the Interdisciplinary Practitioner: a Case Study of Eddie Ladd', *Cyfrwng Media Wales Journal*, 8 (2011), pp. 23–35.

Allinson, J., 'Approaches to multimedia theatre: theory, practice, pedagogy (unpublished PhD thesis, University of Glamorgan, 2011).

Anderson, Benedict, *Imagined Communities, Reflections on the Origin and Spread of Nationalism* (London: Verso and New Left Books, 1983).

Anderson, Jay, *Time Machines: The World of Living History* (Nashville: American Association for State and Local History, 1984).

Assmann, A., 'Re-framing memory. Between individual and collective forms of constructing the past', in K. Tilmans et al. (eds), *Performing the Past. Memory, History and Identity in Modern Europe* (Amsterdam University Press, 2010), pp. 35–50.

Assmann, Aleida, *Cultural Memory and Western Civilization: Functions, Media, Archives* (Cambridge: Cambridge University Press, 2011).

Bachelard, Gaston, *The Poetics of Space* (Boston: Beacon Press, 1994).

Bagnall, G., 'Performance and Performativity at Heritage Sites', *Museum and Society*, 1/2 (2003), 87–103.

Bala, Iwan (ed.), *Certain Welsh Artists: Custodial Aesthetics in Contemporary Welsh Art* (Bridgend: Seren, 1999).

Bala, Iwan, *Here and Now: Essays on Contemporary Art in Wales* (Bridgend: Seren, 2003).

Barba, Eugenio and Nicola Savarese, *A Dictionary of Theatre Anthropology: The Secret Art of the Performer* (London: Routledge, 2005).

Bassett, D. A., 'The Making of a National Museum (Part III)', *Transactions of the Honourable Society of Cymmrodorion* (1984), 217–316.

Baugh, Christopher, *Theatre, Performance and Technology: The Development of Scenography in the Twentieth Century* (London: Palgrave, 2005).

Bauman, Richard, *Folklore, Cultural Performance and Popular Entertainments* (Oxford University Press, 1992).

Bauman, Richard, *Verbal Art as Performance* (Long Grove, Illinois: Waveland Press Inc., 1977).

Bauman, R. and C. L. Briggs, 'Poetics and Performance as Critical Perspectives on Language and Social Life', *Annual Review of Anthropology* 19 (1990), 59–88.

Bennett, Tony, *The Birth of the Museum: History, Theory, Politics* (London: Routledge, 1995).

Bennett, T., 'The Exhibitionary Complex', *New Formations*, 4 (1988), 73–102.

Bennett, T., 'Museum and "the people"', in M. Wallace (ed.), *The Museum Time-Machine* (London: Routledge, 1988).

Berlant, Lauren, *The Queen of America Goes to Washington: Essays on Sex and Citizenship* (Durham: Duke University Press, 1997).

Bhabha, H. K. (ed.), *Nation and Narration* (London: Routledge, 1990).

Bhabha, Homi K., *The Location of Culture* (London: Routledge, 1994).

Billig, Michael, *Banal Nationalism* (London: Sage, 1995).

Billington, M., 'The Persians', *The Guardian*, 13 August 2010.

Blandford, Steve, *Film, Drama and the Break-up of Britain* (Bristol: Intellect, 2007).

Blandford, S., 'Theatre and performance in a devolved Wales', in S. Blandford (ed.), *Theatre and Performance in Small Nations* (Bristol: Intellect, 2013), pp. 53–70.

Blau, Herbert, *The Audience* (Baltimore: Johns Hopkins University Press, 1990).

Bohata, Kirsti, *Postcolonialism Revisited* (Cardiff: University of Wales Press, 2004).

Boswell, D. and J. Evans (eds), *Representing the Nation: A Reader – Histories, Heritages, and Museums* (London: Routledge, 1999).

Bourriaud, Nicholas, *Relational Aesthetics* (Dijon: Les presses du réel, 2002).

Brennan, T., 'The national longing for form', in H. K. Bhabha (ed.), *Nation and Narration* (London: Routledge, 1990), pp. 44–70.

Bromwich, Rachel, *Medieval Celtic Literature: A Select Bibliography* (Toronto and Buffalo: University of Toronto Press, 1974).

Bromwich, R. (ed.), *Trioedd Ynys Prydein. The Welsh Triads* (Cardiff: University of Wales Press, 1978).

Broughton, S., 'Eddie Ladd in conversation with Sarah Broughton', *Platfform: Contemporary Performance Practice in Wales*, 1 (2003), 8–15.

Brunvand, J. H., *The Study of American Folklore: An Encyclopaedia* (London: Taylor and Francis, 1996).

Burke, P., 'Popular Culture in Norway and Sweden', *History Workshop*, 3 (1977), 143–7.

Burke, P., 'A short history of distance', in M. S. Phillips et al., *Rethinking Historical Distance* (Basingstoke: Palgrave Macmillan, 2013), pp. 21–34.

Cantwell, Robert, *Ethnomimesis: Folklife and the Representation of Culture* (Chapel Hill and London: University of North Carolina Press, 1993).

Carbonell, B. M. (ed.), *Museum Studies: An Anthology of Contexts* (Oxford: Wiley-Blackwell, 2012).

Carlson, Marvin, *The Haunted Stage: The Theatre as Memory Machine* (Ann Arbor: University of Michigan Press, 2003).

Casey, Edward S., *Remembering: A Phenomenological Study* (Bloomington: Indiana University Press, 2000).

Celtica visitor's handbook, no date.

Charney, L. and V. R. Schwartz (eds), *Cinema and the Invention of Modern Life* (Princeton, NJ: Princeton University Press, 1995).

Clapp, S., 'The best theatre of 2011 – Susannah Clapp's choice', *Guardian*, 1 May 2011.

Clemons, L., 'Present enacting past: the functions of battle reenacting in historical representation', in S. Magelssen and R. Justice-Molloy (eds), *Enacting History* (Tuscaloosa: University of Alabama Press, 2011), pp. 10–21.

Cochrane, C., 'The Contaminated Audience: Researching Amateur Theatre in Wales before 1939', *New Theatre Quarterly*, 19/2 (2003), 169–76.

Collingwood, R. G., *The Idea of History* (Oxford: Oxford University Press, 1994 [1946]).

Conquergood, Dwight, *Cultural Struggles: Performance, Ethnography, Praxis* (Ann Arbor: University of Michigan Press, 2013).

Conquergood, D., 'Poetics, Play, Process and Power: The Performative Turn in Anthropology', *Text and Performance Quarterly*, 1 (1989), 82–95.

Connerton, Paul, *How Societies Remember* (Cambridge: Cambridge University Press, 1989).

Cooper-Greenhill, E., 'The museum: the socio-historical articulations of knowledge and things' (unpublished PhD thesis, University of London, 1988).

Corsane, G. (ed.), *Heritage, Museums and Galleries* (London: Routledge, 2005).

Crang, M., 'Magic Kingdom or a Magical Quest for Authenticity?', *Annals of Tourism Research*, 23/2 (1996), 415–31.

Crimp, D., 'On the Museum's Ruins', *October*, 13 (1980), 41–57.

Crimp, Douglas, *On the Museum's Ruins* (Cambridge: MIT Press, 1993).

Cubitt, Geoffrey, *History and Memory* (Manchester: Manchester University Press, 2007).

Dafydd, Elain, *Nid Sianel Deledu Gyffredin Mohoni! Hanes Sefydlu S4C* (Cardiff: University of Wales Press, 2016).

Davies, H. W. (ed.), *Y Theatr Genedlaethol yng Nghymru* (Cardiff: University of Wales Press, 2008).

Davies, H. W. 'Case study: refashioning a myth, performances of the tale of Blodeuwedd', in B. Kershaw (ed.), *The Cambridge History of British Theatre, Volume 3, since 1985*, (Cambridge: Cambridge University Press, 2004), pp. 273–87.

Davies, John, *A History of Wales* (Harmondsworth: Penguin, 1994).

Deleuze, Gilles and Félix Guattari, *What is Philosophy?* (Columbia University Press, 1994).

Derfel, R. J., *Brad y Llyfrau Gleision* (Rhuthyn: I. Clarke, 1854).

Dewhurst, C. K., 'Folk museums', in J. H. Brunvand, *The Study of American Folklore: An Encyclopedia* (London: Taylor and Francis, 1996), pp. 575–7.

Dewhurst, C. Kurt, Patricia Hall and Charlie Seemann (eds), *Folklife and Museums: Twenty-First Century Perspectives* (London: Rowman and Littlefield Publishers, 2016).

Diamond, Elin, *Performance and Cultural Politics* (London: Routledge, 1996).

Dicks, Bella, *Heritage, Place and Community* (Cardiff: University of Wales Press, 2000).

Dicks, B. 'Encoding and Decoding the People, Circuits of Communication at a Local Heritage Museum', *European Journal of Communication* (2000), 15/1, 61–78.

Dorson, R. M. (ed.), *Folklore and Folklife: An Introduction* (Chicago: University of Chicago Press, 1972).

Duncan, C. and A. Wallach, 'The Universal Survey Museum', *Art History*, 3/4 (1980), 448–69.

Durning, S., 'Literature – Nationalism's other? The case for revision' in H. K. Bhabha (ed.), *Nation and Narration* (London: Routledge, 1990), pp. 138–53.

Edwards, E., 'Dramateiddio Tirlithriad', *Barn* 405 (1996), *http://www.theatre-wales.co.uk/barn/*

Edwards, Hywel Teifi, *The Eisteddfod* (Cardiff: University of Wales Press, 1990).

Edwards, H. T., *Eisteddfod Ffair y Byd* (Llandysul: Gwasg Gomer, 1990).

Edwards, H. T., 'The Welsh language in the Eisteddfod', in G. H. Jenkins (ed.), *The Welsh Language and its Social Domains 1801–1911* (Cardiff: University of Wales Press, 2000), pp. 293–316.

Elfyn, M. and J. Rowlands (eds), *The Bloodaxe Book of Modern Welsh Poetry* (Northumberland: Bloodaxe Books, 2003).

Escobar, A., 'Culture Sits in Places: Reflections on Globalism and Subaltern Strategies of Localisation', *Political Geography*, 20 (2001), 139–74.

Evans, G. Ll., 'Astudiaeth o'r cysyniad o theatr ôl-ddramataidd yng nghyd-destun gwaith Cwmni Brith Gof a'i ddilynwyr ac Aled Jones Williams' (unpublished PhD thesis, Aberystwyth University, 2012).

Evans, R. P., 'Mythology and Tradition', in T. Herbert and G. E. Jones (eds), *The Remaking of Wales in the Eighteenth Century* (Cardiff: University of Wales Press, 1988).

'Ffarwel Brith Gof?', *Barn*, March, 2007.

Fischer-Lichte, Erika, *The Transformative Power of Performance: A New Aesthetics* (London: Routledge, 2008).

Fisher, Philip, *Making and Effacing Art: Modern American Art in a Culture of Museums* (Cambridge: Harvard University Press, 1991).

Ford, C., 'Theatre as a learning medium in museums', in J. Blais (ed.), *Les langages de l'interprétation personnalisée / The Languages of Live Interpretation* (Québec: Musée canadien des civilisations, 1997), pp. 41–60.

Foster, G. M., 'What is Folk Culture', *American Anthropologist*, 55 (1953), 159–73.

Michel Foucault, 'Of Other Spaces: Utopias and Heterotopias', *Architecture, Mouvement, Continuité* (1984), 1–9.

Francis, H., 'A Nation of Museum Attendants', *Arcade*, 16 January (1981), 8–9.

Fuchs, E. and U. Chaudhuri (eds), *Land/Scape/Theater* (Ann Arbor: University of Michigan Press, 2002).

Fusco, Coco, *English is Broken Here: Notes on Cultural Fusion in the Americas* (New York: The New Press, 1995).

Gardner, L., 'The Passion – review', *Guardian*, 24 April 2011.

Geertz, Clifford, *The Interpretation of Cultures: Selected Essays* (New York: Basic Books, 1973).

Geiriadur Prifysgol Cymru, A Dictionary of the Welsh Language, (Cardiff: University of Wales Press, 1987–2002).

Geliot, E. and C. Gomez, 'What Gives Theatre in Wales its Radical Edge?', British Council website, 2016 *https://theatreanddance.britishcouncil.org/blog/2016/09/what-gives-theatre-in-wales-its-radical-edge*

Gellner, Ernest, *Thought and Change* (London: Weidenfeld and Nicholson, 1964).

Gernsheim, Helmut and Alison, *L. J. M. Daguerre, The History of the Diorama and the Daguerreotype* (New York: Dover Publications, 1968).

Giannachi, G. and M. Luckhurst (eds), *On Directing: Interviews with Directors* (London: Palgrave Macmillan, 1999).

Giebelhausen, M., 'The architecture *is* the museum', in J. Marstine (ed.), *New Museum Theory and Practice* (Oxford: Blackwell, 2006), pp. 41–63.

Gramsci, Antonio, *Selections from Cultural Writings* (London: Lawrence and Wishart, 1985).

Gramsci, Antonio Fo, *Prison Notebooks* (New York: Columbia University Press, 2011).

Griffiths, Rh. (ed.), *Caneuon Ffydd* (Llandysul: Gwasg Gomer, 2001).

Gurian, E. H., 'A blurring of the boundaries', in G. Corsane (ed.), *Heritage, Museums and Galleries* (London: Routledge, 2005), pp. 71–7.

Gwenallt, see Jones, D. Gwenallt

Habermas, Jürgen, *The Structural Transformation of the Public Sphere: An Inquiry into a Category of Bourgeois Society* (Cambridge, Mass.: MIT Press, 1989).

Halbwachs, Maurice, *On Collective Memory* (London: University of Chicago Press, 1992).

Halbwachs, Maurice, *Les cadres sociaux de la mémoire* (Paris: Presses Universitaires de France, 1952).

Handler, Richard, *Nationalism and the Politics of Culture in Québec* (Madison: University of Wisconsin Press, 1988).

Handler, R. and W. Saxton, 'Dyssimulation: Reflexivity, Narrative, and the Quest for Authenticity in "Living History"', *Cultural Anthropology*, 3/3 (1988), 242–60.

Handler, Richard and Eric Gable, *The New History in an Old Museum: Creating the Past at Colonial Williamsburg* (London: Duke University Press, 1997).

Harrison, J. D., 'Ideas of museums in the 1990s', in G. Corsane (ed.), *Heritage, Museums and Galleries* (London: Routledge, 2005), pp. 38–53.

Harvie, Jen, *Staging the UK* (Manchester: Manchester University Press, 2005).

Heidegger, Martin, 'The Origin of the Work of Art' (1950), in *Basic Writings* (London: Routledge, 1993).

Heidegger, Martin, 'The Age of the World Picture', in *The Question Concerning Technology and Other Essays* (Austin: University of Texas Press, 1979).

Henning, Michelle, *Museums, Media and Cultural Theory* (Maidenhead: Open University Press, 2006).

Herbert, T. and G. E. Jones (eds), *The Remaking of Wales in the Eighteenth Century* (Cardiff: University of Wales Press, 1988).

Hewison, Robert, *The Heritage Industry: Britain in a Climate of Decline* (London: Methuen, 1987).

Hobsbawm, E. and T. Ranger (eds), *The Invention of Tradition* (Cambridge: Cambridge University Press, 1983).

Hooper-Greenhill, Eilean, *Museums and the Shaping of Knowledge* (London: Routledge, 1992).

Hughes Jones, L., 'Sand and Milk', Theatre-Women-Lives, *Open Page* 2 (1997), 29–31, *http://www.themagdalenaproject.org/sites/default/files/OP2_Jones.pdf*.

Humphreys, Emyr, *The Taliesin Tradition: A Quest for the Welsh Identity* (London: Black Raven Press, 1983).

Jackson, A., and J. Kidd (eds), *Performing Heritage: Research, Practice and Innovation in Museum Theatre and Live Interpretation* (Manchester: Manchester University Press, 2011).

James, Dafydd, *Llwyth* (Cardiff: Sgript Cymru, 2010).

Jenkins, G. H. (ed.), *A Rattleskull Genius: The Many Faces of Iolo Morganwg* (Cardiff: University of Wales Press, 2009).

Jenkins, J. Geraint, 'The Use of Artifacts and Folk Art in the Folk Museum', in R. M. Dorson (ed.), *Folkore and Folklife: An Introduction* (Chicago: University of Chicago Press, 1972), pp. 497–516.

Jenkins, J. Geraint, 'Interpreting the Heritage of Wales', *Folk Life: A Journal of Ethnological Studies* 25 (1986/7), 5–17.

Jenkins, J. Geraint, *Getting Yesterday Right: Interpreting the Heritage of Wales* (Cardiff: University of Wales Press, 1992).

Jenkins, J. Geraint, *Morwr Tir Sych: Hunangofiant* (Aberystwyth: Cymdeithas Lyfrau Ceredigion, 2007).

Jones, Anwen, *National Theatres in Context: France, Germany, England and Wales* (Cardiff: University of Wales Press, 2007).

Jones, Anwen, 'Cymru, cenedligrwydd a theatr genedlaethol: Dilyn y gwys neu dorri cwys newydd?', in A. Jones and L. Lewis (eds), *Ysgrifau ar Theatr a Pherfformio* (Cardiff: University of Wales Press, 2013), pp. 103–18.

Jones, A. and L. Lewis (eds), *Ysgrifau ar Theatr a Pherfformio* (Cardiff: University of Wales Press, 2013).

Jones, D. Gwenallt, *Eples* (Llandysul: Gwasg Gomer, 1951).

Jones, J. R., *A Raid i'r Iaith ein Gwahanu?* (Talybont: Y Lolfa, 1978).

Jones, J. R., *Prydeindod* (Llandybïe: Llyfrau'r Dryw, 1966).

Jones, J. R., *Ac Onide: Ymdriniaeth mewn Ysgrif a Phregeth ar Argyfwng y Gymru Gyfoes* (Llandybïe: Llyfrau'r Dryw, 1970).

Jones, L. T., 'Datblygiad Theatr Genedlaethol i Gymru, 1964–82', in H. W. Davies (ed.), *Y Theatr Genedlaethol yng Nghymru* (Cardiff: University of Wales Press, 2007), pp. 169–207.

Jones, R. Gerallt, *Writers of Wales: T. H. Parry-Williams* (Cardiff: University of Wales Press, 1978).

Karp, Ivan and Stephen D. Lavine (eds), *Exhibiting Cultures: The Poetics and Politics of Museum Display* (London: Smithsonian Institution Press, 1991).

Kaye, Nick, *Art Into Theatre: Performance Interviews and Documents* (London: Routledge, 1996).

Kershaw, Baz (ed.), *The Cambridge History of British Theatre, Volume 3, Since 1895* (Cambridge: Cambridge University Press, 2004).

Kirby, M., 'On Acting and Not-acting', in P. Zarrilli (ed.), *Acting (Re) Considered: A Theoretical and Practical Guide* (London: Routledge, 2002), pp. 40–52.

Kirshenblatt-Gimblett, Barbara, *Destination Culture: Tourism, Museums and Heritage* (Berkeley and Los Angeles: University of California Press, 1998).

Kirshenblatt-Gimblet, B., 'Afterlives', *Performance Research*, 2/2 (1997), 1–9.

Kirshenblatt-Gimblett, B., 'Objects of Ethnography', in I. Karp and S. D. Lavine (eds), *Exhibiting Cultures* (1991), pp. 386–443.

Kurin, Richard, *Reflections of a Culture Broker: A View from the Smithsonian* (Washington: Smithsonian Institution Press, 1997).

Kurin, Richard, *Smithsonian Folklife Festival, Culture Of, By, and For the People* (Washington D. C.: The Smithsonian Institute, 1998).

Kwon, Miwon, *One Place After Another: Site-specific Art and Locational Identity* (London: MIT Press, 2002).

Lamb, J., 'Historical Re-enactment, Extremity and Passion', *The Eighteenth Century: Theory and Interpretation* 49/3 (2008), 239–50.

Leahy, H. R., 'Watching me, watching you: performance and performativity in the museum', in A. Jackson and J. Kidd (eds), *Performing Heritage: Research, Practice and Innovation in Museum Theatre and Live Interpretation* (Manchester: University of Manchester Press, 2011), pp. 26–7.

Lefebvre, Henri, *The Production of Space* (Oxford: Blackwell, 1991).

Lefebvre, H., 'Reflections on the politics of space' in R. Peet (ed.), *Radical Geography* (London: Methuen, 1978), pp. 339–52.

Lehmann, Hans-Thies, *Postdramatic Theatre*, trans. Karen Jürs-Munby (London: Routledge, 2006).

Lewis, Ceri W., *Iolo Morganwg* (Caernarfon: Gwasg Pantycelyn, 1995).

Lewis, L., 'Cwmni Theatr Cymru ac Emily Davies, 1982–4', in H. W. Davies (ed.), *Y Theatr Genedlaethol yng Nghymru* (Cardiff: University of Wales Press, 2007), pp. 208–51.

Ling, A. G., 'Peasant Architecture in the Northern Provinces of Spain', *Journal of the Royal Institute of British Architects* 3/43 (1935–6), 845–63.

Lippard, Lucy R., *The Lure of the Local, Senses of Place in a Multicentered Society* (New York: The New Press, 1997).

Llancaiach Fawr Manor, guide (2010).

Llwyd, A., 'Yr Eisteddfod', in Moses Glyn Jones (ed.), *Cerddi Prifeirdd, Cyfrol 2* (Swansea: Gwasg Christopher Davies, 1979).

Llwyd, Alan, *Y Gaer Fechan Olaf, Hanes Eisteddfod Genedlaethol Cymru 1937–1950* (Llandybïe: Gwasg Dinefwr, 2006).

Llywelyn, Dorian, *Sacred Place, Chosen People: Land and National Identity in Welsh Spirituality* (Cardiff: University of Wales Press, 1999).

Llywodraeth Cynulliad Cymru, *Iaith Pawb, A National Action Plan for a Bilingual Wales*, Welsh Assembly Government (2003).

Llywodraeth Cynulliad Cymru, *One Wales: A progressive agenda for the government of Wales*, an agreement between the Labour and Plaid Cymru Groups in the National Assembly (2007).

Lord, Peter, *The Aesthetics of Relevance* (Llandysul: Gomer, 1992).

Lord, Peter, *The Meaning of Pictures: Images of Personal, Social and Political Identity* (Cardiff: University of Wales Press, 2009).

Low, S. M., 'Embodied Space(s), Anthropological Theories of Body, Space and Culture', *Space and Culture*, 6/9 (2003), 9–18.

Lowenthal, David, *The Past is a Foreign Country* (Cambridge University Press, 2009).

MacCannell, Dean, *The Tourist* (Berkeley and Los Angeles: University of Los Angeles Press, 1999).

Macdonald, S. J. and G. Fyfe (eds), *Theorizing Museums: Representing Identity and Diversity in a Changing World* (Oxford: Blackwell Publishers / *Sociological Review*, 1996).

Macdonald, S. J., 'A people's story: heritage, identity and authenticity', in C. Rojek and J. Urry (eds), *Touring Cultures: Transformations of Travel and Theory* (London: Routledge, 1997), pp. 155–75.

Macdonald, S. J., 'Museums, National, Postnational and Transcultural Identities', *Museum and Society*, 1/1 (2003).

Macdonald, S. and R. Silverstone, 'Rewriting the museum's fictions: taxonomies, stories and readers', in D. Boswell and J. Evans (eds.), *Representing the Nation: A Reader – Histories, Heritages and Museums* (London: Routledge, 1999), pp. 421–34.

McCalman, I. and P. A. Pickering (eds), *Historical Re-enactment: From Realism to the Affective Turn* (London: Palgrave Macmillan, 2010).

McGrath, J. E., 'Rapid Response', *New Welsh Review* 85 (2009), 9–14.

McLucas, Cliff, 'The Host, the Ghost and the Witness. Some approaches to site in the theatre works of Brith Gof 1989–1999. The Roehampton Remix' (1998), (Brith Gof Archive, National Library of Wales), pp. 12–13.

Machon, Josephine, *Immersive Theatres: Intimacy and Immediacy in Contemporary Performance* (Basingstoke: Palgrave Macmillan, 2013).

Magelssen, Scott, *Living History Museums: Undoing History through Performance* (Maryland: Scarecrow Press, 2007).

Magelssen, S. and R. Justice-Molloy (eds), *Enacting History* (Tuscaloosa: University of Alabama Press, 2011).

Marstine, J. (ed.), *New Museum Theory and Practice* (Oxford: Blackwell, 2006).

Mason, Rhiannon, 'Nation Building and the Museum of Welsh Life', *Museum and Society*, 3/1 (2005), 18–35.

Massey, D., 'Politics and Space/Time', in M. Keith and S. Pile (eds), *Place and the Politics of Identity* (London: Routledge, 1996), pp. 141–61.

Meethan, Kevin, *Tourism in a Global Society: Place, Culture, Consumption* (London: Palgrave Macmillan, 2001).

Minhinnick, Robert, *A Postcard Home: Tourism in the Mid-'Nineties* (Llandysul: Gwasg Gomer, 1993).

Morgan, Kenneth O., *Rebirth of a Nation: Wales 1880–1980* (Oxford University Press, 1981).

Morgan, P., 'Keeping the legends alive', in T. Curtis (ed.), *Wales: The Imagined Nation, Studies in Cultural and National Identity* (Bridgend: Poetry Wales Press, 1986), pp. 19–41.

Morris, Jan, *Wales, Epic Views of a Small Country* (London: Penguin Books, 1998).

Morris-Jones, John, *Cerdd Dafod* (Oxford: Clarendon Press, 1925; Cardiff: University of Wales Press, 1980).

Moss, S., 'National Theatre Wales: Roving Revolution', *Guardian*, 1 March 2010.

Nairn, Tom, *The Break-Up of Britain: Crisis and Neo-Nationalism* (London: New Left Books, 1977).

Nash, Gerallt, *Timber-framed buildings in Wales* (Cardiff: National Museums and Galleries of Wales, 1995).

National Theatre Wales, 'newspaper' pamphlet, 2012.

Nora, P. (ed.), *Realms of Memory: The Construction of the French Past, Volume 1, Conflicts and Divisions* (New York: Columbia University Press, 1996).

O'Neill, R., 'Croesi'r Bar: Archwilio hunaniaeth y mewnfudwr Prydeinig trwy gyfrwng archif yr artist Cliff McLucas' (unpublished PhD thesis, Aberystwyth University, 2013).

Owen, Dafydd, *Cynan* (Cardiff: University of Wales Press, 1979).

Owen, Gary, *Amgen/Broken* (Cardiff: Sgript Cymru, 2009).

Owen, Roger, 'Theatre in Wales in the 1990s and beyond', in B. Kershaw (ed.), *The Cambridge History of British Theatre Volume 3, Since 1895* (Cambridge: Cambridge University Press, 2004), pp. 485–97.

Owen, Roger, 'Theatr Dewi': Ymddiriedolaeth Theatr Dewi Sant a Phwyllgor Cymreig Cyngor Celfyddydau Prydain Fawr, 1959–67', yn H. W. Davies (ed.), *Y Theatr Genedlaethol yng Nghymru* (Cardiff: University of Wales Press, 2007), pp. 129–68.

Owen, Roger, *Ar Wasgar: Theatr a Chenedligrwydd yn y Gymru Gymraeg 1979–1997* (Cardiff: University of Wales Press, 2003).

Owen, Trefor M., *Welsh Folk Customs* (Cardiff: National Museum of Wales, Welsh Folk Museum, 1978).

Parry, C. E., 'Theatre-in-Museum at the National Museums and Galleries of Wales, 1990–2002' (unpublished MPhil thesis, University of Wales Aberystwyth, 2003).

Parry, R. Williams., 'Gwae Awdur Dyddiaduron', *Cerddi'r Gaeaf* (Dinbych: Gwasg Gee, 1952).

Redfield, R., 'The Social Organisation of Tradition', *Far Eastern Quarterly*, 15/1 (1995), 13–21.

Papagiannouli, Christina, *Political Cyberformance: The Etheatre Project* (London: Palgrave Macmillan, 2015).

Parry-Williams, T. H., *Detholiad o Gerddi* (Llandysul: Gwasg Gomer, 1972).

Pearson, Mike, *Brith Gof: A Welsh Theatre Company, 1. 1981–5*, (Aberystwyth, 1985).

Pearson, Mike, 'My balls/your chin', *Performance Research* 3/2 (1998), 35–41.

Pearson, Mike, 'Special Worlds, Secret Maps: A Poetics of Performance', in A. Taylor (ed.), *Staging Wales, Welsh Theatre 1979–1997* (Cardiff: University of Wales Press, 1997), pp. 85–99.

Pearson, Mike, *Site-Specific Performance* (London: Palgrave Macmillan, 2010).

Pearson, Mike, and Michael Shanks, *Theatre/Archaeology* (London: Routledge, 2001).

Peate, Iorwerth C., *Guide to the Collection of Welsh Bygones* (Cardiff: National Museum of Wales, 1929).

Peate, I. C., *Rhwng Dau Fyd, Darn o hunangofiant* (Dinbych: Gwasg Gee, 1976).

Peate, I. C., *Sylfeini* (Wrecsam: Hughes a'i Fab, 1938).

Peate, I. C., 'The Place of Folk Culture in the Museum', *Museums Journal*, 41 (1941), 45–50.

Peate, I. C., 'Folk Studies in Wales', *Welsh Review*, 3 (1944), 49–55.

Peate, I. C., 'Welsh Folk Culture', *Welsh Outlook* (1933), 294–97

Peate, I. C., 'A Folk Museum for Wales', *Museums Journal*, 34 (1934), 229–31.

Peate, I. C., 'Mynydd Epynt', *Y Llenor*, 20/4 (1941), 183–8.

Peate, I. C., *The Welsh House: A Study in Folk Culture* (Liverpool: Hugh Evans / The Brython Press, 1944).

Peate, I. C., 'Gwerth Amgueddfa', *Lleufer: Cylchgrawn Cymdeithas Addysg y Gweithwyr*, 2/1 (1946), 14–16.

Peate, I. C., *Amgueddfeydd Gwerin, Folk Museums* (Cardiff, University of Wales Press, 1948).

Peate, I. C., 'Re-erected Buildings at the Welsh Folk Museum', *Museums Journal*, 52 (1953), 74–6.

Peate, I. C., 'The Study of Folk Life: and Its Part in the Defence of Civilisation', *The Advancement of Science*, 15 (1958), 86–94, reprinted in *Gwerin*, 2/3, (1959), 97–109.

Peate, I. C., *Canu Chwarter Canrif* (Dinbych: Gwasg Gee, 1963).

Peate, I. C., 'Astudio Bywyd Gwerin: a'i ran mewn amddiffyn gwareiddiad', *Syniadau* (Llandysul: Gwasg Gomer, 1969), pp. 9–23.

Peate, I. C., *Diwylliant Gwerin Cymru* (Dinbych: Gwasg Gee, 1975).

Penczer, Peter R., *The Washington National Mall* (Arlington, Virginia: Oneonta Press, 2007).

Phelan, Peggy, *Unmarked: the Politics of Performance* (London: Routledge, 1993).

Pitchford, Susan, *Identity Tourism: Imaging and Imagining the Nation* (Bingley: Emerald Group, 2007).

Preziosi, D. and C. Farago (eds), *Grasping the World: the Idea of the Museum* (Aldershot: Asghate, 2004).

Preziosi, D., 'Narrativity and the museological myths of nationality', in B. M. Carbonell (ed.), *Museum Studies: An Anthology of Contexts* (Oxford: Wiley-Blackwell, 2012), pp. 82–91.

Rayner, A., 'E-scapes: Performance in the Time of Cyberspace', in E. Fuchs and U. Chaudhuri (eds), *Land/Scape/Theater* (Ann Arbor: University of Michigan Press, 2002), pp. 350–70.

Reas, Paul, Stuart Cosgrove and Val Williams, *Flogging a Dead Horse: Heritage Culture and its Role in Post-Industrial Britain* (Manchester: Cornerhouse, 1993).

Rees, Ifor (ed.), *Dŵr o Ffynnon Felin Bach: Cyfrol Dathlu Canlwyddiant Geni Cynan* (Dinbych: Gwasg Gee, 1995).

Reports of the Commissioners of Inquiry into the State of Education in Wales (London: Williams Clowes and Sons / HMSO, 1848).

Ringle, Ken, 'Of Lawyers and Other Folk: Even Barristers Join the Blend at the Smithsonian's Festival of Diversity', *Washington Post*, 25 June 1986.

Ripley, S. D., 'The Festival – A Living Museum', in *Festival of American Folklife Program Book* (Washington, DC: Smithsonian Institution, 1973).

Roach, Joseph, *Cities of the Dead, Circum-Atlantic Performance* (New York: Columbia University Press, 1996).

Robertshaw, A., 'Live interpretation', in A. Hems and M. Blockley (eds), *Heritage Interpretation* (London: Routledge, 2006), pp. 41–54.

Rockefeller, S., 'Where are you going? Work, power and movement in the Bolivian Andes' (unpublished Ph.D. thesis, University of Chicago, 2001).

Rogers, E., 'Deil y Perfformiad i Ysu'r Cof', *Y Cymro* 16 August 1983, 13.

Rokem, Freddie, *Performing History: Theatrical Representations of the Past in Contemporary Theatre* (Iowa City: University of Iowa Press, 2000).

Roms, H., 'Identifying (with) Performance: Representation and Constructions of Cultural Identity in Contemporary Theatre Practice – Three Case Studies' (unpublished PhD thesis, Aberystwyth University, 2001).

Roms, Heike, 'What's Welsh for Performance? Constructing an Archive of Performance Art in Wales', *Cyfrwng: Media Wales Journal*, 5 (2008), 54–72.

Roms, Heike, *What's Welsh for Performance? An Oral History of Performance Art in Wales 1968–2008*, Vol. 1 (Samizdat Press, 2008).

Roms, Heike, 'The lure of the local, the seduction of the global: locating intermediality in Eddie Ladd's *Scarface*', in P. Koski and M. Silva (eds), *The Local Meets the Global in Performance* (Newcastle-Upon-Tyne: Cambridge Scholars Publishing, 2010), pp. 65–80.

Ros, N., '"Llwfrdra" yn Achub Brith Gof', *Golwg*, 27 March 1997.

Ros, N., 'Big Changes in Funding are Inevitable', *New Welsh Review*, Spring (1997).

Ros, N. and G. Harper (eds), *Studies in Theatre and Production*, 24/3 (2004).

Said, Edward, *Orientalism* (Harmondsworth: Penguin Books, 1979).

Said, Edward, *The World, the Text and the Critic* (Harvard University Press, 1983).

Samuel, Raphael, *Theatres of Memory: Present and Past in Contemporary Culture* (London: Verso, 2012).

Sandberg, M., 'Effigy and narrative: looking into the nineteenth-century folk museum', in L. Charney and V. R. Schwartz (eds), *Cinema and the Invention of Modern Life* (Princeton, NJ, Princeton University Press, 1995).

Saunders, Alun, *A Good Clean Heart* (London: Oberon Books, 2015).

Savill, C. C., 'Dismantling the Wall', *Planet* 79 (1990), 20–8.

Schechner, Richard, *Performance Theory* (London: Routledge, 1988).

Schechner, Richard, *Performance Studies; An Introduction* (London: Routledge, 2002).

Schneider, Bernard, *Daniel Liebskind, Jewish Museum Berlin* (London: Prestel, 2007).

Schneider, Rebecca, *Performing Remains: Art and War in Times of Theatrical Reenactment* (London: Routledge, 2011).

Sedgeman, Kirsty, *Locating the Audience: How People Found Value in National Theatre Wales* (Bristol: Intellect, 2016).

Sheehy, D. E., 'Tradition and Change', in *The 2009 Smithsonian Folklife Festival: Giving Voice, Las Americas, Wales* (Washington DC: Smithsonian Institution, 2009).

Shepherd, Simon, *The Cambridge Introduction to Performance Theory* (Cambridge: Cambridge University Press, 2016).

Simon, Nina, *The Participatory Museum* (Santa Cruz, California: Museum 20, 2010).

Singer, Milton, *When A Great Tradition Modernizes: An Anthropological Approach to Indian Civilization* (Chicago: University of Chicago Press, 1972).

Smith, D., 'Labour History and Heritage', *Social History Curators Group Journal*, 18, (1990/91), 3–6.

Smith, Laurajane, *Uses of Heritage* (London: Routledge, 2006).

Smith, L., 'The 'doing' of heritage: heritage as performance', in A. Jackson and J. Kidd (eds), *Performing Heritage: Research, Practice and Innovation in Museum Theatre and Live Interpretation* (Manchester: Manchester University Press, 2011), pp. 69–81.

Smith, Peter, *Houses of the Welsh Countryside: A Study in Historical Geography* (Royal Commission on the Ancient and Historical Monuments in Wales, 1975).

Smith, P., 'A la Ronde: eccentricity, interpretation and the end of the world', in A. Jackson and J. Kidd (eds), *Performing Heritage: Research, Practice and Innovation in Museum Theatre and Live Interpretation* (Manchester: Manchester University Press, 2011), pp. 158–71.

Snow, Stephen Eddy, *Performing the Pilgrims: A Study of Ethnohistorical Role-Playing at Plimoth Plantation* (Jackson: University Press of Mississippi, 1993).

Soja, Edward, *Postmodern Geographies: The Reassertion of Space in Critical Social Theory* (London: Verso, 1989).

Stevens, Catrin, *Iorwerth C. Peate* (Cardiff: University of Wales Press, 1986).

Stoeltje, B. J., 'Festival', in R. Bauman (ed.), *Folklore, Cultural Performance, and Popular Entertainments* (Oxford: Oxford University Press, 1992), pp. 261–71.

Straub, Jürgen (ed.), *Narration, Identity and Historical Consciousness* (New York: Berghahn, 2005).

Szondi, Peter, *Theory of the Modern Drama* (Cambridge: Polity Press, 1987).

Taylor, A. (ed.) *Staging Wales: Welsh Theatre 1979–1997* (Cardiff: University of Wales Press, 1997).

Taylor, Diana, *The Archive and The Repertoire: Performing Cultural Memory in the Americas* (Durham and London: Duke University Press, 2003).

Thomas, M. Wynn, *Internal Difference: Literature in Twentieth-Century Wales* (Cardiff: University of Wales Press, 1992).

Thomas, M. Wynn, *Corresponding Cultures: The Two Literatures of Wales* (Cardiff: University of Wales Press, 1999).

Thomas, M. Wynn, 'Cyfieithu: Cynnyrch Cyffindir Iaith', *Taliesin, Cylchgrawn Llenyddol yr Academi Gymreig*, 118 (2003), 109–13.

Thomas, R. S., *Selected Poems 1946–1968* (London: Granada, 1983).

Tilden, Freeman, *Interpreting Our Heritage* (Chapel Hill: University of North Carolina Press, 2007).

Tillich, Paul, *The Courage to Be* (London: Yale University Press, 1952).

Tilmans, K., et al. (eds), *Performing the Past: Memory, History and Identity in Modern Europe* (Amsterdam University Press, 2010).

Turner, Victor, *The Forest of Symbols: Aspects of Ndembu Rituals* (Ithaca: Cornell University Press, 1970).

Turner, Victor, *From Ritual to Theatre: The Human Seriousness of Play* (New York: PAJ Publications, 1982).

Turner, Victor, *The Ritual Process: Structure and Anti-Structure* (Ithaca: Cornell University Press, 1977).

Uzzell, D., and R. Ballyntyne, 'Heritage that hurts: Interpretation in a postmodern world', in D. Uzzell and R. Ballyntyne (eds), *Contemporary Issues in Heritage and Environmental Interpretation* (London: Stationery Office, 1998).

Van Gennep, Arnold, *Les Rites de Passage* (Paris: Edition A & J Picard, 2011).

Vergo, P. (ed.), *The New Museology* (London: Reaktion Books, 1989).

Vizenor, Gerald, *Manifest Manners: Narratives on Postindian Survivance* (Nebraska: Bison Books, University of Nebraska Press, 1999).

Walker, William S., *A Living Exhibition: The Smithsonian and the Transformation of the Universal Museum* (Amherst and Boston: University of Massachusetts Press, 2013).

Wallace, M. (ed.), *The Museum Time-Machine* (London: Routledge, 1988).

Walsh, Kevin, *The Representation of the Past: Museums and Heritage in a Post-modern World* (London: Routledge, 1992).

Weil, Simone, *L'Enracinement: Prélude a une déclaration des devoir envers l'être humain* (Paris: Gallimard, 1949).

Weil, Simone, *The Need for Roots: Prelude towards a declaration of duties towards mankind* (London: Routledge and Kegan Paul, 1952).

Weil, Stephen E., *Rethinking the Museum* (Washington: Smithsonian Institution, 1990).

White, H., 'The fictions of factual representation', in D. Preziosi and C. Farago (eds), *Grasping the World: The Idea of the Museum* (Aldershot: Ashgate, 2004), pp. 22–35.

Widén, P., 'National museums in Sweden: a story of denied empire and a neutral state', in P. Aronsson and G. Elegnius (eds), *Building National Museums in Europe, 1750–2010. Conference Proceedings from EuNaMus, European National Museums: Identity Politics, the Uses of the Past and the European Citizen*, EuNaMus Report No 1 (Linköping University Electronic Press, 2011).

Wiles, David, *A Short History of Western Performance Space* (Cambridge: Cambridge University Press, 2003).

Wilkie, F., 'Mapping the Terrain: A Survey of Site-Specific Performance in Britain', *New Theatre Quarterly*, 18/2 (2002), 140–60.

Wilkie, F., 'Out of place: the negotiation of space in site-specific performance (unpublished PhD thesis, University of Surrey, 2004).

Williams, Daniel G. (ed.), Raymond Williams, *Who Speaks for Wales?* (Cardiff: University of Wales Press, 2003).

Williams, Daniel G., *Black Skin, Blue Books: African Americans and Wales 1845–1945* (Cardiff: University of Wales Press, 2014).

Williams, Daniel G., *Wales Unchained: Literature, Politics and Identity in the American Century* (Cardiff: University of Wales Press, 2015).

Williams, D. J., *Hen Dŷ Ffarm* (Llandysul: Gwasg Gomer, 1953).

Williams, Gwyn A., *When Was Wales? A History of the Welsh* (Harmondsworth: Penguin, 1985).

Williams, Gwyn A., 'Iolo Morganwg: bardd rhamantaidd ar gyfer cenedl nad oedd yn cyfrif', in G. H. Jenkins (ed.), *Cof Cenedl V, Ysgrifau ar Hanes Cymru* (Llandysul: Gwasg Gomer, 1990), pp. 57–84.

Williams, Gruffydd John, *Iolo Morganwg* (Cardiff: University of Wales Press, 1956).

Williams, Ioan, *A Straitened Stage: A Study of the Theatre of J. Saunders Lewis* (Bridgend: Seren Books, 1995).

Williams, Ioan, 'Towards national identities: Welsh theatres' in B. Kershaw (ed.), *The Cambridge History of British Theatre, Volume 3, Since 1895* (Cambridge: Cambridge University Press, 2004), pp. 242–72.

Williams, Ioan, *Y Mudiad Drama yng Nghymru 1880–1940* (Cardiff: University of Wales Press, 2006).

Williams, Raymond, *Problems in Materialism and Culture* (London: Verso, 1980).

Williams, Raymond, *The Year 2000* (New York: Pantheon, 1983).

Williams, R.aymond, 'Marxism, Poetry, Wales', in D. G. Williams, (ed.), *Who Speaks for Wales? Nation, Culture, Identity* (Cardiff: University of Wales Press, 2003), pp. 81–94; originally published in *Poetry Wales* 13/3 (1977), 16–34.

Williams, Raymond, 'Base and Superstructure in Marxist Cultural Theory', *New Left Review* 82 (1973), 3–16.

Williams, Raymond., 'The Culture of Nations', in D. G. Williams (ed.), *Who Speaks for Wales? Nation, Culture, Identity* (Cardiff: University of Wales Press, 2003), pp. 191–203; originally published in *Towards 2000* (London: Chatto and Windus, 1983), 177, 180–4, 190–9.

Williams, Raymond, 'Wales and England', in D. G. Williams (ed.), *Who Speaks for Wales?* (Cardiff: University of Wales Press, 2003), pp. 16–26; originally published in *New Wales*, 1 (1983), 34–8.

Williams, Waldo, *Dail Pren* (Aberystwyth: Gwasg Aberystwyth, 1957).

Williams, Waldo, *The Peacemakers: Selected Poems*, translated by Tony Conran (Llandysul: Gomer Press, 1997).

Wright, Patrick, *On Living in an Old Country* (London: Verso, 1985).

Zarrilli, P. (ed.), *Acting (Re)Considered, A Theoretical and Practical Guide* (London: Routledge, 2002).

Zimmern, Alfred, *My Impressions of Wales* (London: Mills and Boon, 1921).

Zolberg, V., 'Museums as contested sites of remembrance: the Enola Gay affair', in S. Macdonald and G. Fyfe (eds), *Theorizing Museums, Representing Identity and Diversity in a Changing World* (Oxford: Blackwell Publishers/ *The Sociological Review*, 1996), pp. 69–82.

Websites

freemenofgwent.com (The Freemen of Gwent, medieval re-enactment group).

http://boarsreenactors.wixsite.com/boars (Brotherhood of Aman Re-enactment Society (BOARS), 12th–13th century).

https://cardiffcastlegarrison.wordpress.com (Cardiff Castle Garrison, medieval re-enactment).

http://ironage-history.com/brigantia/ (Brigantia, Iron Age Celtic re-enactment).

http://www.museumwales.ac.uk/our_plans/operational_plan_2014-15/ (Amgueddfa Cymru/Museum Wales operational plan 2014–15).

https://nationaltheatrewales.org/about#ourstory (National Theatre of Wales).

http://www.plh.manchester.ac.uk (AHRC funded 'The Performance, Learning and Heritage Project', 2005–8).

https://sites.google.com/site/historymattersorg/Home/the-montgomery-levy (The Montgomery Levy).

http://.r-i-p-e.co.uk (Marc Rees, *shed * light*).

http://www.webster.uk.net/Hobbies-and-Interests/Re-enactment-WW2 -SWB/Home.aspx (South Wales Borderers WW2 re-enactment group).

thewelshtommies.weebly.com (The Welsh Tommies 39–45 re-enactment group).

www.ageoftheprinces.co.uk (Age of the Princes).

www.blaeddaudu.co.uk (Blaeddau Du Viking re-enactment).

www.cardiffcastlemuseum.org.uk

www.dumnonika.com (Dumnonika Iron Age British (Celtic) re-enactment).

www.bedwyrwilliams.com

www.eddieladd.com (Eddie Ladd).

www.experienceofworship.org.uk (AHRC/ESRC The Experience of Worship project).

www.marcherstuarts.com (The Marcher Stuarts Living History and Military Group).

www.marcrees.com (Marc Rees).

www.sonsofthedragon.co.uk (Meibion y Ddraig/Sons of the Dragon, medieval Welsh archers).

www.waldowilliams.com (Cymdeithas Waldo Williams).

INDEX

local eisteddfodau, 140

locations, 130, 137–8

Maes, y (field), 133, 134, 135–6,
137, 139, 142

and meaning, 124

and memory, 33, 124, 131,
132–8

and national identity, 123,
124–6, 139, 143–4

Pabell y Cymdeithasau (societies'
tent), 142

Pafiliwn, y (Pavilion), 126, 130,
141–2

Pafiliwn Gwyddoniaeth a
Thechnoleg, y (science and
technology pavilion), 142

and participation, 131–2, 134–6,
138, 142–3

and people, 126–32

as performance for the outside
world, 8, 123, 126, 143

performance spaces, 141–2

and place, 124, 133, 137–44

and play, 123–4, 129

and *poiesis*, 144

Prose Medal, 130

and religion, 124, 126, 130

and resolution, 132

and ritual, 123, 126–32, 133–4

school and youth eisteddfodau,
140

social contexts, 124–5

and social space, 138

and symbolism, 127, 130–2,
133–4, 138

Theatr y Maes (theatre of the
Maes), 142

and time, 133–4, 140

and tradition, 33, 124, 127–9,
132–3, 136–7

and transformation, 126, 133,
134–5

and the Welsh language, 123,
124–5, 141

and Welsh-language culture,
123, 124–5, 136–7

national identity
concepts of the nation, 13–17

and culture, 6–7, 47–8, 215–17

and festivals, 121, 123, 124–6,
139, 143–4, 148

and heritage, 83, 91, 100–1,
107–8, 114–16, 217–18

and language, 7–8, 15–16, 47,
49, 190–2, 209

and memory, 21–3, 28–30, 100,
101, 209

and museums, 38, 39–40, 42, 46,
47–58, 68

and the National Eisteddfod,
123, 124–6, 139, 143–4

and place, 28–30, 192–4, 203–7,
217–18

and re-enactment, 114–16

and theatre, 166, 190, 192–4,
203–7, 209–13

see also identity

National Mall, Washington, 45, 144,
146–7, 154, 159

National Museum and Gallery,
73

National Museum of African
American History and
Culture, 146

National Museum of the American
Indian (NMAI), 45–6, 146

National Museum of the Welsh
Woollen Industry, 72

National Museum of Wales, 35, 47,
55–6, 63, 69, 72, 73–4, 88